Mastering Prezi for Business Presentations

Second Edition

Engage your audience visually with stunning Prezi presentation designs and be the envy of your colleagues who use PowerPoint with this book and ebook

Russell Anderson-Williams

J.J. Sylvia IV

[PACKT]
PUBLISHING

BIRMINGHAM - MUMBAI

Mastering Prezi for Business Presentations
Second Edition

First published: July 2012

Second edition: July 2015

Production reference: 1230715

Published by Packt Publishing Ltd.
Livery Place
35 Livery Street
Birmingham B3 2PB, UK.

ISBN 978-1-78217-509-4

www.packtpub.com

Credits

Authors
Russell Anderson-Williams
J.J. Sylvia IV

Reviewers
Marthe Bijman
Mikah J. Pritchard

Commissioning Editor
Ashwin Nair

Acquisition Editor
Kevin Colaco

Content Development Editor
Mamata Walkar

Technical Editor
Rohan Uttam Gosavi

Copy Editor
Pranjali Chury

Project Coordinator
Shipra Chawhan

Proofreader
Safis Editing

Indexer
Mariammal Chettiyar

Graphics
Disha Haria

Production Coordinator
Conidon Miranda

Cover Work
Conidon Miranda

About the Authors

Russell Anderson-Williams is one of Prezi's very own official independent experts, and the founder of the Prezi design and training agency (`http://www.theprezenter.com`). He is dedicated to educating Prezi users on best practices, sharing advice and tips on design, and more than anything, changing the mindset of Prezi users to that of nonlinear thinkers. A wildly creative and visual thinker, Russell has a strong background in visual communication and graphic design, as well as a long career in training and presenting. Russell has designed and delivered hundreds of presentations for some of the world's biggest companies in a variety of sectors. By merging his love and passion for educating people with his joy for all things wonderfully visual, he has designed a course to turn anyone in the business world into a Prezi master through his on-site training programs, and he tirelessly blogs about everything Prezi-related. He resides in the extremely creative city of Bristol in the United Kingdom, where he manages a small team of Prezi-focused designers and trainers.

J.J. Sylvia IV is a PhD student of the communication, rhetoric, and digital media program at North Carolina State University. He also has an MA in philosophy from The University of Southern Mississippi and BA degrees in philosophy and communication from Mississippi State University. His experience spans the fields of business, education, and nonprofits, which has given him the opportunity to develop a unique perspective on the way people use and engage with technology.

His primary research interests revolve around the ways technology affects our understanding and interactions with the world around us. Before graduate school, he managed paid advertising and marketing strategies for an e-commerce site and developed a social media outreach initiative for a nonprofit organization. Recently, he managed the AmeriCorps interns who worked to integrate technology into the classroom, and built a community around an educational outreach blog, www. PhilosophyMatters.org. He can also be found at www.jjsylvia.com.

John has reviewed *Prezi Hotshot and Prezi Essentials*. He has published chapters in the books *Radiohead and Philosophy*, *Doctor Who and Philosophy*, and *Supervillains and Philosophy*, all published by Open Court, and also in *Ethical Issues in E-Business*, published by Business Science Reference.

About the Reviewers

Marthe Bijman is a writer, literary critic, and communications specialist in mining engineering. She has worked extensively in the mining and information technology industries. She holds a BA degree, BA honors in literature, BA honors in journalism, H.Dip.Ed in language teaching, and an MA in applied linguistics and literary sciences. She is the president of Red Pennant Communications Corp (`www.red-pennant-communications.com`). She has nurtured a lifelong interest in language and literary analysis, and is an astute and prolific reader and literature reviewer. She publishes her reviews and thoughts on the written word on her blog and website, `www.sevencircumstances.com`. In collaboration with her husband, she is the author and designer of self-published photography, and reference and poetry books featured on `www.blurb.com`. Born in South Africa, she now lives and works in Vancouver, Canada.

Mikah J. Pritchard is currently an instructional designer at Eastern Kentucky University. She is pursuing a PhD in educational psychology at the University of Kentucky. Her primary research interests revolves around student motivation and student persistence in distance education courses. Mikah has an M.S. Ed. in instructional systems technology from Indiana University and a BS in psychology from Oakland City University. Her areas of expertise are instructional design, e-learning, educational psychology, technical writing, instructional technology consulting, and graphic design. Mikah enjoys exploring, learning, and implementing new technologies and strives to produce engaging instructions with a strong theoretical base.

www.PacktPub.com

Support files, eBooks, discount offers, and more

For support files and downloads related to your book, please visit www.PacktPub.com.

Did you know that Packt offers eBook versions of every book published, with PDF and ePub files available? You can upgrade to the eBook version at www.PacktPub.com and as a print book customer, you are entitled to a discount on the eBook copy. Get in touch with us at service@packtpub.com for more details.

At www.PacktPub.com, you can also read a collection of free technical articles, sign up for a range of free newsletters and receive exclusive discounts and offers on Packt books and eBooks.

https://www2.packtpub.com/books/subscription/packtlib

Do you need instant solutions to your IT questions? PacktLib is Packt's online digital book library. Here, you can search, access, and read Packt's entire library of books.

Why subscribe?

- Fully searchable across every book published by Packt
- Copy and paste, print, and bookmark content
- On demand and accessible via a web browser

Free access for Packt account holders

If you have an account with Packt at www.PacktPub.com, you can use this to access PacktLib today and view 9 entirely free books. Simply use your login credentials for immediate access.

Table of Contents

Preface   **ix**

Chapter 1: Understanding the Prezi Frame of Mind   **1**

Thinking about nonlinear presentations   **2**
Linear presentations   3
Nonlinear presentations   3
The best of both worlds   4
Think for Prezi   5
Planning your Prezi   **6**
The three Prezi design steps   7
Step 1 – planning your Prezi   7
Step 2 – getting the style right   8
Step 3 – building in layers   12
The steps, again   15
Mind Mapping   **16**
Writing a list   17
Starting with the tool   17
Working efficiently with Prezi   19
Map your journey   19
Deciding the BIG picture   **20**
The science behind it   20
Neural networks in action   21
How to find your BIG picture   25
Common Prezi mistakes   **26**
Motion sickness   26
The blank canvas challenge   27
Going too big   27
Summary   **28**

Chapter 2: Hands-on with Prezi Mechanics	29
Templates	**29**
Using templates	30
Getting the most from templates	31
Paths	**31**
Creating motion	32
Adding, removing, and editing	34
Shapes	**36**
Get creative	37
Editing shapes	39
Editing lines	40
Styled symbols	41
Highlighter	41
Grouping	**42**
Prezi text editor	**45**
Spell checker	45
The text drag-apart feature	45
Font colors	47
Bullet points and indents	47
Animations	**48**
3D backgrounds	**50**
A single 3D background	50
Multiple 3D backgrounds	52
The Present button	**54**
Summary	**55**
Chapter 3: Consistent Branding for Business	**57**
Color schemes	**58**
Customizing Prezi graphics through CSS	**62**
Editing fonts	64
Editing a frame	66
My Content	**71**
Custom logos	**73**
Summary	**75**
Chapter 4: Importing Slides into Prezi	**77**
The importance of slides	**77**
Slide-based software and businesses	78
Converting colleagues to Prezi	78
Importing slides into Prezi	**79**
The Insert PPT function	80

Prezify your slides	84
Checking the import	85
Positioning content	85
Missing content	87
Placing slides on to a Prezi canvas	91
Zooming in and out on slides	91
No time to Prezify	93
Importing your slides as PDF files	94
Potential problems	**96**
Low-resolution imagery	96
Pixilation	97
Text	97
Spell check	98
Animations	98
An alternative solution	100
Summary	**100**
Chapter 5: Best Practices with Imagery	**101**
Raster and vector images	**101**
What are raster images?	102
Raster file formats	103
What are vector images?	104
Vector file formats	105
Benefits of Prezi	**105**
Finding great imagery	**107**
Direct upload	107
Prezi insert	108
Limitations of the Insert from web function	111
Using Google image search outside of Prezi	111
Advanced image search	111
Standard search	113
Google image search limitations	114
Other online sources for imagery	114
Time versus quality	115
Vectorising your imagery	**116**
Using software to vectorize	116
The quick way to create a vector image	121
Creating your vector images	**122**
Hand-drawn images	123
Working with images – quick tips	124
Prezi effects and animations	**126**
Effects	126
Fade-in animations	130
Summary	**134**

Chapter 6: Using Audio   135
Why use sound in Prezi?   135
How to find sound files   136
Creating your own sounds   137
Adding audio in Prezi   140
Background music   140
Voice-over   143
Using the audio during presentation   145
Common problems   145
Uneven volume levels   146
Background music for only one path step   149
Music only   149
Music and voice   150
Working on mobile devices   152
Android   153
iPhone   156
Getting the audio into Prezi   158
Example uses   159
Less text   159
Translation   159
Narration   159
Customers   160
Testimonials   160
Example   161
Summary   162

Chapter 7: Inserting a Video   163
The technical bit   163
File size restrictions   164
Online or offline?   164
Will your Prezi be viewed online?   164
Will colleagues want a copy of your Prezi?   165
Determining your design   165
Playing videos   165
Playing along a path   166
Letting the user play   166
Positioning videos   168
Videos – the easy way with YouTube   169
Searching for the right clip   169
Creating your own YouTube account   170
Uploading your own videos to YouTube   171

Editing videos on YouTube	172
Enhancements	173
Audio	175
Annotations	176
Captions	177
Other sources for videos	181
Vimeo	181
Using Windows Live Movie Maker or iMovie	181
Fun with videos in Prezi	**182**
Questions	183
Experts	183
Customer scenarios	183
Summary	**184**
Chapter 8: Using Projectors with Prezi	**185**
Advantages of Prezi	**186**
Planning your Prezi	**187**
Beware of overlapping content	187
Changing the aspect ratio	190
Why do you need to know about ratios?	193
What this means for your Prezi?	193
Building your Prezi at the correct ratio	195
Sharing your Prezi	**196**
Sharing the online link	197
Sharing portable Prezis	199
Screen blackout	**200**
Interactive Prezis	**201**
How it works	201
How will you use it?	203
Summary	**204**
Chapter 9: Prezi for Online Delivery	**205**
Your Prezis	**206**
Private Prezis	206
Sharing your Prezi	208
Search engines	209
Embedding your Prezi	**210**
Sizing your Prezi	211
User experience	211
Embedding the code	211
The online design approach	**214**
The three Prezi design steps	214

Giving instructions	214
Narration	217
Highlighting	217
Highlighting with frames	218
Highlighting with color	219
Timing	221
The BIG picture hook	**221**
Summary	**224**
Chapter 10: Customized Interactions	**225**
Benefits of interactive Prezis	**226**
The Prezi API	**227**
Preparation	228
Web servers	228
The HTML editor	229
Basic operations	231
Creating menus	**232**
The base HTML file	232
JavaScript implementation	233
Coding the menu	238
Styling the menu	240
Creating submenus	245
Summary	**249**
Chapter 11: Prezi for Tablets and Phones	**251**
The Prezi iPad application	**252**
Using the Prezi viewer	254
Edit mode	257
Show mode	258
Prezi for iPhone and Android	**259**
Presenting with a tablet	**267**
Using a tablet to project your Prezi	268
A bit of fun	269
Summary	**270**
Chapter 12: Online Collaboration	**271**
Shared folders	**271**
Creating a folder	272
Managing folders	274
Adding viewers	274
Removing viewers	276
Deleting a folder	277

Cocreating Prezis   **278**
  Sharing the Prezi   278
  Avatars   282
Presenting remotely   **284**
  The remote presentation setup   285
  The presentation   288
  Tips to present remotely   291
Video presentations   **292**
Summary   **295**

Chapter 13: Case Studies   **297**
  Collaboration and brainstorming   **297**
    Getting visual   297
    The perks of digital presence   298
    Easy sharing   298
  Marketing and web presence   **298**
    Prezume   298
    Storytelling   299
    Easy incorporation   299
  Sales   **300**
    The pitch   300
    In the field   300
  Example case studies   **301**
  The sales pitch   **301**
    The multimedia tie-in   308
    Visual appeal   309
  Summary   **313**

Chapter 14: Getting Prezi through the Door   **315**
  PowerPoint's grip on business   **315**
  The hard truth   **316**
  The first hurdle   **317**
  Opportunities to zoom   **319**
  Be prepared   **319**
    Using Theme Wizard   320
    Frame templates   321
    Backing it up   323
  Using PowerPoint to introduce Prezi   **323**
    Inserting PowerPoint slides   324
    Building a PowerPoint presentation   326

Slide Dynamic   327
  Offline Prezis   328
  Online Prezis   331
Educating your business   332
Company's how-to guide   333
Summary   **334**
Index   **335**

Preface

If you've discovered Prezi in the last few years or even very recently, you have become a part of an interesting movement that's rapidly changing how ideas are shared. If you're reading this now, then there's no doubt in our minds that you're completely sold on the fact that business presentations need to change. You're probably also sold on the fact that Prezi is exactly what's needed to make that change. In this book, you'll find all the tools and guidance to take your business presentations to the next level and build on what you already know about Prezi. Our aim is to take you from being a Prezi user to a Prezi master, and we hope you enjoy the ride.

What this book covers

Chapter 1, Understanding the Prezi Frame of Mind, will show you how to start thinking about presentations through the Prezi frame of mind, which affords a nonlinear approach. We will also discuss three Prezi design steps that will help you to craft the perfect Prezis every time.

Chapter 2, Hands-on with Prezi Mechanics, introduces the basic mechanics of Prezi that are required to start creating a new Prezi of your own. Although we call these basics, even frequent Prezi users are likely to find some new ideas here.

Chapter 3, Consistent Branding for Business, explains how to create reusable elements that can be easily used in multiple Prezis to create consistent branding for an organization. We'll also explore how to customize the style sheets for your Prezi in order to get a completely custom style that will best suit your business brand.

Chapter 4, Importing Slides into Prezi, helps you understand the insert PPT feature and gives great tips on how to truly turn linear slides into nonlinear presentations. With PowerPoint being so dominant in business presentations for such a long time, there's no doubt you'll need to Prezify slides for your organization.

Chapter 5, *Best Practices with Imagery*, shows you two different types of imagery. It will help you understand the pros and cons of using them within the Prezi canvas. You will also get some useful tips on where to find imagery for your Prezi designs and how to create some of your own.

Chapter 6, *Using Audio*, teaches you how to add audio to your canvas and understand when this technique should and shouldn't be used. Audio can bring a whole new dimension to your Prezi designs and creates an engaging experience for anyone viewing it online.

Chapter 7, *Inserting a Video*, explores the benefits of using video files that are stored offline or online. We will also look at how to create our own YouTube account to edit and manage our files online.

Chapter 8, *Using Projectors with Prezi*, helps you understand why some of your Prezi designs don't look the same when projected onto a big screen and discusses how to plan for and navigate these issues. This is an extremely useful chapter that will help keep each and every frame of your Prezi looking useful.

Chapter 9, *Prezi for Online Delivery*, gives you some simple tips to help you to engage with your audience and keep them focused when exploring a Prezi on their own. Some of your Prezis will be accessed by colleagues and customers online, and because of this, you'll need to take a slightly different approach that really takes your audience into account.

Chapter 10, *Customized Interactions*, demonstrates how to create a custom menu for your Prezi designs. These menus can increase engagement and allow viewers to navigate directly to specific points within a Prezi. Allowing this type of interaction can really help your Prezi brand stand out from the crowd and works well when embedded on a company's webpage or blog.

Chapter 11, *Prezi for Tablets and Phones*, explains how Prezi works on mobile devices and gives tips for presenting with the devices themselves. If you're already using these devices, why not use them to present your new ideas to colleagues, managers, and clients?

Chapter 12, *Online Collaboration*, helps you work together with your colleagues to share ideas in an exciting and engaging way. There are lots of step-by-step instructions to help you to set up this collaboration and useful tips to ensure that you get the most out of these collaborations.

Chapter 13, *Case Studies*, looks at some of the ways other businesses have used Prezi. This chapter is meant to give you real-world examples that will get your creative juices flowing as you brainstorm ways in which you can implement Prezi in your own business.

Chapter 14, Getting Prezi through the Door, explores some of the barriers you may face when introducing Prezi to your business. This is going to be just as hard as mastering the tool itself, but we've given you lots of useful tips to help get Prezi through the door and into the hands of your colleagues.

What you need for this book

This book will allow you to advance your own Prezi skills. In case you're new to Prezi, we start with the basics, but even regular users will benefit from the ideas and techniques described in this book. It is aimed at helping you think, plan, approach, and build Prezis that engage and inspire your colleagues and customers like never before.

Who this book is for

If you use Prezi in business and want to take your presentations to the next level, or if you want to become the office Prezi master, this book is for you.

Conventions

In this book, you will find a number of text styles that distinguish between different kinds of information. Here are some examples of these styles and an explanation of their meaning.

Code words in text, database table names, folder names, filenames, file extensions, pathnames, dummy URLs, user input, and Twitter handles are shown as follows: "You can save your file as `blooms.html`."

A block of code is set as follows:

```
<script type="text/javascript">
var player = new PreziPlayer('prezi-player', {
  preziId: "sk845xdbl9dn",
  width: 640,
  height: 480,
  controls: true,
  explorable: true
});
</script>
```

New terms and **important words** are shown in bold. Words that you see on the screen, for example, in menus or dialog boxes, appear in the text like this: "From the new sharing settings dialogue box, you can choose either the **Copy link** or **Add people** option to share the presentation."

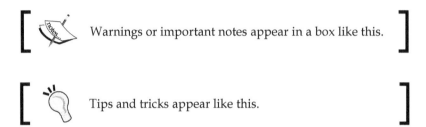

Warnings or important notes appear in a box like this.

Tips and tricks appear like this.

Reader feedback

Feedback from our readers is always welcome. Let us know what you think about this book—what you liked or disliked. Reader feedback is important for us as it helps us develop titles that you will really get the most out of.

To send us general feedback, simply e-mail feedback@packtpub.com, and mention the book's title in the subject of your message.

If there is a topic that you have expertise in and you are interested in either writing or contributing to a book, see our author guide at www.packtpub.com/authors.

Customer support

Now that you are the proud owner of a Packt book, we have a number of things to help you to get the most from your purchase.

Errata

Although we have taken every care to ensure the accuracy of our content, mistakes do happen. If you find a mistake in one of our books—maybe a mistake in the text or the code—we would be grateful if you could report this to us. By doing so, you can save other readers from frustration and help us improve subsequent versions of this book. If you find any errata, please report them by visiting http://www.packtpub.com/submit-errata, selecting your book, clicking on the **Errata Submission Form** link, and entering the details of your errata. Once your errata are verified, your submission will be accepted and the errata will be uploaded to our website or added to any list of existing errata under the Errata section of that title.

To view the previously submitted errata, go to https://www.packtpub.com/books/content/support and enter the name of the book in the search field. The required information will appear under the **Errata** section.

Piracy

Piracy of copyrighted material on the Internet is an ongoing problem across all media. At Packt, we take the protection of our copyright and licenses very seriously. If you come across any illegal copies of our works in any form on the Internet, please provide us with the location address or website name immediately so that we can pursue a remedy.

Please contact us at copyright@packtpub.com with a link to the suspected pirated material.

We appreciate your help in protecting our authors and our ability to bring you valuable content.

Questions

If you have a problem with any aspect of this book, you can contact us at questions@packtpub.com, and we will do our best to address the problem.

1
Understanding the Prezi Frame of Mind

Although it is certainly possible to use **Prezi** in a similar way to other presentation tools, such as **Microsoft PowerPoint**, Prezi opens up new ways of presenting that simply aren't possible with the other tools. While teaching others how to use Prezi, we have discovered that the biggest learning curve is not usually the technical aspect of how to use the tool itself, but rather how to understand and start thinking in what we call the Prezi frame of mind. Many of us have become so accustomed to the slides made prominent by PowerPoint that it's difficult to think outside of the box — literally outside of the box that makes up the slide. Prezi opens up our presentational possibilities in new and exciting ways. Just as important as learning *how to use* the technical aspect of Prezi is learning *how to think* Prezi. As we work through the technical elements, we will also reinforce how these elements can help us think differently about how to present.

In this first chapter, we will get an overview of what these different types of presentations look like, covering the following topics:

- Thinking about nonlinear presentations
- Planning your Prezi
- Mind mapping
- Deciding the BIG picture
- Common Prezi mistakes

Thinking about nonlinear presentations

As Prezi is so different to other presentation tools both technically and aesthetically, we need to ensure that we approach it in a very different way compared to how we might go about designing a PowerPoint presentation.

It goes without saying that a presentation designed in any media should have a good degree of planning first, but even more so in Prezi. The reason is that Prezi's infinite canvas gives you such a huge expanse of space that it is very easy to lose elements of your design within it.

By simply planning your Prezi in the right way, you can save lots of time in the design stage and really take advantage of this space.

Forget Slides

It's easy to keep using the term slides when building a Prezi, but slides don't exist in this software, and this kind of thinking will keep you stuck in the old way of presenting. Force yourself and your colleagues to use Prezi terms such as canvas and frames to break the mold and get yourself focused on the right type of approach.

You probably moved over to Prezi because you were getting tired and fed up with the rigid nature of PowerPoint or some other slide-based tool. You felt trapped and confined by the slides that only allowed you to deliver your presentations in one way, that is, in a linear fashion from beginning to end. Then, you saw Prezi and were blown away by the fact that it is a completely open canvas that doesn't have any walls or restrictions like slides do. In other words, it has a three-dimensional canvas as opposed to the traditional two-dimensional slide.

For some though, this fact can be very difficult to embrace and they very quickly return to the comfort of their slide-walled prisons because too much freedom scares them. They simply don't know how to use the space well to deliver their message. If you watch them closely, you will see that they try to build a **slideshow** in Prezi, and the way they think just doesn't match up with the way Prezi works.

These prisoners can easily be freed if they learn how to think and plan for Prezi, and we believe there are three key steps to master your Prezi designs, which we will explore later in this chapter.

If you ask any Prezi master why they love it so much, you might hear the words "nonlinear presenting" quite a lot. In order to master Prezi, it's important to know what a nonlinear presentation exactly means.

Linear presentations

If we want a presentation that teaches someone how to drive, then we will need to start with the absolute basics and build from there. This type of presentation will have to be linear and might have a flow similar to the following:

1. Unlock the driver's side door.
2. Get in and put your seat belt on.
3. Put your foot down on the clutch to check whether you are in gear.
4. Put the keys into the ignition.
5. Start the car.

The instructions would follow in a similar manner so that the task is carried out in the right way. This is a linear path, and any presentation built to visually represent it would have to start at step one and then move on to step two, and so on.

Information of this kind always needs to be presented in a linear fashion, so you can use PowerPoint's slide-based design or build a Prezi that uses a series of paths. Both will have clear start and end points.

Nonlinear presentations

What if your subject matter had several different areas or modules that didn't have to be presented in a certain order? Who decides where the *start* and *end* should be? You? Your manager? The CEO? We'll give you a clue. They're going to be sitting right in front of you during your presentation.

One of the main reasons why presentations don't hit the mark is because they don't consider which elements of the content are most important to their audiences. So why not ask them where they'd like to start? Or at least start your presentation with some friendly introductions; start a conversation and then find out what is the most important part of the topic to them. If enough people agree on the same area, then zoom straight into that area and get going.

This is a nonlinear and more conversational approach to presenting, and it is extremely easy to implement with Prezi.

The beauty of using this approach in Prezi is that it engages your audience more and lets the conversation you have with them unfold very naturally. Following is an example template of how you can structure your nonlinear presentation to cover five separate modules:

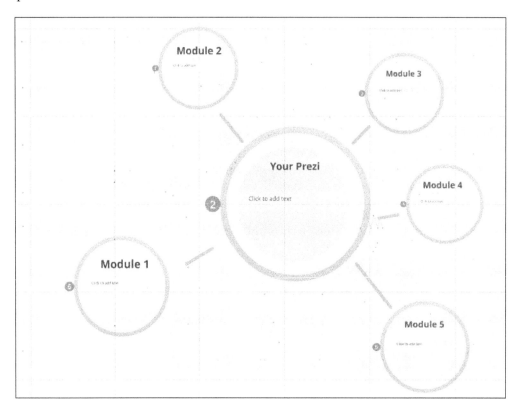

All of the modules are contained inside one giant circular frame, and each module's content is contained inside its own frame within that.

The best of both worlds

Even though a nonlinear approach is much more creative, there may be elements to your presentation that are best explained in a linear order for your audience to make sense of them.

If this is the case, you can join the different elements of your Prezi together with paths. This gives you the benefit of allowing your audience to decide the direction of your presentation (nonlinear), but also the opportunity to break down key points into a logical order (linear).

Using Prezi's paths tool with this method, your presentation might look similar to the one shown in the following screenshot:

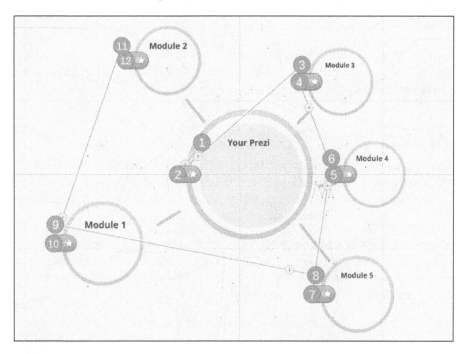

If your audience decides that they would like to start on **Module 3**, simply zoom in to that frame using your mouse. This can be done quickly by clicking on the desired frame or title. After this, you can let the paths take over so that you flow through the content of **Module 3** in a linear manner if needed.

Think for Prezi

We already mentioned previously that Prezi can (and should) be used in a nonlinear way, but most of us are so used to the linear method of PowerPoint and other slide-based tools that we find it very hard to break out of that mold and use this crazy nonlinear concept.

By thinking in the old linear slide-by-slide way, you can end up with what looks like a PowerPoint presentation, but with some fancy transitions in between slides. If you end up with a presentation like this, then you might as well have continued using PowerPoint because you're not taking full advantage of what Prezi has to offer. Realizing that your presentation's movement doesn't just have to go from left (slide 1) to right (slide 2), but that it can also zoom in to detail and back out to show an overview of everything, will unlock a whole new world of presentation mastery to you.

There's no doubt that to master Prezi you need to learn two things:

1. The Prezi software
2. The Prezi mindset

Simply knowing what all the buttons do isn't enough to become a Prezi master. You must ensure that you take the time to train your brain to think differently as well. Failing to do so will kill a Prezi design.

Planning your Prezi

If your boss asks you to build a presentation on that new business idea you mentioned to them at the Christmas party, you are bound to get very excited indeed. Then, if they ask whether you can present the idea to the board in an hour's time, you slowly start to melt in your chair.

Most people would grab a strong coffee, open up their copy of Prezi, insert images, text, video, and anything else they can find to help explain their idea. They would then link the key elements together with paths and be happy that their Prezi will really communicate their idea enough to get a good result.

A Prezi master, on the other hand, would not even dream of touching the Prezi software until they knew exactly how their Prezi was going to deliver their idea, which imagery to use, and what the key messages are. In fact, if they had one hour to build a Prezi, they would probably spend the first 15-20 minutes planning and the rest of the time actually building their Prezi. This is because they've taken the time to learn the three design steps to build a Prezi presentation.

One of these employees will get booted out of the boardroom for giving their senior management team motion sickness, and the other gets commended for delivering a wonderfully clear picture of their business idea. We're pretty sure you know who belongs to which category.

 Ensure that you master the design steps explained in the following section. It is one thing to know the software, but to build really great presentations, you must go about the design in the right way.

The three Prezi design steps

The three-step approach explained over the next few pages is aimed at helping you get the most out of Prezi. By ensuring that you follow the three steps, you'll start to think in the right way, understand the key messages in your design, and also build the Prezi in a sensible and time-efficient way.

The three steps are:

1. Planning your Prezi.
2. Getting the style right.
3. Building in layers.

Failure to use this approach can get you frustrated during the design process and will make you lose track of everything on your canvas, waste valuable time, and/or you end up creating something that's sure to deliver motion sickness to your audience.

To master Prezi, you must master these steps.

Step 1 – planning your Prezi

The first design step is without a doubt the most important of all. Taking the time to plan your Prezi will give you a clear vision of exactly what it is that you need to say or show to your audience in order to deliver your message.

Things you need to know

There are some questions you should always ask yourself at the start of any Prezi design:

1. What's the overall message I'm trying to get across?
2. What must people know by the end of my Prezi?
3. Are there any smaller key messages along the way that will help to make my point?
4. Will my Prezi be led by a presenter such as myself, or will it be accessed by people online?

Answering these questions before you start can give you a really good understanding of what your Prezi needs to say and how it can be said.

Step 2 – getting the style right

Have you ever been in a presentation and spent too much time trying to figure out what the image on screen means rather than what the actual message from the presenter is? Anything visual in your presentation can be extremely powerful for the audience, or it can be extremely distracting and can cloud the importance of your message.

Let's briefly look at some of the unique features of Prezi that can help us start planning from a Prezi perspective.

Zooming

Prezi's **zooming** feature can help you deliver your message in a powerful way when it's used correctly. It's simple to create such a zooming effect technically, and we'll look at how to do that. However, first, it's even more important to think about why you're zooming. You don't want to simply zoom in and out just because you can easily do so. What will your zoom communicate? Let's take a look at an intentionally strong use of zoom to understand how this can be done:

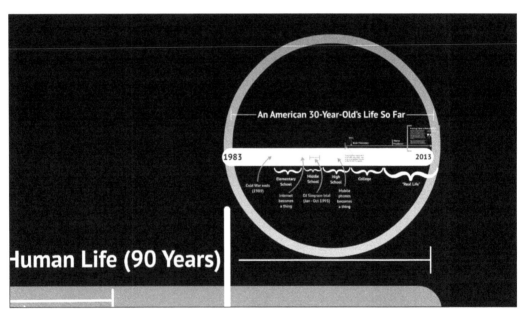

Screenshot from Putting Time into Perspective by Prezi Jedi

In this Prezi, the viewer starts by seeing the events that have shaped the life of a contemporary American who is 30 years old. The Prezi then zooms out further through each step of the presentation, revealing a larger time frame with each step. It finally ends with the time frame of the **Behaviorally Modern Humans**:

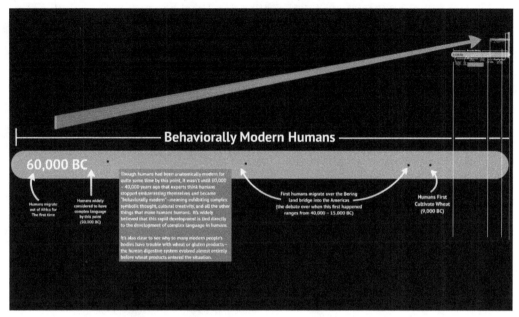

Screenshot from Putting Time into Perspective by Prezi Jedi

The original frame from Prezi is way up at the very top right corner now, way past the tip of the gray arrow—so small that you can't even see it. Here zoom is used intentionally to demonstrate how difficult it is for humans to conceive of time. You can see this effect in action and get the full impact at `https://prezi.com/veychlhwrdgz/putting-time-in-perspective/`.

Obviously, not every Prezi will be able to use the zoom feature in this way, but this style of zooming reflects the Prezi frame of mind that is so important to the design process. As part of your design process, ensure that you ask, "How will I use zooming in my Prezi?"

Frames

In *Chapter 3, Consistent Branding for Business*, we will look at how we can create templates that will allow us to reuse elements of the design we create for our Prezi. For now, though, the important thing is to start thinking in terms of **Frames** rather than slides. Although there are a lot of similarities, Prezi has decided to use the name frames to help emphasize the **3D** nature of their canvas.

Prezi offers a few different ways to create frames. If you are looking to completely custom design your frame, you can use the **frame menu** option near the top-left corner of the Prezi window:

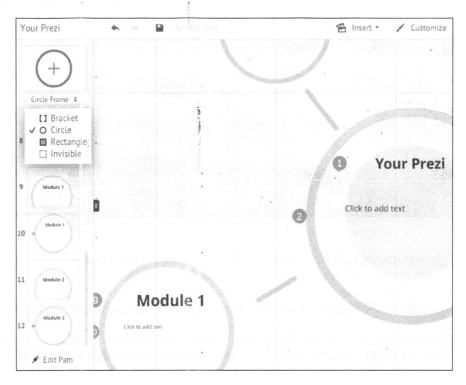

Prezi offers four different default frame styles: **Bracket**, **Circle**, **Rectangle**, and **Invisible**. The **Invisible** frames can be used to help determine the path layout of a presentation, but won't be seen by when the Prezi is used in presentation mode. All of the others will be visible at all times. You can see grey circle frames used in the preceding example of Prezi.

If you're looking for a bit more direction, Prezi offers the option to insert a layout, which is a frame with predefined areas to insert elements such as text and images. To access this, go to the top tool bar menu and navigate to **Insert | Layouts...**. This brings up a tool bar on the right that allows you to insert either single or multi-frame layouts.

Multi-frame layouts offer a wide range of options that have been used in popular Prezi templates. These include layouts that can be used either as part of a larger Prezi, or even as an entire presentation in itself, such as the timeline frame or the tip of the iceberg frame pictured here:

This template actually makes great use of both the frame and zooming features because the presentation can start as zoomed in at the very top, showing a more straightforward understanding of an issue, and then zoom out to the entire iceberg to reveal that there's actually much more complexity to an issue below the surface.

The key to your planning process is to realize that frames are liberated on a **3D** canvas in a way that slides in PowerPoint are not.

In a PowerPoint presentation, slides are sequential and always have to be just to the right or left of one another. However, frames can be placed anywhere, and their actual positions relative to one another can help create meaning in your presentation, as with the tip of the iceberg shown earlier. Making use of this new space can be challenging but it's also an opportunity to allow your creativity to flourish.

Step 3 – building in layers

Now comes the easy part. Taking the Prezi design, you've designed in *step 1 – Planning your Prezi*, add all of the imagery and styles from *step 2 – Getting the style right*, and put it all together on the Prezi canvas. It's a piece of cake right?

We're pretty sure that every Prezi user comes unstuck now, and this is again because they rush into the canvas and try to add everything at once. This can lead to certain elements getting lost because you zoomed in too far and then back out again, or you might find that your Prezi doesn't end up looking quite like you'd planned.

A piece of cake

In order to help you in this final step, we want you to think of making your Prezi in the same way that you'd make a delicious Victoria sponge cake like the one shown in the following image:

Once you've got all of your ingredients from *step 1 – Planning your Prezi*, and *step 2 – Getting the style right*, you should build your Prezi in the layers listed here.

The bottom layer of sponge

If you're going to have some kind of background image that sits behind everything in your Prezi, then you must insert this onto your canvas before anything else. You may want to start your Prezi by zooming in to a small part of a much larger image that will be revealed at the end. In this case, ensure that it's the first thing you insert.

In the example shown in the following image, the Prezi starts in the top-left corner of the **iPad** screen at path points **1** and **2**. The audience is then taken through the Prezi path, which is all contained inside the screen of the iPad. It is only when the audience reaches path point **12** that the Prezi zooms out to reveal the background image:

This example can be viewed online at http://prezi.com/yl9_u5si57pp/prezi-ipad-freedom/.

 The technique of revealing an eye-catching background image at the end of your Prezi is known as the **BIG picture technique** and is explained further at the end of this chapter.

Cream and jam

Now that you have your first layer of sponge in place, you can start to add those tasty ingredients and spread them right across your Prezi canvas. Yummy!

The cream and jam of your Prezi might include some or all of the following items:

- Text
- Images
- Graphs
- Video files (including sound)
- YouTube clips
- Flash animations
- Frames

If you've planned your Prezi well enough in *step 1 – Plan your Prezi*, then you should have a good idea of where to place each of these elements on your canvas.

We'd encourage you to place the separate elements at slightly different angles from one another so that the canvas turns a little during transition. Again, try not to overcook this as too much spinning can make people feel ill.

If you do need to adjust the position of any object at this stage, just right-click on it and use the **Send Backward** or **Bring Forward** options, as shown in the following screenshot:

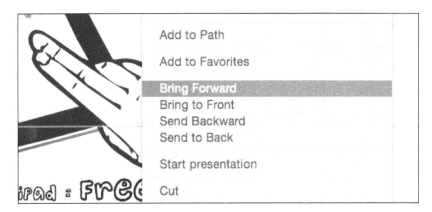

The top layer of sponge

Once you have your background imagery (bottom layer) and your different elements (cream and jam) on the same canvas, the only thing left to do is join them all together with paths so that your Prezi flows in the correct order.

 As we already mentioned, your Prezi design might not need a path if you're using a conversational presentation method. So, for some, this step might be optional.

It can be extremely difficult and frustrating to try to adjust paths when things need to be moved around on your canvas, so ensure that you are totally happy with the position of your cream and jam before adding this top layer of sponge.

Once you've added your paths, we strongly recommend that you take your Prezi into show mode and test that everything looks and tastes great.

The steps, again

We highly recommend that you master these three design steps as they will really help you to achieve great results and visualize the design before you even touch the Prezi software.

Knowing what you want to achieve from your Prezi at the start is crucial. It's extremely easy to get lost in the Prezi canvas and waste time looking for missing objects, so adding this very structured and logical approach will really help.

As a reminder, the three Prezi design steps are as follows:

1. Planning your Prezi.
2. Getting the style right.
3. Building in layers.

Once you master these steps, building any Prezi will be a piece of cake.

Don't get caught out

When building a Prezi for your business, you'll no doubt be under serious time constraints, have other work that needs your attention, and probably have a number of distractions around you. Don't allow yourself to skip over these steps because you think there isn't time. They'll actually save you time in the long run if used correctly.

Mind Mapping

You may be familiar with the term **Mind Mapping**, and if not, we'd definitely recommend that you look it up to get help with designing your Prezi. We'll explain it in the following screenshot in more detail, but it's definitely a subject that Prezi masters will want to explore more in their own time.

In essence, Mind Mapping is a way of spreading your ideas onto a piece of paper or any canvas available instead of just writing a very dull (and linear) list of what's needed in your Prezi presentation. You can see a very simple example of Mind Mapping in the following diagram, which we created to help us understand how to best communicate the three Prezi design steps in this chapter:

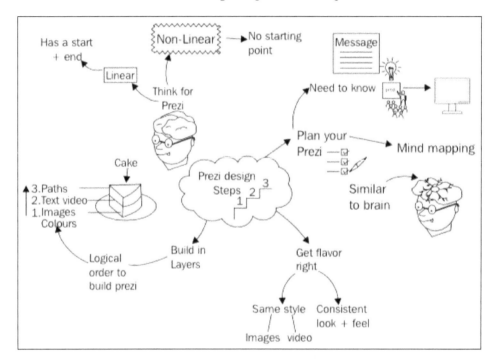

 You can see that this Mind Map uses words and pictures to make associations. This is extremely important when planning a Prezi because the more visual, the better it is for your audience.

Writing a list

If you aren't used to using the Mind Mapping technique, it can be a little hard to understand why you should start now and not just write a list of what needs to go into your Prezi.

We already mentioned that Prezi is a nonlinear presentation tool, so it makes perfect sense to plan your Prezi in a nonlinear way. Forcing yourself to plan in this way and spread your ideas out onto one page will start to give you a great idea of how your Prezi will look because Prezi itself is one giant canvas.

[Writing a list to plan your Prezi will encourage you to construct it in a very linear fashion like you would construct a PowerPoint presentation]

Starting with the tool

Mind Mapping is an amazing tool for generating and planning ideas, but it does take practice. If you haven't done it before, then start now by following the instructions given here:

1. Grab a pen and paper, and start by writing the subject of your Prezi, that is, *My business*, in the center of your page.

2. Circle the title and link any subheadings or important subjects that spring to your mind around it with arrows. These could be your company departments or products.

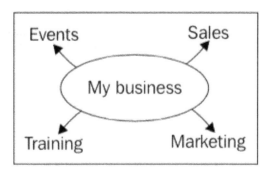

3. Then, focus on one sub heading at a time and write any key information you can think of around that. Again, link each point back to its heading with arrows or lines.

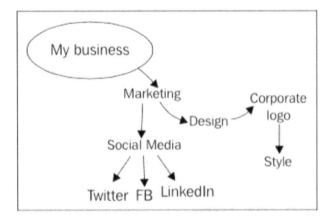

4. Keep repeating these steps until you either run out of things to write, or you find the key points to explain in your Prezi.

 Try to avoid using ruled paper as it may encourage you to start writing a list instead of a Mind Map.

5. Once you identify the key points that need to be presented in your Prezi, underline them or highlight them in some way so that they stand out from everything else.

6. For each of the key points, try to think of an image that will help visualize it and do a quick sketch of the image. It doesn't have to be a work of art!

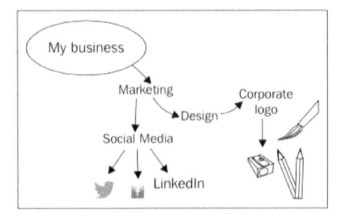

If you aren't familiar with the Mind Mapping technique, then try to go through the preceding steps as many times as you can, and for as many subjects as you can think of.

This form of mental exercise will help you think in the right way for Prezi, and will also help your brain make connections between the text and imagery on your map.

There are also plenty of great free digital Mind Mapping tools that you can find through a quick Internet search. Even better — you can use the Prezi canvas itself as a Mind Map along with the arrows and shapes you can insert.

Working efficiently with Prezi

We already mentioned that Mind Mapping is great for planning Prezi because they both use a canvas in the same way. However, there is another more scientific explanation as to why this technique and Prezi work so well in communicating ideas.

This connection is related to the way that our brains retain information. While the inner workings of the human brain aren't yet fully understood, we do know that ideas form when the brain creates neural networks between the vast amounts of information that goes into our heads every day.

When presenting to an audience, the best way to get them to remember something is to zoom in on individual details one at a time, then try to show them some kind of link between these details, or at least show them all of the details in one single view and frame them for our audience.

This simple trick is called the **BIG picture technique** and is explained in the next section. In short, it is simply a way of allowing your audiences' brains to connect the dots and retain the information you want them to.

Map your journey

Ensure that you spend enough time as is needed to fully plan out your Prezi in a Mind Map. Some people will find this very easy and natural to do, while others may struggle to think in this way. Whichever end of the spectrum you fall into, ensure that you keep doing it and never approach the Prezi software until you have your map in front of you. This will help to ensure that you approach your design from a Prezi frame of mind.

By doing this, you'll know:

- What are your key points?
- What are the images you need to tell the story?
- How big your Prezi might be?
- Where you will need to zoom in to explain details?
- What could visually link everything together (your BIG picture)?

Change your mind

To help you perfect the art of Mind Mapping, try to use it to plan other things in your work and life, not just your Prezi designs. It is such a powerful tool and can really help you explore possibilities in any area that you decide needs a little focus.

Deciding the BIG picture

By taking all of the skills you learned so far and combining them with a great way of delivering your Prezi, you're bound to be viewed as a Prezi master by colleagues and bosses alike.

The BIG picture technique is a way of presenting your information to an audience so that they can understand how different elements link together. It enables you to structure your message in a way that will be more memorable to your audience, giving your business Prezi a much higher impact than the traditional presentation tools.

The science behind it

The brain is made up of tiny nerve cells called neurons, these neurons have tiny branch-like structures that reach out and connect with other neurons. Each place where a neuron connects with another neuron is called a synapse or synaptic connection. The pattern and ways our neurons connect to each other form our neural network. These networks form our ideas, thoughts, and memories.

Think of these neural networks in the same way as the mind maps we looked at earlier. Our brains take in thousands of tiny stimuli every second. In a presentation, the stimuli would normally be images, words, and sounds from the presenter and the group we might be sitting with. Our brains take everything in and connect the dots with neural networks between each piece of stimuli. Where a connection is made, an idea is formed.

In the traditional slide-by-slide approach to presenting, it is more difficult for the brain to make connections. This is generally a downside to the way presentations are put together, that is, it's hard to connect a concept on slide 2 to something on slide 50 an hour later.

As Prezi gives us such freedom to move around the canvas and zoom in and out of different elements, it's very easy for us to present in a way that aids the brain in creating neural networks. This, in turn, leads to our Prezi's messages being remembered for longer and in more detail than by using slides.

Neural networks in action

In order to explain how Prezi can help build neural networks, what better tool to use than Prezi itself? If you have an Internet connection while you're reading this, you can go to http://prezi.com/vuf5fbirwjke/big-picture-thinking/ and refer to a Prezi explaining this concept. If you don't have an Internet connection, refer to the screenshots we added of the same Prezi.

If you follow the steps explained here when constructing your Prezi, you are bound to deliver a much more powerful message:

1. Show your audience the first piece of information.

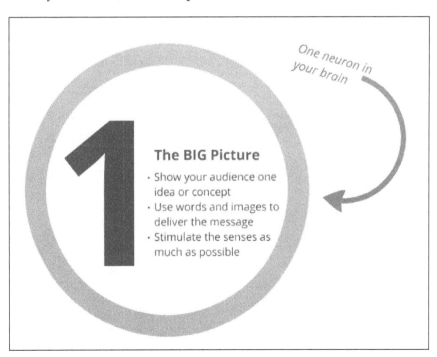

2. Move to the next piece of information; don't rush things.

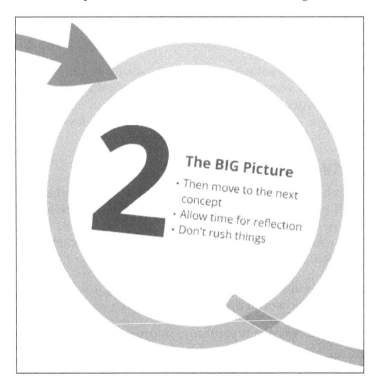

3. Move along again until you've covered all the key elements.

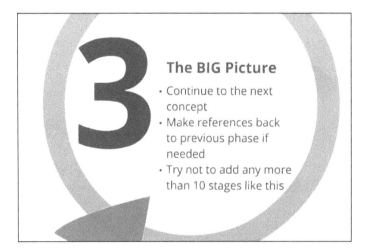

4. Zoom out to show all of the key elements and their relationships in one view.

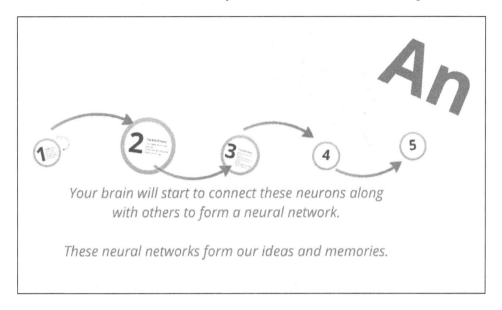

5. You can zoom out again to display even more relationships between the information.

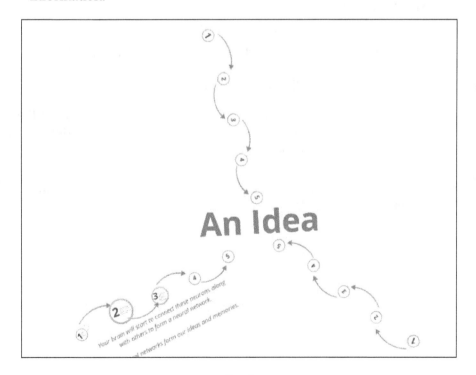

6. Your audience will remember the relationships and understand the BIG picture.

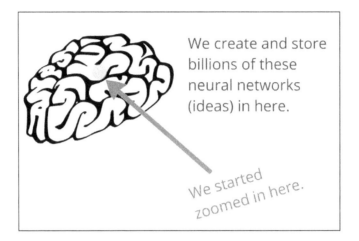

 You can create a copy of the preceding Prezi online at `http://prezi.com/vuf5fbirwjke/big-picture-thinking/` to store it in your own Prezi account.

This Prezi explains how to help create the neural networks discussed using the BIG picture technique itself.

You can see how at the start we are already zoomed in to one neuron of the brain, and then we slowly move outwards. The previous two images clearly show the connections between everything that we previously saw in the Prezi.

In the final frame of the Prezi, we zoomed out completely to see an image of the brain. This is the BIG picture view for this particular Prezi, as it clearly demonstrates that everything we've been seeing happens inside the human brain.

 If you can deliver every message in your presentation in this way, then you will truly be a Prezi master.

How to find your BIG picture

If done correctly, you should start to see your BIG picture form in the planning stage of your Prezi (*step 1 – Planning your Prezi*). By using the Mind Mapping techniques explained earlier, you will start to see connections between the different elements of your Prezi. At this stage, you should ask yourself the question "What single image could sum up the links between everything?"

It might be difficult to find the right image, and in some cases, it might need a combination of images together. However, the key messages along the way should all be delivered inside of the BIG picture.

The BIG picture in reverse

You can also try using the BIG picture technique in reverse order. Show the BIG picture at the very start of your Prezi, then zoom in to the details and explain the relationships.

To help you practice finding images that sum up a series of different elements and link them together, have a go at completing the following table. Hopefully, you'll start to get much better at this with time—if you master the three Prezi design steps, of course!

				What image would you use to connect everything?
Book	Cream	Glasses	Towel	
Mushrooms	Dough	Tomatoes	Cheese	
Revenue	Client base	Contract	Projects	
Employees	Salaries	Sick Leave	Grievances	
Club	Tee	Ball	Sand	

Common Prezi mistakes

Now that you're starting to think in the Prezi frame of mind, you'll be able to pull together some of these strategies to start creating your own BIG picture Prezis. Before you do so, we have one last note of caution. It's incredibly easy to get carried away by excitement with some of the awesome Prezi tools at your disposal. We inevitably see some of these things popping up during every Prezi training session. If you can avoid these common mistakes, you'll be one step closer to becoming a Prezi master.

Motion sickness

One of the biggest attractions to Prezi is the zooming and spinning that happens when transitioning from one element to another. This movement is so smooth and fluent that it's normally the first thing to make people sit up straight and say *Wow this is great, how do you do that?*

The danger with this is that people then go off and create their own Prezi with as many spins and zooms as they can because they think it looks so great that their presentation is bound to be talked about for ages by their colleagues.

Their Prezi will only be talked about for one reason, and that's because after 20 minutes of all the spinning and zooming, people had to leave the room because they fell ill. Especially when viewed on large screens, this extreme use of zooming and spinning has been known to literally cause actual motion sickness.

The spins and zooms you can create in Prezi can be very useful in helping you to tell your story, especially if used cleverly by slowly revealing words or zooming in to find hidden details, as we discussed earlier. On their own, they have no impact at all and do not help the audience retain any information.

 Don't rely on the zoom to tell your story. You, your content, and some subtle clever use of Prezi will do that, not a 360 degree rotation between each key point!

The blank canvas challenge

Staring at a blank canvas can be much more intimidating than a blank slide. Precisely because there is more freedom, there is also much more to consider. When you're sitting there with the blank canvas staring back at you, it can be easy to resort to a style with which you're more comfortable. We've seen too many new Prezi users to count who have performed either of the following actions:

- Resorted back to laying out their presentation exactly as if it were a PowerPoint.
- Just started placing text and images randomly across the canvas, with no plan.

In the first scenario, you're falling back into a linear way of thinking, and not taking advantage of the additional opportunities afforded by the Prezi platform. In the second, it's easy to think you're designing a great nonlinear presentation, but without a solid plan, you end up zooming, panning, and rotating around the screen for no good reason. Many people who claim they don't like Prezi have only seen it used in these ways.

 Don't even open the Prezi canvas until you have a plan ready. This will help ensure you're not overwhelmed or distracted by staring at the blank canvas.

Going too big

It's easy to get so excited about the new presenting opportunities afforded by Prezi that you want to make use of every single one of them and create the single best presentation in all of history. Slow down, though.

That may happen in time, but if you're creating your first business presentations, it's much better to keep things simple in the beginning. Use some of the features you're most comfortable with first. Your Prezi will look much better if it uses one Prezi design strategy well, rather than many of them poorly. Keep it simple and expand to try new things as and when you're comfortable with them.

Summary

This chapter introduced us to Prezi, and gave us a chance to master some of the nontechnical elements. This is an element of the software that is either forgotten or just not given any thought at all by most Prezi users. However, it is just as important as learning what each button does inside the software itself and some people would even argue that it's more important than knowing the software.

As you start working on your Prezi, remember that you'll need to think ahead about the purpose of your Prezi, make sure that you achieve the appropriate style, and utilize the 3D features of the Prezi canvas as you build your own Prezi.

Using the Mind Mapping technique to help you plan your nonlinear Prezi will get you on the right track for the BIG picture thinking that we've practiced in this chapter. Ensure that you master the techniques in this chapter and align the way you think and plan a presentation to the way that Prezi works. Once you've created a Prezi using these steps, you'll be able to serve up a delicious, multilayered Prezi that makes you look like a total superstar to everyone in your business.

In the next chapter, we will transition to the technical side of Prezi with a hands-on look at the technical mechanics of Prezi.

2
Hands-on with Prezi Mechanics

Now that you have got a feel for the Prezi frame of mind and what it's like to design on this new canvas, you're probably ready to start trying out some of your ideas. In order to achieve this, we'll take a look at some of the main tools Prezi offers to build a presentation using their software. These tools really make up the core of what Prezi is, and they help it stand out from the other presentation software options. You'll learn how to bring your Prezi to life with paths that connect your content and create motion in your presentation. We will discuss:

- Templates
- Paths
- Shapes
- Grouping
- The Text editor
- Animations
- 3D backgrounds
- The present button

Templates

We always face constraints when creating a business presentation, most often in the form of an impending deadline. If you do find yourself against the clock when building a Prezi, then why not give yourself a slight advantage and use one of Prezi's templates to get your design started? There are lots of templates you can choose from and we'll consider how to make the most out of them when the clock is ticking.

Additionally, using these templates is also a great way to start familiarizing yourself with Prezi and its mechanics. Filling in some elements in a template is much less daunting than creating something new from a blank canvas. The basic design and structure of the presentation is already created, and you can fill in the details and make changes to the structure where needed. Although the very best Prezis are typically the ones created from scratch, it makes sense to familiarize yourself with the capabilities of Prezi by creating at least a few that are based on templates.

Using templates

When you create any new Prezi online or in the desktop editor, you'll be presented with a choice of templates, as shown in the following screenshot:

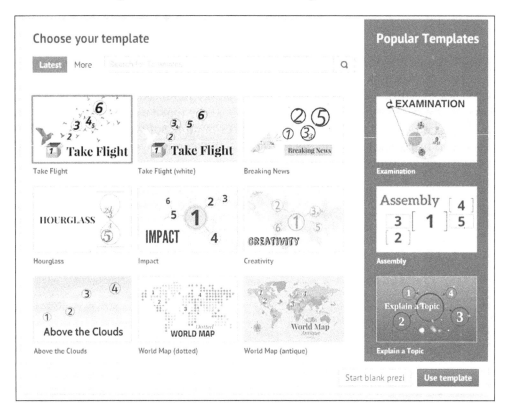

By default, the newest templates are displayed on the left, and the most popular templates on the right. However, you can also click on the **More** button to get the full list of available templates, or search for a template based on a key word.

When you see a template you'd like to use, you can either double-click on it to open it or click on it once, followed by clicking on the **Use template** button. From here, you can also opt out of any template by clicking on **Start blank prezi**.

Unfortunately, it is no longer possible to preview a template beyond its thumbnail image before you select one. However, if you open up a new Prezi theme and decide it's not for you, it's easy to delete your selection and create a new one. When you're at the **Your Prezis** tab, you can delete any Pezi by hovering over it and clicking on the Trash Can icon in the upper-right corner of the Pezi you'd like to delete:

Getting the most from templates

Once you go into edit mode, don't think that you're stuck with how everything is laid out. You can (and should) move things around to fit with the message you're trying to deliver to your audience.

Paths

The **path** is the tool in Prezi that helps you arrange the order you will move through your presentation. In PowerPoint, you can only move from one slide to the one immediately following or preceding it. If you're moving through paths in Prezi, you still go in order, but you can move anywhere in the Prezi, rather than being forced to stay in close spatial proximity to the last point on your path. Additionally, it is possible to revisit a previous point in the path without having to duplicate the content in order to expand on or emphasize something that may already have been covered. In addition, you can stop following a path at any time and choose to freely scroll or zoom around the canvas.

Creating motion

Paths are incredibly important in Prezi because this is the tool that actually allows us to create the motion for which Prezi is so well known:

This presentation is available at: https://prezi.com/hddprjo5hc5a/running-amooc/

In the preceding example, each number represents the order of the path that has been created. The first point is a frame that surrounds the entire presentation. So when this presentation is started, you would see everything pictured, as shown in the preceding screenshot. Step **2** of the path is the first circular frame. In moving from path step **1** to path step **2**, Prezi automatically creates a zoom effect, as it moves from the full view, shown in the preceding image, to just the frame, as shown here:

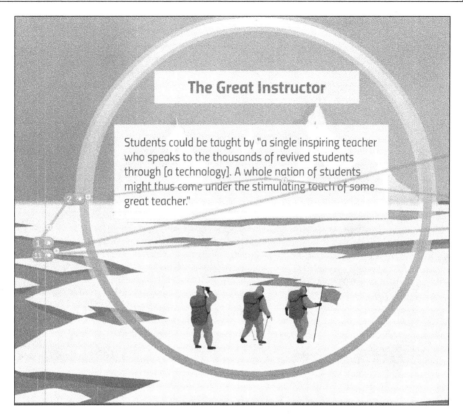

The Great Instructor

Students could be taught by "a single inspiring teacher who speaks to the thousands of revived students through [a technology]. A whole nation of students might thus come under the stimulating touch of some great teacher."

The spinning effect can be created in a similar fashion. If you rotate the element in one of the paths of the step, Prezi will rotate the entire canvas as it moves between the path points so that the content is displayed upright. This creates the **spin** effect.

 Just remember not to overuse these features, or else you'll be at a risk of inducing motion sickness, which we discussed in the last chapter.

Note the rotated content here:

Adding, removing, and editing

The very first thing we would suggest when opening a template is clicking on the **Edit Paths** button and taking a look at how the Prezi flows. The whole reason you're using a template is because you're pushed for time, but you should know how many frames you need and how many different areas you'll want to focus on in your presentation before you get started. If you do, then you can adjust the paths, add new path points, or delete some that are there already.

To add a path, you can simply click on any frame or content. When you hover over one of these elements before clicking on it, it will show a slightly lighter path step, as step **13** appears here. Once you click, it adds it as a new step at the end of your current path:

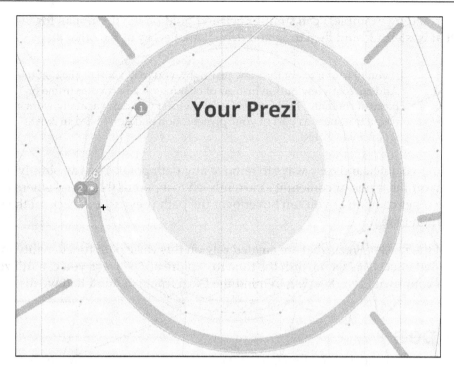

If you want that step in the path placed somewhere else, you can simply drag and drop it in the **path editor** on the left-hand side of the screen:

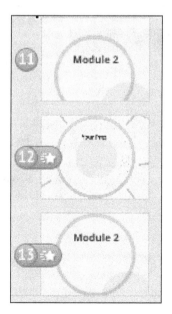

In the preceding example, I can simply click and hold on the thumbnail for the new step, that is, step **13** , and then drag and drop it above any of the other steps.

 If you're trying to get the view just right, you may want to click on the **Add current view** button instead of clicking on a particular frame or piece of content. This is particularly useful if you don't actually want a frame to appear as part of your presentation and don't need to create an invisible frame.

There are two quick and easy ways to remove any path point. You can simply drag the point off the frame or content it's currently on to a part of the screen where there isn't any other content, or you can hover over the path preview and click on the red cross button to remove it.

Many of the master Prezis that are created rely on this basic path functionality to create good effects. It's well worth the time to explore all the ways you can utilize paths in your own Prezi, keeping in mind the Prezi frame of mind that we discussed.

Shapes

A very simple element of the Prezi that gets overlooked a lot is the **Symbols & shapes...** option, which is available in the **Insert** menu. In this part of the chapter, we'll look at some things you may not know about how shapes work within Prezi.

After clicking on the **Symbols & shapes...** option, a new menu will appear on the right-hand side of your screen, allowing you to select from various types of symbols and shapes. If you click on **Shapes** from here, you'll be able to access and easily add the standard shapes such as triangles, circles, and rectangles.

 Using these shapes along with the **Draw arrow** and **Draw line** option available in the **Insert** menu in Prezi can allow you to create custom designs or **doodles** in Prezi that can help your presentation stand out. Try to create your own simple drawings whenever you can, as these can be reused over time and will, in turn, save you lots of time searching for imagery via other means.

Get creative

In the following screenshot, I've created a very basic doodle of a male character using the shapes available in Prezi:

 You can also use empty circle frames in place of the actual circle shape if you don't want it filled with a particular color.

Let's say that we want to add some more detail to the male character. Maybe we'll give him a more exciting hairstyle to replace the boring one that he has at the moment.

1. First, select the current hairline and delete it from the character's head.

2. Now, select the Draw line tool from the Insert menu and give this guy a flat top, straight from the 80's, as shown in the following screenshot:

3. One of our lines is too long on the right. To adjust it, simply click on the line to enter edit mode and drag the points to the right position as shown in the following screenshot:

So, there we have a great example of how to quickly draw your own image on the Prezi canvas by just using lines. It's an excellent feature of Prezi, and as you can see, it's given our character a cute new look.

 If you want to reuse any shape, it's easy to copy and paste. For example, once I created the line for the longest piece of hair on the left, I copied the line and moved it to the right-hand side of his head so I could reuse it.

Editing shapes

In step 3 of giving our character a new haircut, you saw the edit menu, which is accessed by a simple click. You can use the edit function on all items in the **Shapes** menu. Any shape can be clicked to change its size and color, as shown in the following screenshot:

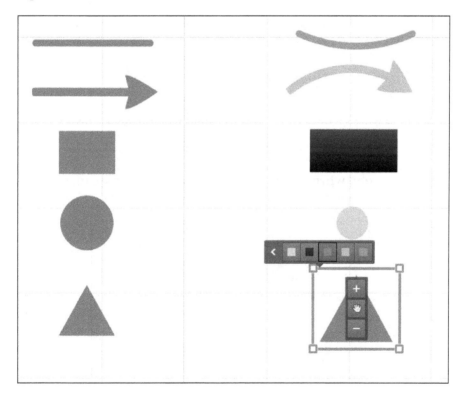

You can see that all of the shapes on the left have been copied and then edited to change their color and size. The edited versions on the right have all been clicked and one of the five extra available colors has been selected. The points of each shape have also been clicked on and dragged to change the dimensions of the shape. To make a shape larger or smaller, you can click and drag one of the corners, or click on the plus or minus buttons as seen in the preceding figure.

Editing lines

When editing lines or arrows, you can change them from being straight to curved by dragging the center point in any direction:

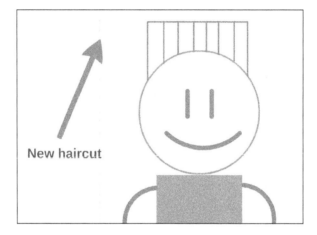

This is extremely useful when creating the line drawings we saw earlier. It's also useful to get arrows pointing at various objects on your canvas:

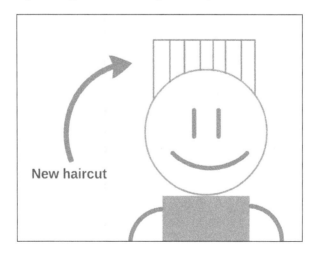

Styled symbols

If you're on a tight deadline, or trying to create drawings with shapes simply isn't for you, then the styles available in Prezi may be of more interest to you. These are common symbols that Prezi has created in a few different styles that can be easily inserted into any of your presentations. You can select these from the same **Symbols & shapes...** option from the **Insert** menu where we found the symbols. You'll see several different styles to choose from on the right-hand side of your screen.

Each of these categories has similar symbols, but styled differently. There is a wide variety of symbols available ranging from people to social media logos. You can pick a style that best matches your theme or the atmosphere you've created for your presentation.

Instead of creating your own person from shapes, you can select from a variety of people symbols available:

 Although these symbols can be very handy, you should be aware that you can't edit them as part of your presentation. If you decide to use one, note that it will work as it is – there are no new hairstyles for these symbols.

Highlighter

The highlighter tool is extremely useful for pointing out key pieces of information such as an interesting fact. To use it, navigate to the **Insert** menu and select the **Highlighter** option. Then, just drag the cursor across the text you'd like to highlight. Once you've done this, the highlighter marks become objects in their own right, so you can click on them to change their size or position just as you would do for a shape.

To change the color of your highlighter, you will need to go into the Theme Wizard and edit the RGB values. We'll cover how to do this later when we discuss branding.

Grouping

Grouping is a great feature that allows you to move or edit several different elements of your presentation at once. This can be especially useful if you're trying to reorganize the layout of your Prezi after it's been created, or to add animations to several elements at once. Let's go back to the drawing we created earlier to see how this might work:

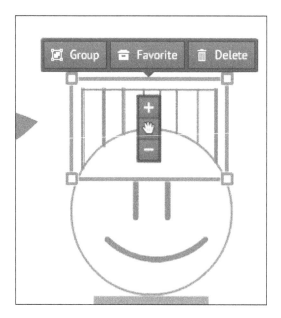

The first way to group items is to hold down the *Ctrl* key (*Command* on Mac OS) and to left-click on each element you want to group individually. In this case, I need to click on each individual line that makes up the flat top hair in the preceding image. This might be necessary if I only want to group the hair, for example:

Another method for grouping is to hold down the *Shift* key while dragging your mouse to select multiple items at once. In the preceding screenshot, I've selected my entire person at once. Now, I can easily rotate, resize, or move the entire person at once, without having to move each individual line or shape.

If you select a group of objects, move them, and then realize that a piece is missing because it didn't get selected, just press the *Ctrl+Z* (*Command+Z* on Mac OS) keys on your keyboard to *undo* the move. Then, broaden your selection and try again. Alternatively, you can hold down the *Shift* key and simply click on the piece you missed to add it to the group.

If we want to keep these elements grouped together instead of having to reselect them each time we decide to make a change, we can click on the **Group** button that appears with this change. Now these items will stay grouped unless we click on the new **Ungroup** button, now located in the same place as the **Group** button previously was:

 You can also use frames to group material together. If you already created frames as part of your layout, this might make the grouping process even easier.

Prezi text editor

Over the years, the Prezi text editor has evolved to be quite robust, and it's now possible to easily do all of your text editing directly within Prezi.

Spell checker

When you spell something incorrectly, Prezi will underline the word it doesn't recognize with a red line. This is just as you would see it in Microsoft Word or any other text editor.

To correct the word, simply right-click on it (or *Command* + Click on Mac OS) and select the word you meant to type from the suggestions, as shown in the following screenshot:

The text drag-apart feature

So a colleague of yours has just e-mailed you the text that they want to appear in the Prezi you're designing for them? That's great news as it'll help you understand the flow of the presentation. What's frustrating, though, is that you'll have to copy and paste every single line or paragraph across to put it in the right place on your canvas.

At least, that used to be the case before Prezi introduced the drag-apart feature in the text editor. This means you can now easily drag a selection of text anywhere on your canvas without having to rely on the copy and paste options. Let's see how we can easily change the text we spellchecked previously, as shown in the following screenshot:

In order to drag your text apart, simply highlight the area you require, hold the mouse button down, and then drag the text anywhere on your canvas.

Once you have separated your text, you can then edit the separate parts as you would edit any other individual object on your canvas. In this example, we can change the size of the company name and leave the other text as it is, which we couldn't do within a single textbox:

Company:
My Great Presentation

Building Prezis for colleagues

If you've kindly offered to build a Prezi for one of your colleagues, ask them to supply the text for it in Word format. You'll be able to run a spellcheck on it from there before you copy and paste it into Prezi. Any bad spellings you miss will also get highlighted on your Prezi canvas but it's good to use both options as a safety net.

Font colors

Other than dragging text apart to make it stand out more on its own, you might want to highlight certain words so that they jump out at your audience even more.

The great news is that you can now highlight individual lines of text or single words and change their color. To do so, just highlight a word by clicking and dragging your mouse across it. Then, click on the color picker at the top of the textbox to see the color menu, as shown in the following screenshot:

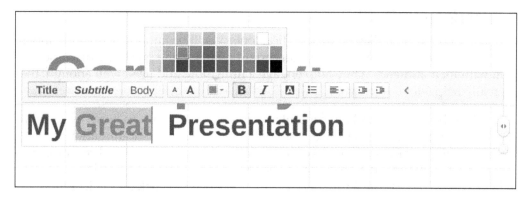

Select any of the colors available in the palette to change the color of that piece of text. Nothing else in the textbox will be affected apart from the text you have selected. This gives you much greater freedom to use colored text in your Prezi design, and doesn't leave you restricted as in older versions of the software.

Choose the right color

To make good use of this feature, we recommend that you use a color that completely contrasts to the rest of your design. For example, if your design and corporate colors are blue, we suggest you use red or purple to highlight key words. Also, once you pick a color, stick to it throughout the presentation so that your audience knows when they see a key piece of information.

Bullet points and indents

Bullets and **indents** make it much easier to put together your business presentations and helps to give the audience some short, simple information as text in the same format they're used to seeing in other presentations. This can be done by simply selecting the main body of text and clicking on the bullet point icon at the top of the textbox.

This is a really simple feature, but a useful one nonetheless. We'd obviously like to point out that too much text on any presentation is a bad thing. Keep it short and to the point.

 Also, remember that too many bullets can kill a presentation.

Animations

If you've used any slide-based presentation tools, you'll be familiar with animations. They are normally used to slowly reveal certain points as the presenter discusses them with their audience. They help engage a little more and used well enough, they can really help tell your story.

Prezi offers the option to fade in content as a functionality that can be accessed while editing the path. And that's it—users can only fade in as no other animations are available. This can be done from two different locations, either the path thumbnail previews on the left-hand side of the screen, or from the path step displayed on the main canvas. To access the animation features, you need to click on the icon that looks like a shooting star, as seen here:

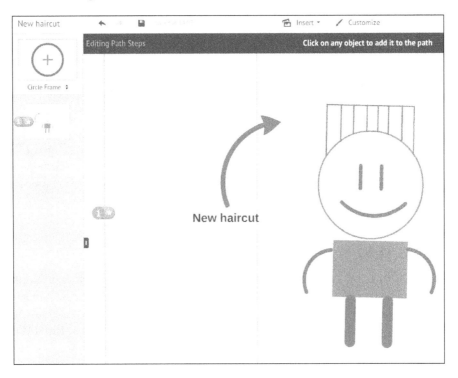

Now, when you hover over an item, a green shooting star appears. You can click on each element in the order that you want it to fade in. Let's take a look at an example here:

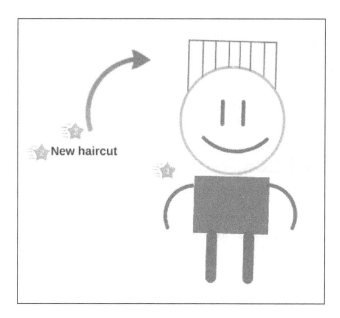

In the preceding example, our character has already been grouped, and I clicked to make him fade in first. You can see the text **New Haircut** will fade in second, and with one more click, the arrow will fade in last.

If you click on things in the wrong order, you can simply click on the **Reset** button and start over. To see if the animation works as you planned, you can click on the blue play button in the top-right corner to see a preview. Once you're happy with the animations you created, you can click on **Done**.

When you're presenting your Prezi in presentation mode, Prezi will move through each path point as normal when you click to advance, but then it will fade in each element one at a time with the click of the advance button. Once all of the elements in that step have been faded in, it will move to the next step of the path when you press the advance button again.

Animating bullet points

If you'd like to animate bullet points, you need to ensure that you create each bullet point in a separate textbox. Then you add an animation effect to each box.

3D backgrounds

You can easily add instant atmosphere to any Prezi using a 3D background. The hardest part is selecting one or more images that will work well. Once you upload the images, Prezi takes care of the 3D effect and parallax movement for you. Let's take a look at how to do this.

 You should use images that are at least 3000 pixels so that the background doesn't become pixelated as you zoom in on it.

A single 3D background

Creating a single 3D background is quick and easy:

1. Click on the **Customize** button on the Prezi menu. This will create a new menu on the right-hand side of the screen.

2. The first option on this new menu is for a background image. Click on the **Choose file...** button to bring up the file selection screen.

3. Select the file you would like to use as the background and either double-click on it or select **Open**.

4. Voilà! You now have your first background image.

As you scroll around the canvas, you'll be able to see that there is now a parallax effect. The items you've added to your Prezi move more quickly in relation to the background image.

The following is the *Save the Ocean* by *Guilherme Criscuolo* Prezi:

This Prezi *Save the Ocean* by *Guilherme Criscuolo* uses an ocean floor background to create atmosphere. In this screenshot, the text and turtle are elements that have been added to the presentation. Everything else is part of the background. When moving between path points, it almost looks like the turtle is moving through the ocean.

 To see this for yourself, visit `https://prezi.com/pgh5a3xbuicm/save-the-ocean`.

Multiple 3D backgrounds

If you want to use more than one background image, Prezi will automatically layer them for you. The process is similar to adding just one image, but requires a few extra steps:

1. Click on the **Customize** button on the Prezi menu. This will create a new menu on the right-hand side of the screen.

2. Scroll down to the very bottom of this new menu and click on the **Advanced...** button. This brings up a new **Theme Wizard** menu.

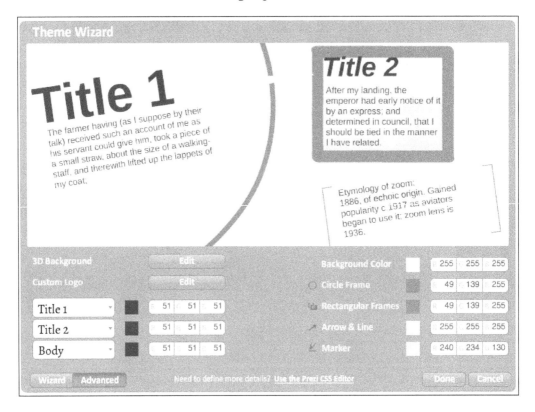

3. Ensure that you are in the **Advanced** menu section by clicking on the button at the bottom-left of this menu.

4. Next, go to the **3D Background** text and click on **Edit**. You're now at a screen where you can upload up to 3 background images.

5. Click on **Upload** to browse for your first file to upload. You will see a thumbnail of the background once it's uploaded, and can now upload a second image.

6. Once you've uploaded at least two backgrounds, you can click on the **Done** button to finish. You'll need to click on **Done** in the Theme Wizard as well to return to the canvas and view your new background.

These new background images will be layered based on the level of zoom used. In other words, the first image is displayed when you are zoomed out. As you zoom further in, this background image will fade into the next one.

Using backgrounds

Changing backgrounds can be particularly effective when you're trying to highlight a point or change in the story, or affect the atmosphere of your presentation. This is achieved particularly well by background images that are significantly different in color. For example, moving from a dark background to a light background can create a strong impact at an important turn of events in your presentation.

3D backgrounds can quickly and easily add a professional polish to any presentation. Yet, there is also a lot of room to be creative in more advanced uses of these backgrounds, such as hiding surprise elements that can only be found if a user manually moves around your Pezi.

The Present button

While you're still editing a Prezi, the present button is located near the top-right corner of the menu and is what we use to put our Prezis into show mode to check whether they look okay during the design phase. It is used later, of course, when our Prezis are actually being presented. One helpful option is the ability to have the Prezi move automatically through each of the path points.

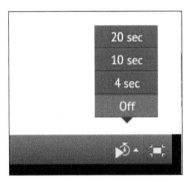

Once in presentation mode, the bottom-right corner of your Prezi will have a full screen button and a play sign on top of a stopwatch icon. Clicking on this stop watch icon will give you the following options:

- 4 seconds
- 10 seconds
- 20 seconds

You can use these to select the timing you'd like your Prezi to play at.

This is useful for presentations that don't have a presenter to talk through them. They might be shown in your company's reception on a flat screen, or at a trade show for people to see. However and whenever you decide to let your Prezi play on its own, ensure that you get the timings right so that people can see and read everything without having to wait until it loops again. Additionally, these timings will be applied to any animation effects that have been added. If, for instance, you have animated bullet points, viewers will need to wait for the selected number of seconds before each bullet point comes into view.

 When designing Prezis to play on their own in this way, ensure that you pay close attention to the amount of zooming and spinning in your design. Motion sickness can be intensified when someone is overly focused on the screen in front of them.

Summary

In this chapter, we discussed the basic mechanics of Prezi. Learning to combine these tools in creative ways will help you to move from a Prezi novice to a Prezi master. Templates allow you to use the designs created by the Prezi team and edit them to your liking. Paths link together your content and determine the order of the information you will present. Shapes can be used creatively to create content and drawings, and can be grouped together for easy movement and editing. Prezi also features basic text editing and fade-in animations that can add an extra layer of polish to your presentation. A 3D background can also help your presentation stand out. Finally, the present button is what makes all of this magic come to life!

One great thing about being a Prezi user is that there is a lot to look forward to in the future. Prezi has consistently added new features and tweaked its design capabilities based on user feedback. As Prezi is accessed via the Internet, it's very likely that some of its functionality may have changed by the time you have this book in your hands! Just ensure that you put every new feature to good use, and make it work for you to save as much time as possible. Also, if there's a feature you'd really like to see, don't hesitate to send your suggestion in to Prezi!

In the next chapter, we'll look at how to create a consistent branding in Prezi for your business.

3
Consistent Branding for Business

Now that we've had some hands-on experience with some of the mechanics native to Prezi, it's time to start thinking about how we can reuse some of the elements that we design. Most businesses, for example, have logos and color schemes that are applied consistently to media such as documents and websites.

In PowerPoint, you might create a template slide that can be reused for all business presentations. A very common template might have a bar across the bottom of the slide in one of the company colors, with the company name in the bottom-right corner.

As Prezi can be so much more dynamic than the traditional slide, we're not going to have a template that is quite that straightforward. However, there are many reusable elements that we can create to help bring consistent branding to our presentations. In this chapter, we'll discuss the following topics:

- Color schemes
- Customizing Prezi graphics through CSS
- My Content
- Custom logos

Color schemes

The first thing you'll want to tweak in your Prezi when you're tailoring it for your business is the color scheme. Clicking on the **Customize** button on the Prezi menu will bring up a menu on the right that allows you to select from several color themes that have already been created. For many presentations, these may work well enough:

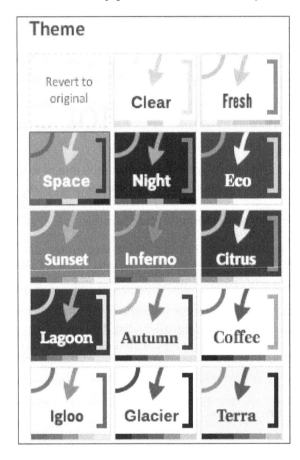

Despite these options, you might find that none of the themes offered by Prezi match the colors that are used by your business. Luckily, we can create our own color scheme rather easily.

The steps to create our own color scheme are as follows:

1. If you scroll past the generic color schemes created by Prezi, you can click on the **Advanced...** button that will allow you to tweak the colors for your presentation. This will bring you to the Wizard version of the advanced theme settings. On the first screen, you will be able to change the background color or upload a 3D background or custom logo. We'll come back to the custom logo a bit later.

2. By clicking on the **Wizard** button, then selecting **Next**, you can access options to change the fonts and colors for text. On this Wizard screen, you can change colors by clicking on a standard menu. On the **Advanced** menu, you can change the colors by changing the **RBG** values. Clicking on **Next** one final time allows you to edit colors for frames, arrows, lines, and the highlighter:

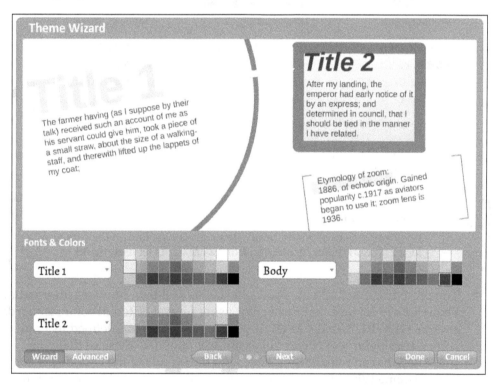

3. In the **Theme Wizard** menu, you are limited to selecting from only 30 different colors, and these will likely be sufficient for many uses. However, large businesses and organizations often specify color palettes in order to ensure consistent branding across various media. For example, my university wants to ensure that the same shade of red is used in all official material created for the university, and they specify the exact parameters of that shade on the website:

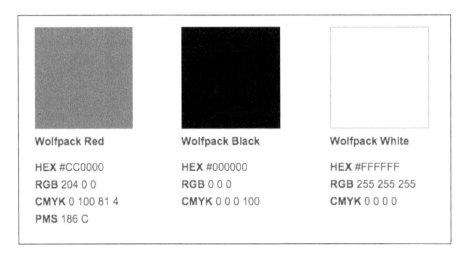

Wolfpack Red

HEX #CC0000
RGB 204 0 0
CMYK 0 100 81 4
PMS 186 C

Wolfpack Black

HEX #000000
RGB 0 0 0
CMYK 0 0 0 100

Wolfpack White

HEX #FFFFFF
RGB 255 255 255
CMYK 0 0 0 0

Color scheme for North Carolina State University taken from `http://brand.ncsu.edu/color/`

Color Selection

If your brand doesn't specifically define its colors, look at the company logo and draw color inspiration from what has been used there!

4. The preceding color scheme shows the colors and then provides information about how to achieve that exact color using several different color standards such as **HEX**, **RGB**, and **CMYK**. If your organization has defined its branded colors in a similar way, Prezi can easily accommodate these so that your presentations can remain consistent with the brand. At the bottom-left corner of the **Theme Wizard** menu, you'll need to click on the **Advanced** button:

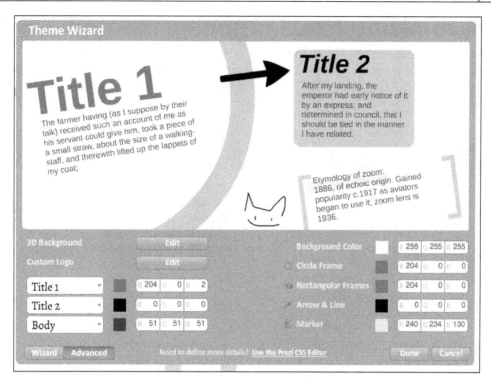

5. This menu allows you to enter colors by their RGB value, which was one of the standards specified in the branded colors shown earlier. Here, I entered these values into the **Advanced** menu for the titles and frames. The basic color scheme for any text or frames in this Prezi now reflects the branded color scheme for my university.

If you really want your presentation to stand out, we can customize the standard Prezi graphics even further using the Prezi CSS editor linked at the bottom of the Theme Wizard!

Customizing Prezi graphics through CSS

In the preceding screenshot, you may have noticed the link at the bottom of the window that allows you to define more details through the Prezi **CSS** editor. Don't worry if you're not familiar with CSS—we're going to walk through the basics together.

CSS stands for **Cascading Style Sheets**. It is a markup language that allows the style of a page to be coded separately from the content of the page. So, for example, one style sheet file can be applied to every page of a particular website.

 If a website does not use CSS and you decided to change a design element, such as the color used for headings, someone would need to edit the HTML code for each heading. However, if those headings were designed with reference to a style sheet, one would simply need to change a single line in the style sheet, and every heading on the site would automatically be updated. Style sheets make the design process easier and more flexible.

CSS works with Prezi in a very similar way to how it would with any other website. You can change just a few lines of CSS to change the style of an entire Prezi. This is so much easier than going through and making style changes to every single element that you would like to appear differently.

 Editing the CSS for your Prezi can really help your presentation stand out. Not only is this something that the average Prezi user is unlikely to use, but it allows you to make changes that would not be possible within the graphical interfaces Prezi has designed for editing.

Let's take a look at a couple of examples so that we can understand the potential impact of editing the CSS and hopefully get some creative ideas flowing.

When you click on **Use the Prezi CSS Editor** from the **Theme Wizard** menu, you'll see a new window on the right-hand side of your screen:

```
Edit CSS                              ✕
@font-face
{
src: url('Arimo-Regular.keg');
font-class: body;
fontFamily: body;
font-style: normal;
font-weight: normal;
}

@font-face
{
src: url('Arimo-Bold.keg');
font-class: head;
fontFamily: head;
font-style: normal;
font-weight: bold;
}

@font-face
{
src: url('Arimo-BoldItalic.keg');
font-class: strong;
fontFamily: strong;
font-style: italic;
font-weight: bold;
}

@font-face
{

Help on Prezi CSS                  Apply
```

Here, you'll see the actual code for the style sheet being applied to Prezi. Don't worry if you've never coded before. CSS uses some keywords that are fairly easy to recognize. For example, you probably noticed the word font in the preceding screenshot. Even if you don't know exactly what all of the code means, you can determine that this section of code is related to styling the font. Let's take a look at how we can change the font using the preceding code.

Be extra careful when you're editing the CSS. There's no **undo** button for the coding changes you make. A good idea is to copy the text you're editing into a text editor so you can refer to it if something goes wrong, or if you want to change back to the original code. However, don't stress too much! In the worst case scenario, you can always create a new Prezi and copy the original CSS code from that into the one you're working on, restoring it to default.

Editing fonts

Prezi uses four different styles for the font in the presentations. You can tell what these styles are by looking at the `font-class` property that's defined under each `@ font-face` section. In the preceding screenshot, you can see `body`, `head`, and `strong` font classes. If you scroll down, the fourth and last defined font class is actually an undefined class, which covers everything else.

Here's what a frame looks like with the default font for its heading:

Let's change this to something that's not normally available in the *16* default fonts that Prezi allows us to choose from in the **Theme Wizard**. You will find the following code in the editor, which is for the `font-class: strong`:

```
@font-face
{
  src: url('Arimo-BoldItalic.keg');
  font-class: strong;
  fontFamily: strong;
  font-style: italic;
  font-weight: bold;
}
```

We're going to change the actual font that's being used by editing in a new one:

```
@font-face
{
    src: url('TVBS-Handwritting.keg');
    font-class: strong;
    fontFamily: strong;
    font-style: normal;
    font-weight: normal;
}
```

You can see that on the `src: url` line, I replaced `Arimo-BoldItalic.keg` with `TVBS-Handwritting.keg`. Clicking on **Apply** will then change the font used in my frame:

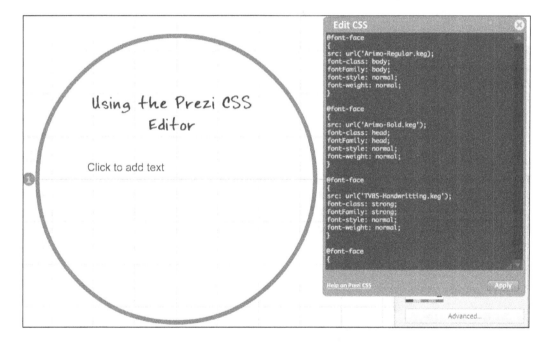

For a list of 1,000 different fonts that are available for use in Prezi, visit `http://www.vandijkcomputeropleidingen.nl/prezi-fonts`. You can try the different font names in the CSS code and see what they look like when you apply changes.

Editing a frame

We can also edit many other elements of our Prezi, though some of these changes require a little deeper understanding of the code. We'll explore how to add a border to a frame as a way to dig a little deeper into the CSS code. If you scroll further down the CSS sidebar, you'll find some code related to the circle frame that should look like this:

```
frame.circle
{
  borderAlpha: 0;
  borderColor: #333;
  borderThickness: 3;
  gradEndAlpha: 1;
  gradEndColor: #318bff;
  gradStartAlpha: 1;
  gradStartColor: #318bff;
  padding: 1.03;
  thickness: 3;
}
```

The name of this section of the code helps us understand that it relates to the circle frame, and some of the settings for the frame are also intuitive. Thickness, for example, will represent how thick the frame itself will be.

In order to add a border to our frame, the first thing we will have to do is change the value of borderAlpha. This setting affects how transparent the border is. The default setting of 0 means that the border is completely transparent, so even if we changed the color or made it thicker, we would still not be able to see it. You can set this to any value between 0 and 1. This means that 0.5 would be 50 percent transparent. In our example, if we change this value to 1, we can see that a black border appears on the frame:

After changing the value of borderAlpha, the code looks like this:

```
frame.circle
{
  borderAlpha: 1;
  borderColor: #333;
  borderThickness: 3;
  gradEndAlpha: 1;
  gradEndColor: #318bff;
  gradStartAlpha: 1;
  gradStartColor: #318bff;
  padding: 1.03;
  thickness: 3;
}
```

The output of the preceding code is as follows:

In order to match our earlier color scheme, let's create a white frame with a red border. You may have noticed that the CSS code doesn't use the same RGB color values that we used earlier, and instead uses the hexadecimal format. This is simply a different way to generate colors. It uses six numbers and characters as opposed to three sets of three numbers like RGB. Luckily, our corporate brand information also included the hex version of its colors.

 If you don't have or don't know the corresponding hex color code, you can use a search engine to easily find a hex color converter, for instance, http://www.color-hex.com is a useful place to start.

Next, let's change the border color to red. We'll do this by inserting the hex code #CC0000 as seen in the following code:

```
frame.circle
{
  borderAlpha: 1;
  borderColor: #CC0000;
  borderThickness: 3;
  gradEndAlpha: 1;
  gradEndColor: #318bff;
  gradStartAlpha: 1;
  gradStartColor: #318bff;
  padding: 1.03;
  thickness: 3;
}
```

The output of the preceding code is as follows:

Next, we will make the inner color of the frame white instead of blue. This will actually require two steps because we have to change both the `gradEndColor` property and `gradStartColor` property. If we change `gradEndColor` to #FFFFFF for white, we will see that the bottom half of the frame turns white and uses a gradient to fade in to the blue at the top:

```
frame.circle
{
    borderAlpha: 1;
    borderColor: #CC0000;
    borderThickness: 3;
    gradEndAlpha: 1;
    gradEndColor: #FFFFFF;
    gradStartAlpha: 1;
    gradStartColor: #318bff;
    padding: 1.03;
    thickness: 3;
}
```

The output of the preceding code is as follows:

Finally, we can change the `gradStartColor` property to #FFFFFF in order make the entire inside of the frame white:

```
frame.circle
{
  borderAlpha: 1;
  borderColor: #CC0000;
  borderThickness: 3;
  gradEndAlpha: 1;
  gradEndColor: #FFFFFF;
  gradStartAlpha: 1;
  gradStartColor: #FFFFFF;
  padding: 1.03;
  thickness: 3;
}
```

The output of the preceding code is as follows:

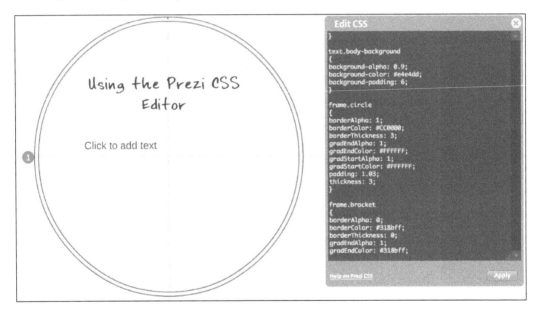

After clicking on **Apply**, you can see just how different the frame looks. You now have a look that wouldn't be possible through the **Theme Wizard** alone.

Of course, these changes are just the tip of the iceberg, and scrolling through the code you'll see you can edit other elements such as arrows, shapes, and even the highlighter. Using this CSS code, you can completely customize the Prezi to match your organization's brand and create a custom look not found in any other presentations.

My Content

The easiest way to get a consistent look and feel throughout different Prezis is to simply reuse frames that you've already created. The My Content feature of Prezi allows you to do exactly this. Why would you want to reuse something? Perhaps you've created a frame that summarizes your business and lists contact information. This is a frame that you can potentially use over and over again, especially if it's branded to match your business. Let's take a look at the following example to get a better idea:

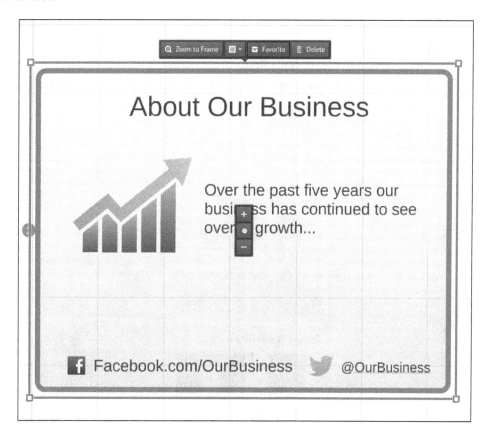

By clicking on a frame and then clicking on the the **Favorite** button, you will add the frame and all of its content to your collection that can be reused. From now on, you can navigate to **Insert** menu and select **My Content...** option to bring up a new menu that will allow you to access everything you have added as a favorite. Simply double-click on it to add it to the current Prezi.

As you can see here, the frame we added as a favorite earlier is now available to add to any future Prezi that we create. This feature, added in the updated version of Prezi released in Summer 2014, makes creating a consistent brand across Prezis very easy.

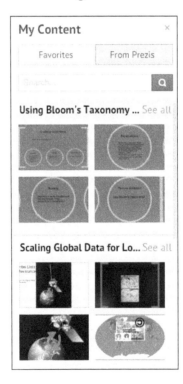

Note you don't even have to save something as a favorite to be able to reuse it. If you click on the **From Prezi** tab, you can pull up frames from any past Prezi that you've created.

Even More Favorites

In addition to frames, you can create favorites from almost any element that can be used in Prezi, including shapes, symbols, images, and even videos. However, remember that elements such as shapes and lines will default to the current CSS style assigned to your Prezi.

Custom logos

Uploading a custom logo can instantly add your brand's presence to any Prezi you create. Even better, it's quick and easy to do.

You need to have an Enjoy, EDU Enjoy, Pro, or EDU Pro account to be able to add a custom logo.

In order to add a logo, you'll need to click on the **Customize** menu, scroll to the bottom and click on the **Advanced...** button, and then click on the **Edit** button next to the **Custom Logo** menu.

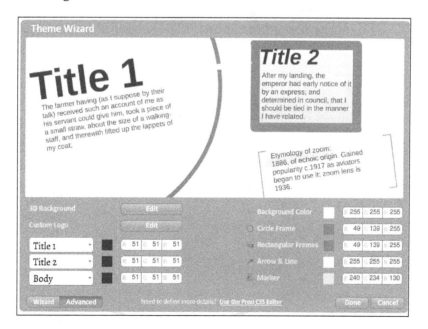

From here, you can simply browse your computer to select the file that you would like to upload. After uploading, you'll see a preview of your logo appear on the screen. Click on **Done** to go back to editing mode:

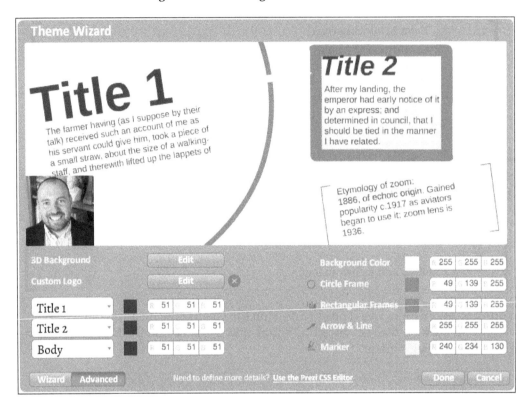

In this example, I have uploaded a picture of myself in lieu of a branded logo. Hopefully, you can see that there's also a lot of room for creativity with this logo element. A business's style guide often also defines the logo. The images that you can get from these guides are often of better quality than if you were to simply do an Internet search for the logo and upload the result. You won't be able to see the logo while you're editing, but it will stay in the bottom corner of your Prezi the entire time you are in the present mode.

Summary

In this chapter, we looked at how you can consistently brand your Prezis by changing the color scheme, editing the CSS code, using the My Content collection, and adding your logo. Each of these tools offers a way to create and reuse your branded content. Changing the color scheme is a quick way to include your company specific brand colors across an entire Prezi. The CSS code, in particular, offers an outstanding way to customize your Prezi and allows it to stand out. The My Content Collection and custom logo offer easy ways to reuse common graphics in your Prezi.

Going back to our discussion of BIG picture Prezi thinking, one last consideration for incorporating your brand is to design the structure of the Prezi itself around an element related to your business.

At this point, you might be excited about all that Prezi has to offer, but hesitant about fully make the switch because you have already spent a lot of time creating great PowerPoint presentations. In the next chapter, we'll look at how to import slides and use elements that you've already created using both PowerPoint and Keynote.

4
Importing Slides into Prezi

In this chapter, we'll look at importing slides into your Prezi canvas. The Prezi master in you is probably shuddering at the thought of importing those nasty linear slides into your beautiful non-linear infinite canvas, but in business, this is a necessary evil. Knowing how to deal with it, and also how to deal with colleagues who don't use Prezi, is a useful tool to have. If your business has relied heavily on PowerPoint slides in the past, there may be a great deal of excellent content within those slides. Rather than recreating everything from scratch or abandoning that wealth of information, it's important to learn how to best use it with Prezi.

The chapter will cover the following:

- Why you'd import slides
- How to import slides
- *Prezifying* your slides
- Things to look out for

The importance of slides

Every now and then, a colleague may ask you if you can import some slides into a Prezi canvas for them. It may be because they have a very important sales pitch to a big client, they're presenting to the board, they want to impress others with the new technology, or they just want to look good when presenting this quarter's figures to their team. However, they may not know how to use Prezi themselves.

If they have the slides already in **PowerPoint** or **Keynote**, then why oh why don't they just use those? Do they really think that importing slides into Prezi is somehow going to magically make their presentation better than it was without any extra time or effort?

If anyone ever asks you to do this, just smile and politely tell them you'll help, but then add the words "bear in mind that slides are still slides in any medium". When they then ask what you mean, you'll be glad you read this chapter.

Before we look at how to deal with this situation and *Prezify* slides, let's understand exactly why we won't be able to escape this in business.

Slide-based software and businesses

As upsetting as it may sound to us Prezi masters, it's true that slide-based software is entrenched in businesses. Slide-based presentations have been around for so long that businesses rely on them heavily to deliver important messages every day.

Because of this, we have to accept that your business isn't going to ban the use of PowerPoint overnight and roll out your new Prezi initiative tomorrow. If it did, our advice would be to run away very fast. Trying to convert just one person over to non-linear thinking is difficult enough!

Slides are definitely here to stay, but as a Prezi master, you have a great chance to convert colleagues to Prezi and slowly introduce it into your business.

 There's more advice on getting Prezi into your business in *Chapter 14, Getting Prezi through the Door.*

As someone who will need to put together presentations for your business, you are going to need data and information. If your business is like most, then chances are that you'll find all the facts and figures you need on a PowerPoint file somewhere.

It's for this reason you should appreciate the fact that all your colleagues use PowerPoint or Keynote. If something appears on a slide, then it's entirely possible to bring that element into your Prezi canvas.

 If you haven't already, then create a library of your colleagues' presentations and store them in one central location. That way, you'll always have useful data for your Prezis.

Converting colleagues to Prezi

Bob, the CEO, saw a presentation created in that Prezi thing you like and he wants you to 'jazz up' his slides for next week's product launch.

Sound familiar?

Another reason why you'll definitely have to work with slides is because Prezi's popularity is growing fast but your bosses and colleagues having time to learn and appreciate Prezi is not going to happen as quickly! However, some businesses are interested in moving toward 3D presentations because they are closer to reality.

We've heard lots of stories like this from Prezi users all over the world, so take some joy in knowing that you aren't alone out there. A lot of business users just see Prezi as something a little more eye-catching than the usual presentation and don't understand the principles of non-linear formats or BIG picture thinking.

You may be asked to *jazz up* some slides with Prezi from time to time, and, using the tips in this chapter, you'll be able to do just that. In addition to showing you how it's done, we've also highlighted some things to look out for along the way.

Importing slides into Prezi

Prezi lets you import PowerPoint slides from the **Insert** menu. To help explain how to use this feature, we'll use the PowerPoint slides shown in the following screenshot. They are very simple slides that have imagery, graphs, and text:

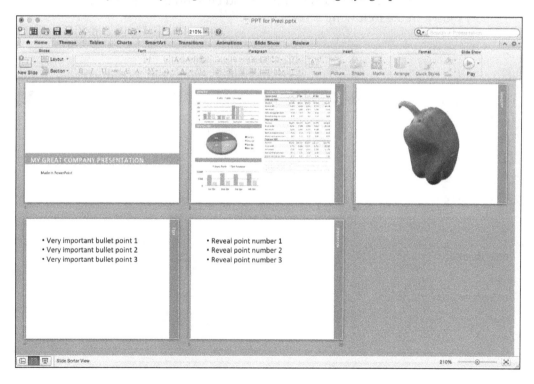

Once these slides are inserted onto the canvas, we will be able to manipulate all of the individual elements, such as text, images, and graphs. This is something that Prezi users weren't able to do for a long time and is another great example of Prezi listening to the needs of its users.

There are several different ways that one might go about importing PowerPoint slides into Prezi, and we will discuss each of these. By far the easiest, if it works correctly, is the built-in insert feature in Prezi. We will start with this method and then consider alternative options that can be used if the method does not work well. If you don't have a lot of time, you may want to skip directly to the later section on importing PowerPoint slides as **PDF** files.

The Insert PPT function

To import your PowerPoint slides into Prezi, follow these steps:

1. Click on the Insert menu and then the PowerPoint... option.

2. Select the PowerPoint slides to import and click on the **Open** button, as shown in the following screenshot:

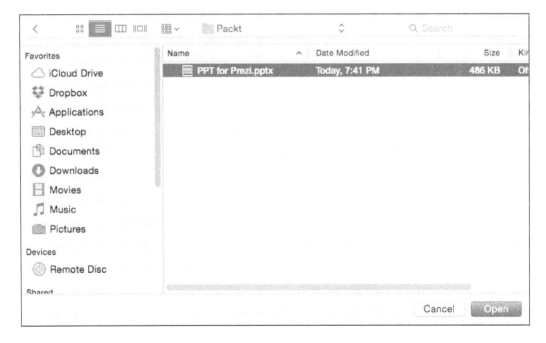

3. You will then see a sidebar appear on the right-hand side of your Prezi screen like the one in the following screenshot:

Do things look different?

Sometimes, imported PowerPoint slides won't look quite the same, especially if they are based on a template, as in the example we're using here. If that's the case for you, don't worry. We will discuss strategies for how to deal with these changes. You may also want to experiment with changing the template into a blank template before inserting it into Prezi.

4. Once all of your slides are loaded into the right-hand panel, you can either drag individual slides onto the canvas or click on the **Insert All** option at the top of the screen, as shown in the following screenshot:

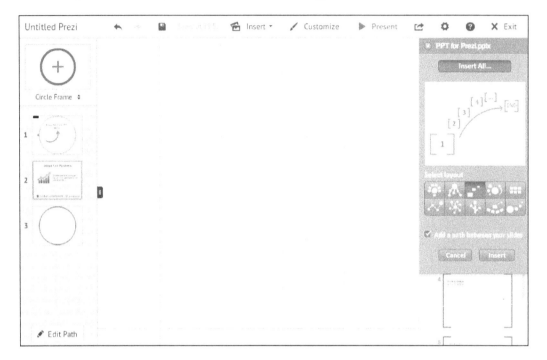

 Tick the box **Add a path between your slides** to save yourself some time later. You can also choose a layout for the frames that will be created based on these slides, creating an instant structure for your Prezi.

5. Now, position the slides container in the correct position on the canvas, as shown in the following screenshot:

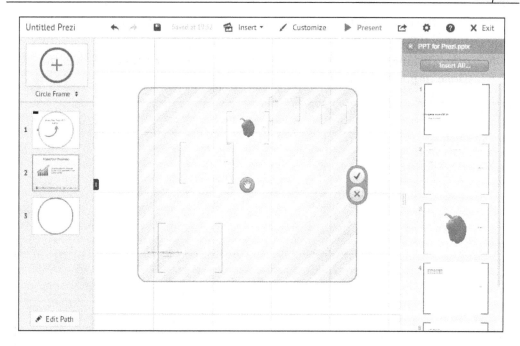

6.   When you are happy with the slides' positioning, click on the green checkmark to insert your slides:

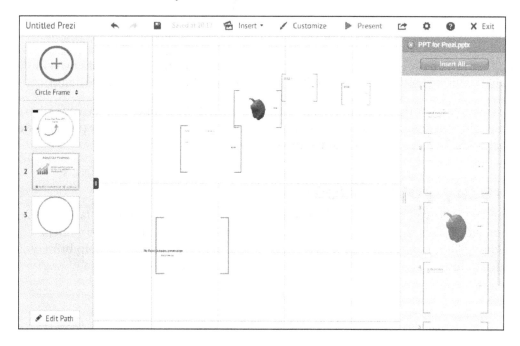

7. Close the import window by clicking on the **x** option that appears in the import menu.

8. After clicking on the **x** option, the following window appears. Select the **Close import** option:

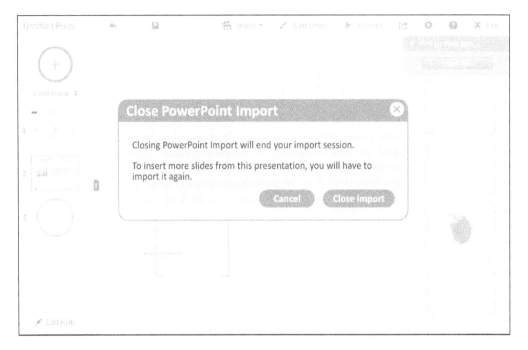

Make sure you only close the import once you have all of the slides that you will want positioned; otherwise, you will need to upload the PowerPoint file again.

Please remember that it is possible to drag individual slides onto the canvas rather than using the Insert All function. Clicking the green tick will finish the process and place slide 2 and all of its elements into our Prezi.

Prezify your slides

If you've followed the steps in the preceding screenshot, you can now start to Prezify your slides. This simply means adding a new dimension to what are very linear (slide-by-slide) presentations. Here, we'll look at a few simple tips to help bring your slides to life.

Checking the import

Looking at the frames that were created in the preceding import, one of the first things to jump out at you is how different these look from the slides that appeared in PowerPoint. At this point, you should take a minute to go through each frame and note the differences.

In the following example, most of the content is there, although the majority of the formatting has been removed:

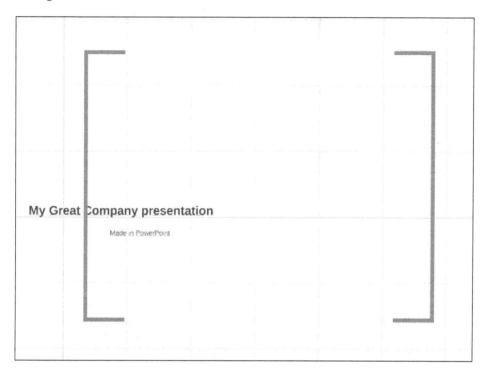

Here you can see that our first frame, based on the title slide, has text of two different sizes; however, all of the color formatting has been removed and the text is not placed within the correct area of the frame. As we'll see, some of the other slides did not fare as well.

Positioning content

You can see, on closer inspection of slide 1 in the preceding screenshot, that the frame is actually on top of the heading text as well. The title should read **My Great Company presentation**, but the **C** in **Company** is being overlapped by the frame.

This will likely be the case for all of your slides, so the very first thing you should do is make sure that all the content is positioned correctly. The simple use of right click and the Bring Forward or Bring Backwards options will enable you to get everything as it should be. I'm also going to make the text bigger. The final outcome can be seen in the following screenshot:

 If you have a large number of slides, this task will take a long time to complete. If your time is limited, you might want to skip to the last half of this chapter and look at the *Importing slides as PDF* files section.

Missing content

Depending on how the PowerPoint that you imported was formatted, you may have some content that did not survive the import to Prezi. In this case, you have a few options. You could import the slides as PDFs instead or manually important the elements that are missing. We'll show you how to do the manual import, but this decision should really be based on how many imports need to be done, how much time you have available, and how important it is to have maximum flexibility within Prezi.

Our second slide was supposed to contain all of the graphs from our PowerPoint template, as shown in the following screenshot:

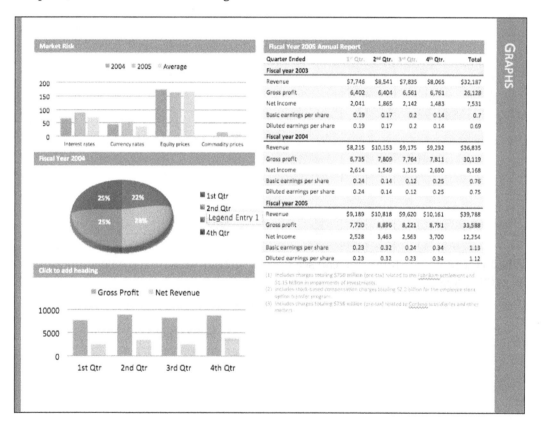

However, what we got from the Prezi import looks nothing like that:

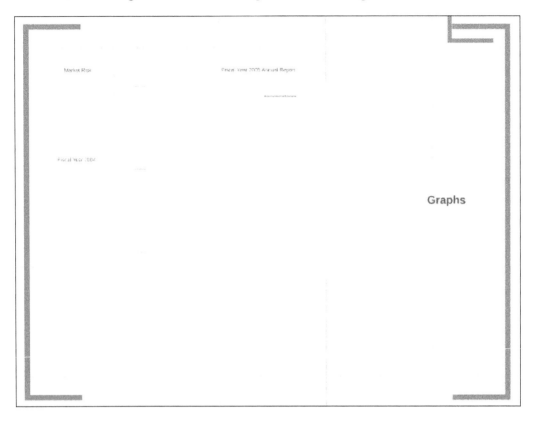

When you zoom in a little, you can see that the graphs seem to have been imported as garbled text:

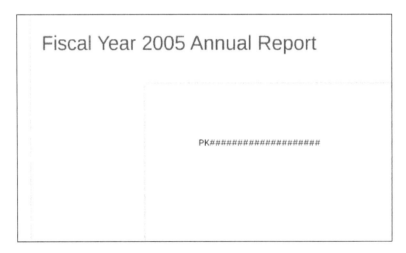

Let's fix this broken import:

1. First, we'll need to delete the elements that were imported incorrectly into Prezi.

2. Take a screenshot of the original PowerPoint content. You can either grab the whole slide at once or capture individual graphs, depending on how much flexibility you'd like in arranging them. Another option is to use the Save As feature in PowerPoint to export the slide as an image. This can work well if you want to capture the entire slide rather than just a particular portion of it.

> On a Mac OS, you can press *Command + Shift + 4* to allow you to draw a box and screen capture only what's in that box. In Windows, the way to take a screenshot can vary greatly depending on what version you're using, so you should use a search engine to determine what works best for your version. You may be limited to taking a screenshot of the entire screen rather than a particular portion, in which case you'll need to use image editing software to crop it to just the area you need.

3. Insert the screenshot by clicking on **Insert** menu and then select the **Image...** option.

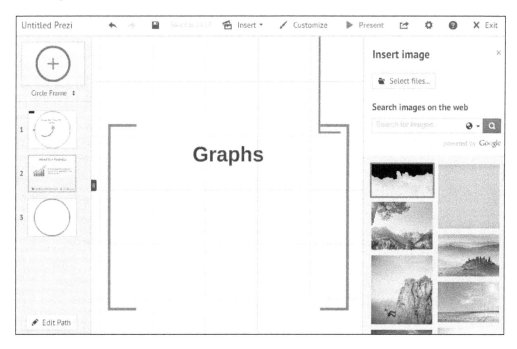

4. Next, click the **Select files...** option.

5. Reposition the images where you want them.

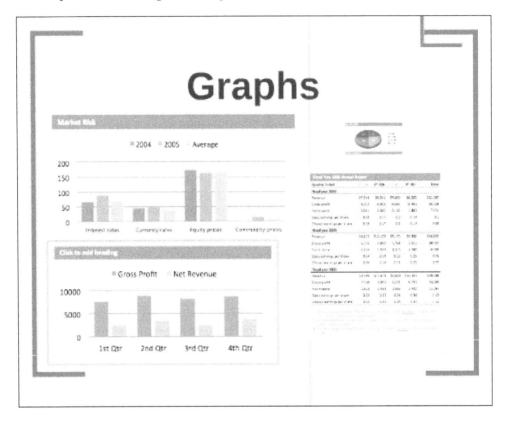

 The graphs don't all have to be sized so you can see them well at the initial zoom level. Remember, when you're setting the path, you can choose to zoom in on each individually if you'd like. Watch out though, because if you use a low-resolution screen shot, it might look fuzzy when you zoom in. Make sure you test your presentation!

Placing slides on to a Prezi canvas

At this stage in becoming a Prezi master, we hope you're starting to think about your presentations more in the non-linear sense and less in the straight lines of linear slide-based presentation techniques.

If that is the case, we'd like to think that the first thing you want to do when you see those slides appear is to move them around and spread them out a bit. You may have already selected a frame layout that works well, but this layout also may need some tweaking to work perfectly for your presentation.

> Remember you might want to zoom out and give an overview (a BIG Picture view) to your audience, so place the slides well in order to show any relationships between them.

The Prezi Insert PowerPoint... function will automatically place a bracket frame around each slide for you. This is extremely useful for moving slides around, and of course, linking them to a path. If your presentation can logically be broken up into different sections, then we'd recommend you group the slides for each section together in another bracket frame as well. This will make it very easy for you or whoever is presenting to zoom out and give an overview and then zoom into a particular section of interest.

Zooming in and out on slides

Of course, we'd recommend that you zoom into details as this will help give your slides an extra dimension. You might want to zoom in on imagery or text, but zooming can work particularly well with graphs that have been created in PowerPoint. It might also be beneficial to your audience if you use the fade-in transitions for graphs so that they aren't all displayed at once in a way that is overwhelming to the audience. This will give them the opportunity to digest each graph one at a time.

As we mentioned earlier, it's important to make sure that each of your graphics is of a high quality so that you can zoom in without creating a fuzzy effect.

High quality screenshots

Notice the difference in the crispness of the text from the first graph and the second one below it in the preceding screenshot? I zoomed in to 300 percent magnification in PowerPoint before taking the first one to make sure I got a higher quality image. If you're going to be zooming in on the graphs you've had to import as images, this is especially important.

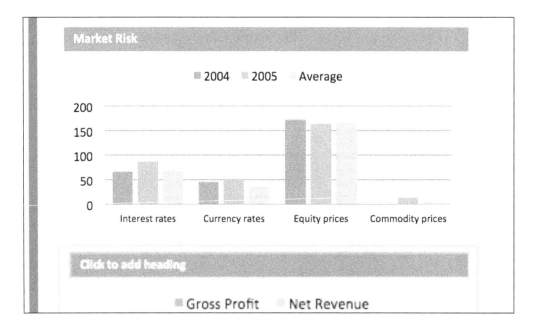

In the preceding screenshot, you can see how a graph looks on the Prezi canvas. In the following screenshot, we've used an invisible frame so that the presenter can zoom into a specific point on the graph:

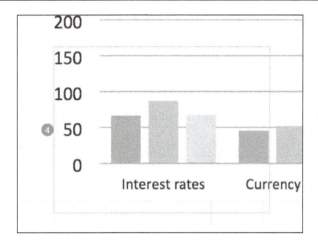

Graphs are great for displaying sales figures and other important management information, but they normally have too much detail and stay onscreen for 20 to 30 minutes while the presenter explains everything. Using the method explained here can really keep the audience engaged and give meaning to what is normally very dry content.

If a graph has been imported into PowerPoint as an image, it will be a raster image and not a vector image (see *Chapter 5, Best Practices with Imagery*) once it has been inserted into Prezi. Therefore, you will get some pixilation if you zoom in too close.

No time to Prezify

Hopefully, you'll have time to use the Insert PowerPoint… function to the best of your abilities and turn those once-linear slides into something much more interesting. However, not all of us will have the time to reposition content for 50 or so slides and spend the time required to fully Prezify our PowerPoint content.

If time really is of the essence and you can't afford to waste a single second, you might want to try the following technique to insert your slides as PDF files. This will mean that, once imported, everything will stay in exactly the same place that it was in PowerPoint, but on the flip side of that, you won't be able to manipulate the individual elements of the slide.

Importing your slides as PDF files

If you don't want to go to all the effort of rearranging the content of your slides in Prezi and simply wish to import the slides as PDF images, then follow these steps:

1. Open the PowerPoint or Keynote file you'd like to import.

2. In PowerPoint, go to the File menu and click the **SaveAs** option, then save as a PDF file:

3. In Keynote, select the Share option, then select the Export option, and then select PDF.

4. Now open Prezi and select **Insert** menu and then select the **Image...** option.

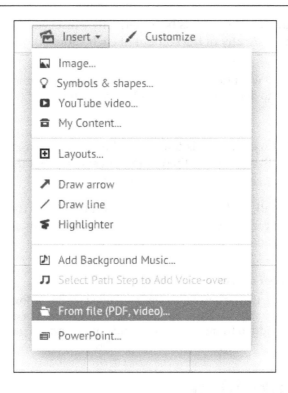

5. Select the PDF file you created in step 2 or 3, and then click the Open button.

6. Your slides will then be placed in order on the Prezi canvas:

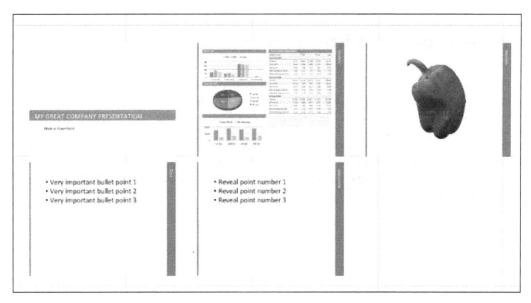

You'll notice all of the formatting has been perfectly preserved here; however, you cannot edit or manipulate any of the content of each slide.

 If you only want to insert a specific slide from your presentation, you will have to delete all the other slides and then save or export the file as a PDF.

A classic mistake that we see a lot is that, once the slides are in Prezi, people simply link them together with a path and then brag to everyone that they've created a Prezi.

This is not the case at all, and as far as we're concerned, slides that have just been linked together on a Prezi canvas are still just slides and might as well have stayed in PowerPoint or Keynote.

 Remember to Prezify

Make sure that you use the steps explained earlier to Prezify your slides and utilize the space you have on the Prezi canvas. For example, you can use hidden frames to zoom in and out on various parts of each slide.

Potential problems

Inserting and Prezifying your slide is great, but make sure to look out for the following items and don't let them catch you out and ruin your lovely Prezi.

Low-resolution imagery

Because PowerPoint and Keynote don't have the functionality to zoom like Prezi does, they don't have to rely on such high-resolution imagery. So long as the images on a slide look good enough when projected, that will usually work fine for the presentation.

Once these images are placed onto a Prezi canvas, you might decide that you want to zoom into them. If the quality isn't good enough, you could end up with pixilation problems, which we will be covering in more detail in the next chapter. You can see an example of this here:

Pixilation

If you are worried about the quality of images once they have been inserted into your Prezi, just use the zoom feature and check for pixilation. If you lose quality and you know things just don't look good, then delete the image and use Prezi's Insert from web function to find a new image of better quality.

Text

You are bound to have lots of important text on your slides. Before you import slides into Prezi though, there is one thing you'd really benefit from. Can you spot the problems the our following slide?:

Text

· Very important bullet point 1
· Very important bullet pint 2
· Very important bullet point three

Hopefully, you've spotted that line two has a spelling mistake at the end (*pint* instead of *point*) and that the end of the third line is formatted differently to the rest. These things are easily done, but they could also be easily missed once inserted into Prezi.

Spell check

Always run the spell checker in PowerPoint before exporting your slides to the PDF format. It will save you lots of time and effort and only takes a minute to do:

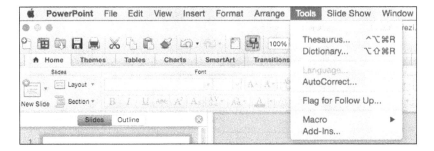

Animations

If you've used any slide-based presentation tool, you'll be familiar with animations. They are normally used to slowly reveal certain points as the presenter discusses them with his/her audience. They help to engage a little more, and if used well enough, they can really help tell your story.

In the PowerPoint slide shown in the following screenshot, you can see that each bullet point is animated so that the presenter can slowly reveal them:

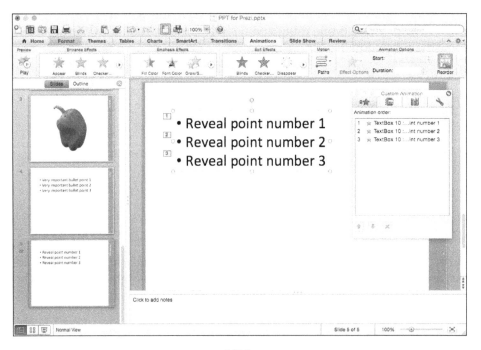

Any animation you've added in your slides will not transfer into Prezi. You can see, in the following screenshot, that once the same slide is inserted into Prezi all of the points are revealed at once:

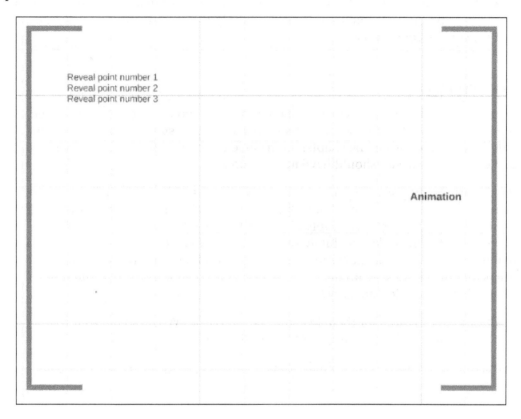

This may not be an issue for simple text animation but may be very important if your animation is a complex one that involves imagery. Due to popular demand by users, Prezi has added the ability to create animations, as discussed in *Chapter 2, Hands-on with Prezi Mechanics*.

 You'll only be able to fade in point by point if you've imported the Prezi directly rather than as PDF files because the entire slide is treated as one element if it is imported as a PDF file.

An alternative solution

If your animation is a complex one, we'd suggest that you take it apart in PowerPoint. Lay the elements out on your slide in an order that makes sense. When you then bring the slide into Prezi, you can simply move from one part to the next and explain the connections.

Summary

By using all of the ideas we've mentioned previously, your presentation won't be recognizable from the PowerPoint or Keynote slides you started off with. As we mentioned at the start of the chapter, being able to Prezify slides is a necessary evil that every Prezi master should have in their toolkit.

Prezi's popularity is growing at a huge rate, so if you're the company Prezi expert, then expect to deal with slides a lot. While you're jazzing up your colleague's slides for them, try to explain why simply importing slides into Prezi doesn't make a good presentation. Make absolutely sure they know just how much time might be required to Prezify their slides, and maybe even send them a little checklist they can use before they send you anything: Did you: Check spelling? Remove animations? Supply high resolution imagery?

That should be enough for them to come back and ask, "Why do you need this done?", at which point you can start to educate them.

In the next chapter, we'll focus in depth on using images in Prezi.

5
Best Practices with Imagery

First and foremost, Prezi is a tool for storytelling. If an image really can say a thousand words, then it's crucial that you use the right kind of imagery in Prezi to deliver your message in the most powerful way possible.

In this chapter, we will explore two different kinds of imagery, and look at how Prezi copes with each. You'll also get some advanced tips on how to create your own imagery that works well with Prezi. By the end of the chapter, you will understand the benefits of using certain types of imagery within your Prezi, and be well on the way to mastering this element of your Prezi designs. In this chapter, we will cover:

- What raster and vector images are
- Benefits of raster and vector images in your Prezi
- Places to find great imagery
- How to create your own vector imagery
- Creating illustrations for Prezi
- Prezi effects and animations

Raster and vector images

You may not have come across the terms raster and vector before, but they are used to describe two different types of imagery. If you've been building presentations for a while in Prezi or another piece of software, chances are that you have scanned through hundreds and hundreds of raster and vector images without even realizing it. After all, why would you need to know these terms? All you need is to make great presentations for your business, right?

While we totally agree that you don't need to be a professor of the arts to build great presentations, we do believe that knowing the difference between your raster and vector imagery will benefit you massively and help you become a true master of Prezi.

We hope you'll agree that the best Prezis are always the ones that have obviously been planned very well from the start. We believe that planning is of the utmost importance before you even touch the Prezi software. A part of that early planning should be deciding what type of imagery you're going to use and whether there is a particular style you want your Prezi to have. You might also want your Prezi to be small in file size, which is another reason why choosing the right imagery will help.

Let's explore raster and vector imagery together, and you can make up your own mind as to which would be right for you and your Prezis.

What are raster images?

A raster image is simply an image made up of tiny pixels of color. Depending on the size of the image, there may be hundreds or even thousands of different pixels placed together in the right way to form the image you see.

In the following raster image, you can see that it looks great at normal size and that there is lots of different shading. However, you can see on the the right-hand side that, when you zoom into this image using Prezi, you will start to see the individual pixels that make up the shaded areas. This degrades the quality of the image when viewed at this size:

The preceding image has been saved as a **Portable Network Graphics (PNG)** file using the much-loved Adobe Photoshop.

Some other raster graphics editors you could use to create raster images are:

- KolourPaint
- GIMP
- GrafX2
- Microsoft Word
- Microsoft PowerPoint

 Each of the preceding raster graphics editors has its own advantages over another, so I recommend that you take 15 minutes out of your day to research them and see which one you would prefer.

Raster file formats

I have mentioned that the example image shown previously was saved as a PNG file, which is one of the formats Prezi will accept through the **insert image** menu option. You probably know already that Prezi will also accept **Joint Photographic Experts Group (JPEG)**, **Graphics Interchange Format (GIF)**, and **Portable Document Format (PDF)** images but you may wonder what these different files mean.

The following table shows raster formats within Prezi:

File format	Uses	Tips
JPEG	This uses 16 million colors, so it is perfect for photographs and images with lots of shading.	Compression can be adjusted so you get to decide how much of a trade-off you want between image size and quality.
GIF	This is great at compressing images that have large blocks of the same color, that is, logos or shapes; also supports transparency.	Avoid using this format for photographs and images with shading. This file format also allows for animation.
PNG	This has many of the same qualities as the GIF format but compresses images in a much better way.	This supports transparency, which is extremely useful when overlaying images in Prezi.
PDF	This format preserves all visual elements within the file and compresses the file size very effectively. This format is useful when importing PowerPoint slides. This was discussed in *Chapter 4, Importing Slides into Prezi*.	Prezi desktop player will need to convert the PDF files, so an Internet connection is needed for this.

What are vector images?

Vector images are not made up of pixels as raster images are. Instead, they are created using points, lines, curves, and shapes to represent a computer graphic. They use mathematical functions to determine where everything sits in the image.

All of this sounds very technical, doesn't it? Here's what you really need to know about vector images to determine whether or not you'll use them in your Prezi's:

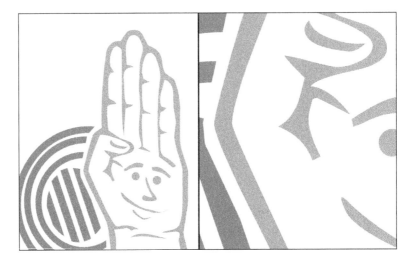

The preceding image has been created in Adobe Illustrator and is saved as a PDF file. You can clearly see in the zoomed section on the right that there is absolutely no loss of image quality. I'll come back to this point later.

You can probably tell by now that I'm a big fan of Adobe products, but I do appreciate that there are other (less expensive) pieces of software for working with vector images. Here are a few you should look into:

- Inkscape
- DrawIt (Mac format only)
- DrawPlus

 Later in this chapter, I'll show you how to create your own vector images using Inkscape. Keep reading though because there's more you need to know before you get to that stage.

Vector file formats

Vector graphic editors, such as the ones mentioned previously, will allow you to export your images in many different file types. The only ones that matter to us though are PDF and **Small Web Format** (**SWF**) because these are the only two file types that can handle vector images and are supported by Prezi. The following table gives a quick explanation of each file format along with some tips on using them in Prezi.

The following table describes the vector formats within Prezi:

File format	Uses	Tips
PDF	This format preserves all visual elements within the file and compresses the file size very effectively.	Prezi desktop player will need to convert .pdf files, so an Internet connection is needed for this. Additionally, PDFs are not susceptible to viruses.
SWF	A very fast-loading format with excellent compression for small file size, this also supports animation (if you know how!).	It supports transparency, like in .png and .gif files, so is very useful in Prezi.

 I should state that PDF is not strictly a vector file format, but exporting vector images to this format preserves the image details for inserting into Prezi. This means that you won't get any pixilation as you can in that of a raster image.

Benefits of Prezi

I hope you're now starting to understand the roles that these two very important image types play in getting your Prezi to look great and load fast.

This book is all about you mastering Prezi, so it's vital that you understand the impact that everything explained so far has on your Prezi designs.

Imagery types	Benefits in Prezi	Drawbacks in Prezi
Raster (JPG, GIF, and PNG)	There are virtually thousands of imagery types available to you online, so with some patience, you should be able to find some great imagery for your Prezi. Most raster images will be photographs, which give more life to your Prezi. Zooming in and out of details is very effective when using raster images saved at a high resolution. You can use Prezi's built-in Google search feature to quickly find raster images.	It's difficult to find lots of raster imagery in the same consistent style unless you pay for it from an online library. Zooming in too close to raster imagery will cause pixilation in Prezi. Big raster images can be slow to load when users first open a Prezi. Lots of raster images in Prezi will mean a larger file size for your presentation.
Vector (SWF and PDF)	Vector images will always have good compression, so file size is extremely small. You'll be able to zoom into a vector image without any loss of quality or pixilation. Vector images are scalable, so enlarging them will not affect the quality of the image at all. It is possible to take a raster image and vectorize it to get all of the benefits mentioned previously.	Quality vector images will not show up in the Prezi image search feature detailed. Vector images have a cartoon-like feel to them, and this can sometimes be a distraction to anyone viewing your Prezi.

 By now, you must have started to understand the benefits listed previously and may already be in favor of either raster or vector. If not, keep on reading, and I'm sure you'll come to a conclusion very soon.

Finding great imagery

One thing we all struggle with when creating presentations is finding the right image to deliver our message. You know exactly what you want to say, and if you could just find the right image to accompany your words, then your whole presentation will have a much bigger impact on its audience.

The problem is, of course, that we all have tight (and usually unrealistic) deadlines to meet, and we are probably trying to work on several different projects at once. There isn't enough time in the day to spend it looking at images, but you do want your Prezi to look great.

The following are a few ways of finding the right images, starting with the least time-consuming methods. If you live on some strange planet other than earth and have the luxury of time to seek out the perfect images, you'll definitely want to take a look at the latter half of this section. For the rest of us earthlings, to whom time is precious, I'm sure you'll find some useful tips at the start.

Direct upload

If you're very lucky, you'll already have all the images that you need for your presentation, and all you need to do is load them into Prezi. In that case, you need to take the following easy steps:

1. Click on **Insert** on the Prezi menu.
2. Click on **Image**.
3. Click the **Select files...** button that appears on the right-hand side of your screen:

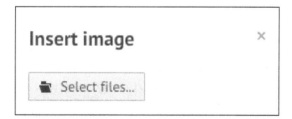

4. Click on **Open** to insert the file into Prezi.

When you're using your own imagery, there are file size restrictions that you'll need to be aware of. Prezi cannot accept any images larger than 2880 x 2880 pixels. Most image editing software will display the number of pixels to you, but you can also find this by viewing the details or properties of the image by right clicking the filename. However, you can upload images larger than this and Prezi will offer to resize them for you.

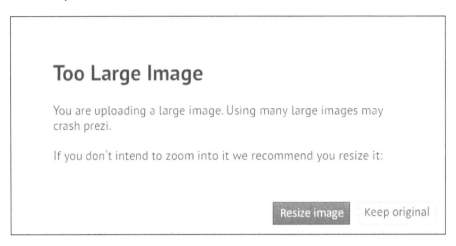

It is possible to select **Keep original** and upload the large file as it is; however, you should use caution when taking this route as it can cause problems with editing and even zooming, later on.

 Unless there is a very specific reason you need to keep the file in its original large size, your safest option is to click **Resize image** and have Prezi automatically resize the image for you.

Prezi insert

The most time-efficient method for finding new imagery is, without a doubt, by starting in Prezi itself and using the Insert image function:

1. To access this function, click on **Insert** on the Prezi menu.

2. Then click on **Image** to open the **Insert image** dialogue box on the right, as shown in the following screenshot:

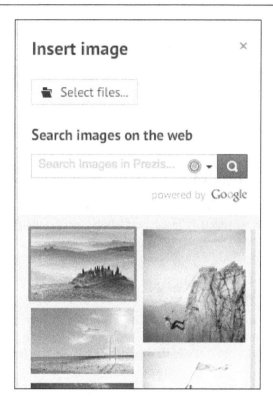

3. If you look closely, you can see that that there is a drop-down arrow next to the box where you can search terms, and if you click it, you get several options, as pictured here:

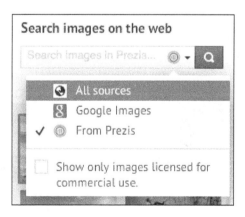

4. You can select any of the options, but if you're looking for the widest variety of sources for images, you'll want to select **All sources**.

5. This will bring in results from images that have been used in other Prezis as well as those from a Google image search. Simply enter a keyword into the search box.

Pre-licensed image checkbox

The checkbox marked **Show only images licensed for commercial use** should be ticked. Removing the checkmark will allow copyrighted images to appear in your search. These images cannot be used unless you gain permission from the image owner, usually at a cost. This is especially important when creating images for businesses and not personal or academic use.

6. Enter the word **Chocolate** into the search box and click on the magnifying glass button to perform a search.

7. You'll then see a series of images linked to that keyword, which you can scroll through and then insert by either double-clicking or dragging and dropping onto the canvas, as in the following screenshot:

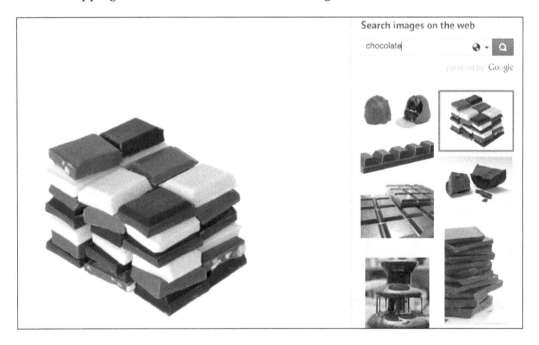

The zoom test

If you see an image that you like, insert it and use the zoom button to take a closer look at the image. If you zoom in a little and the image starts to lose quality and is pixilated, then it has probably been saved at a very low resolution.

Always zoom in and check the quality of the image you're using, especially if you know you're going to zoom into it at some stage in your Prezi.

Limitations of the Insert from web function

There's no doubt that using the **Search images on the web** function is the fastest way to find images for your Prezi, but it does have its limitations. Here are some of the things you won't be able to do:

- Check the image dimensions, that is, width and height in pixels
- See whether the image is a .jpeg, .gif, or .png file
- Your search will only return raster images

Using Google image search outside of Prezi

If you have a bit more time available when searching for imagery, you might decide to open a web browser and run a Google image search outside of Prezi. If so, the tips in the following sections will definitely help.

Advanced image search

Most non-Masters will simply go to the Google images home page, type in a keyword and click search. Those of us in the know, however, will normally always click on the cog wheel option on the right-hand side of the screen, which allows us to access the **Advanced search** option and fine-tune our search before selecting an image. See the following screenshot:

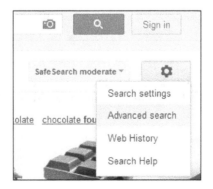

This can actually save you time in the long run because you can be very clear about what you want to see.

Some options I would definitely take advantage of in the advanced image search are:

- **Image size**: This should be set to larger than 800 x 600 pixels. Chances are that these images won't be pixilated as much when zoomed into in Prezi.

- **Type of image**: This should be set to **Photo** to save you from scrolling through hideous clip-art images.

- **Usage rights**: This should be set to free to use or share, even commercially. This mirrors the copyright issues within Prezi we discussed earlier:

 A Prezi master will never use clip art. Unless your Prezi is titled "Look how bad clip art is!", I'd recommend you stay well away from it.

- **Colors in image**: This is extremely useful if you're trying to create a particular style throughout your Prezi and want all imagery to use the same color scheme.

- **File type**: This can be set to only look for PNG, JPG, or GIF formats, which are useful if, for example, you want to take advantage of transparent backgrounds in PNG files.

Standard search

If you decide not to use the advanced search option and simply type your keyword, cross your fingers, and hope for the best, then make sure you look at the following image before saving and inserting an image into Prezi:

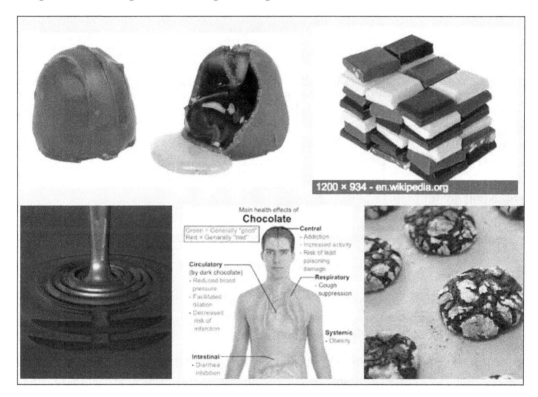

By simply rolling your mouse over one of the images in your Google search, you can reveal some key information about that image file. For our purposes, the **dimensions** will be the most important.

The file also has a dimension of 1200 x 934 pixels. This means it should be large enough to do some zooming in on it within Prezi, if we'd like to.

Google image search limitations

You will need to save the image somewhere on your PC and then go back into Prezi to insert it. This obviously takes time.

You cannot use Google image search to find vector files compatible with Prezi, that is, SWF or PDF files.

Other online sources for imagery

If getting that perfect image in your prezi is important to you (as it should be), then there are other sources you may want to turn to other than Google images. The web has hundreds of online image libraries just waiting to be tapped into. If you still want your images completely free, then `www.freeimages.com`, `www.morguefile.com`, and `www.flickr.com` are definitely worth checking out. There are also some outstanding premium resources available that give the highest quality images taken by professional photographers. Obviously, such resources aren't going to be free, but if you're building your Prezi for business use, I'm hoping you might have some budget for a small spend to get your Prezi looking great.

Here are some things you should know about using online image libraries.

Deciding on the best image source

A simple online search for image library will bring up the most popular resources. These will no doubt include the following:

- `www.shutterstock.com`
- `www.gettyimages.co.uk`
- `www.istockphoto.com`

There are obviously many other that you may wish to look into, but if you are going to invest in the right image, then make sure you get the biggest bang for your buck and compare the following before signing up to any of these sites:

- Is there a "pay per download" option? You don't want to be paying a monthly subscription unless you're a designer and need tons of images regularly.
- Do you get access to any free images when signing up?
- How expensive are the highest resolution images?

Most sites will use a credits system, so make sure you know how many credits you need for the top quality images, as it's these that you'll want to use in Prezi.

The big advantage

When you read that these online resources need to be paid for, you might have instantly thought, "Oh well, I'll skip this part", and I wouldn't have thought any less of you. However, I'm glad you're still reading this because there are some major benefits that these resources can bring to your Prezi designs:

- **Time-saving**: These sites make their money by giving you fast access to the images you want, so the advanced search facilities are usually very detailed and you won't end up scrolling through hundreds of images that aren't related to your original search.

- **Vector images**: All of these libraries will allow you to search for vector images as well as raster. This is obviously a massive advantage if you're planning to zoom in on images and want to keep everything looking great.

- **Other media**: Although their main focus might be imagery, these resources will no doubt stock video, music, and animations as well. All of which can really bring your Prezi to life, which we'll discuss in later chapters.

Time versus quality

To summarize this section, the following chart shows you the three methods mentioned previously and the effects that using each of them will have on your Prezi design.

Method for finding imagery	How this affects your Prezi
Prezi from web function	Fastest method of finding imagery but only searches for raster imagery without displaying the file type or size
Google image search online	Allows for a more advanced search, but it means that you have to save the image outside of Prezi and then insert it, which can take time
Online image library	Will have a price attached but gives the option of searching for vector and raster images that have been produced by professional photographers and/or designers, giving your Prezi a stunning look and feel

Vectorising your imagery

Hopefully, this far into the chapter, you understand the obvious benefits that both raster and vector imagery bring. But what if you could combine the best of both worlds and have realistic-looking imagery, such as photographs, at a very small file size and with the ability to zoom into them as far as you like with no pixilation at all? Well guess what, you can!

In the rest of this chapter, you'll learn how to become a true master and create imagery that has amazing style as well as being perfect for use in Prezi. You don't need to buy any expensive software to do this or have a degree in graphic design.

In the following sections, two separate methods are explained for turning raster images into vector so that they look great and load quickly in Prezi. The only difference between these methods is that one is completely free and the other has a small price attached.

Using software to vectorize

In the steps that follow, you'll learn how to turn a raster image into a stunning-looking vector version. You'll be able to do this without spending a penny on expensive software, so it's a great benefit to your Prezis and your budget. For this you need to perform the following steps:

1. First of all, you'll need a good raster image to vectorize. If you don't already have something to use, then we'd suggest a quick search on Google Images for something interesting.

2. To continue with the current theme (and to give you another sugar rush), we'll use a raster image of chocolate squares. This should look even yummier once it's turned into a vector graphic and inserted into Prezi:

3. Now you need to download and install Inkscape, which is a great piece of vector editing software mentioned earlier in this chapter. It's completely open source which makes it free for anyone to download and use. Inkscape is available on the Windows and Macintosh platforms and has very similar capabilities to its more expensive cousin Adobe Illustrator!

 If you'd like to learn more about Inkscape, you can purchase a copy of *Bethany Hiitola*'s book, *Inkscape Beginners Guide*, from *Packt Publishing*.

4. Go to `http://www.inkscape.org/` and enter the **Download** section to install the correct version of Inkscape for your operating system.

5. Once the software is installed, you should see the Inkscape icon in your programs list or on your desktop.

6. Now for the fun bit. Obviously, we won't go into detail on all of Inkscape's many features, but it's time to open the software and vectorize your image.

7. Double-click on the Inkscape icon from your list of programs.

8. When the software opens, go to the **File** menu and click on **Import**.

9. Select your raster image and click on **OK**.

10. Make sure the **Embed** option is selected on the next screen and click on **OK**.

11. When your image appears on the Inkscape page, make sure it is selected and surrounded by arrows as shown in the following screenshot:

12. Now go to **Path** and select **Trace Bitmap**. The pop-up box that appears will allow you to create a vector trace of your raster image.

   ○ If your image is a simple line drawing without much color, adjust the settings in the top half of the screen under **Single scan**. Click on **Update** to see a preview, and then on **OK** to create the vector trace.

   ○ If your image is a color photo such as the one in the previous step, you'll need to concentrate on the lower half of the Trace Bitmap screen. Select Colors, click on Update, and adjust settings further until you are happy with the preview. Click on **OK** to create your trace.

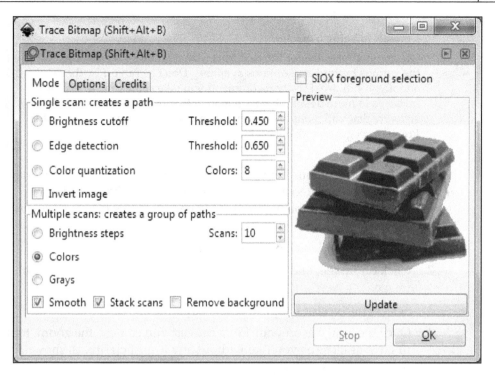

13. Back on the main screen, you will see the new vector version of your image. Hold the *Ctrl* key and use your mouse wheel to zoom in, or click the up arrow in the **z** box bottom-right corner of the screen.

14. If you aren't happy with the vector, just delete it and repeat the steps. Adjust the settings on the **Trace Bitmap** screen until you are happy.

15. Once you are happy with the trace, click on the new vector and move it to one side. You'll see the original raster below. Delete the raster image, leaving only the vector onscreen.

16. Now go to **File** and select **Save As**. Select **Portable Document Format (*.pdf)** from the **Save as type** drop-down list, and save your new vector image to your desktop.

Commit to being a master

On opening Inkscape for the first time, you might be overwhelmed by the various buttons and options available. Don't be put off by these, and if you can, we'd really recommend you take some time to explore Inkscape in more detail. There are many other useful tools within the software that will really make you into a master of creating imagery for Prezi. Don't get scared; get curious.

17. Now it's time to insert your new vector image into Prezi. Our guess is that you probably got so excited at the end of step 3 that you've already done it, but just in case you need the instructions to complete this process, you need to perform the following steps:

    1. Open Prezi and click on **Insert** from the menu.

    2. Click on **Image**, and then click on **Select files** to find your vector image.

    3. Select your vector image and click **Open**.

    4. Once the image is on your Prezi canvas, you can use the zoom tools to go in as close as you like without any loss of clarity, as shown in the following screenshot:

The quick way to create a vector image

Hopefully you enjoyed the last exercise, and learned lots during the process. You might be sitting at your desk now thinking, "That's amazing, but will I have time to do this for 20 images?" We appreciate that you are probably working to very tight deadlines forced upon you by your business. If you really don't have the time to go through the preceding steps every time you need to create a vector image, then follow the next set of steps. It's much quicker, but unfortunately, it comes at a cost. Although there is a small cost involved, the time saving will pay off in the long run.

Just as in the previous steps, you'll need another raster image to vectorize. You can either use the same image as you did before or carry out another Google Image search for something interesting, for this, you need to perform the following steps:

1. Go to `http://www.vectormagic.com` and click on the **Upload Image To Trace** button.

2. Select the raster image you'd like to vectorize and click on **Ok**.

3. Vector Magic will then perform a trace for you and compare the raster and vector images onscreen, as shown in the following screenshot:

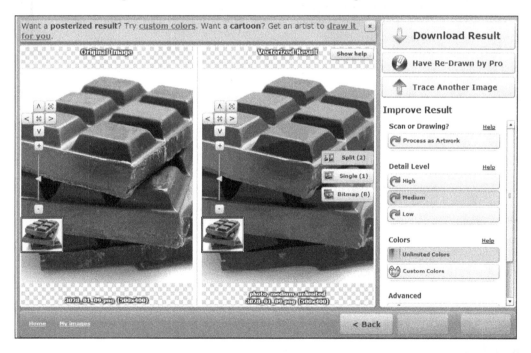

4. The default settings of Vector Magic are normally very good, so if you are happy with them, click on **Download Result** button.

5. You'll be asked to enter an e-mail address so that you can set up a free account.

6. Once you have verified the account, select the **PDF** option for download and save to your desktop.

7. Open Prezi and click on **Insert** on the menu.

8. Click on **Image** and then click on **Select files** to find your vector image.

9. Select your vector image and click on **Open**.

10. Once the image is on your Prezi canvas, you can use the zoom tools to zoom in as close as you like, without any loss of image.

As you can see from the previous two methods, there are some clear benefits for each, but an obvious difference in the amount of time and effort it will take. Only you will be able to decide which method suits you and the demands of your business.

One thing is for sure, though. Vector imagery lends itself much better to building presentations in Prezi, and you should try to use it wherever you can.

Creating your vector images

If you have even the tiniest creative bone in your body, then you might be able to take your Prezi designs to an even higher level by creating your very own illustrations and vectorizing them for Prezi.

Just like you, we've also been shackled by the time restraints of business at some point in our careers. Let's pretend the boss of your company BIG Mechanics is giving an important presentation in an hour's time and he's kindly tasked you with putting together something really eye-catching that explains how the company is like a giant machine with lots of dials and cogs that all work together in unison to get results. As you know, the same old business talk we've heard a million times before.

So once he's finished telling you what he needs, you now only have 40 minutes left. What would be perfect is an image of a giant machine with the company name on it, but can you find a decent enough raster image in time? You'll then need to vectorize it, add the company name to it somehow and then insert it into Prezi. That's going to be a challenge, so why not use your imagination, and create the exact image you need from scratch?

Hand-drawn images

While we can't teach you how to be a world class illustrator in this chapter, we do hope to give you enough confidence to at least have a go at this. When vectorized and inserted into Prezi, illustrations look great, and the fact that they are your own work gives your Prezi a much more human touch. Here's how to vectorise your own illustrations:

1. Grab a decent pen that isn't going to run out of ink and has a fairly thick nib. Try and use your company's corporate color if you can.

2. Draw your image on plain white paper.

3. Get the image onto your PC using a scanner or digital camera.

4. Use Inkscape or Vector Magic to trace the image and create a vector version.

5. Save this as a PDF file.

6. Insert the PDF into Prezi.

Obviously, we are all going to be at different skill levels when it comes to drawing our own illustrations, but even a badly drawn image seems to look a little nicer once vectorized and inserted into Prezi, as shown in the following image:

Make sure you have a try at vectorizing your own illustrations. If you get even slightly good at it, you'll save time and also have one-of-a-kind imagery for your prezis.

Working with images – quick tips

If your Prezi is using lots of images, here are a couple of tips worth knowing:

1. If there are areas of the image you don't want your audience to see, click on the image and select **Crop Image**:

2. Next, simply drag the corners that appear to crop the unwanted area out, as shown in the following screenshot, and press *Enter* to confirm:

3. To place images on top of one another in the correct order, you can simply right-click (for PC) or press *Ctrl* +click (for Mac) on an image and select one of the four available options to change its position:

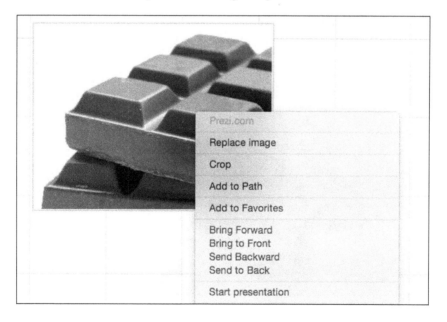

Prezi effects and animations

Due to popular demand, Prezi has recently added new features that allow for effects and animations to be added to images directly inside of Prezi. The animations actually mirror some of the animations that are available in PowerPoint.

Converting PowerPoint advocates

Many PowerPoint gurus resisted moving to Prezi because it did not offer any animations, because this is the key to one of the most used features in PowerPoint: revealing one bullet point on a slide at a time. Although this feature is now available in Prezi, it may not reflect the very best design practices. However, if this is a feature that's very important to a colleague who is considering making the move to Prezi, it may be worth demonstrating how this works in Prezi.

Effects

After clicking on any image, one of the options that appear is a button labeled **Effects**. Clicking this button will open up a new photo editor window:

From here, you'll see that you have three options for working with the image:

- **Enhance**
- **Effects**
- **Frames**

If you've used basic photo editing apps such as Instagram before, these should look familiar to you. Clicking on **Enhance** will bring up three new options, which offer a basic automatic editing functionality:

- **Hi-Def**: This sharpens the image and tweaks the lighting and color.
- **Illuminate**: This brightens the image.
- **Color Fix**: This adjusts the colors.

The following screenshot illustrates the basic automatic editing functionality:

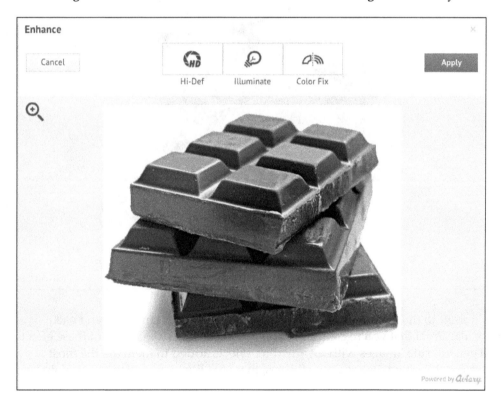

[If you're using high-quality stock images that you've paid for before, these have likely already been carefully edited into the best version. Using automatic tools such as these could actually decrease the quality. However, if you're using your own images or those taken by someone else in your company, these filters may be helpful.]

Clicking on **Effects** will bring up a menu that allows you to apply many different filters. Most of these are basic color tweaks that have fun names:

You'll want to think through the aesthetic feel of both your company and each particular Prezi that you're creating if you're considering using some of these effects. As a general rule, images without any filter effects added to them are the most professional looking, but as with all rules, there are likely exceptions for certain brands.

The final option for editing is adding **Frames**. As with the other effect, these will likely have limited use in a business presentation; however, you never know when a frame might perfectly fit a certain aesthetic look you're trying to achieve, so it's good to know the option is available, as shown in the following screenshot:

Fade-in animations

Let's see how the fade-in animations work by creating an example that PowerPoint advocates will love: fade-in bullet points. First, we'll create the content that we want to animate:

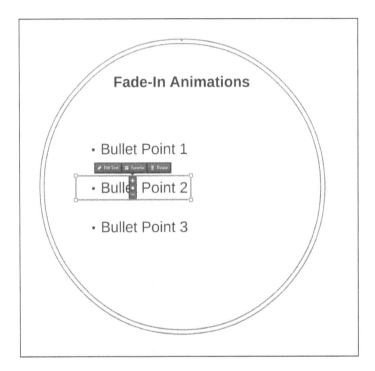

There are a couple of important requirements that we need to make sure we accommodate as we're designing the content we would like to animate:

- The content has to appear inside of a frame.
- If we want the bullet points to fade in individually, we need them to each appear in their own individual text box, rather than all together in the same box. You can see in the preceding image that I have clicked on **Bullet Point 2** and that it is completely separate from the other bullet points.

Now, let's get started animating these bullet points:

1. Click on the **Edit Path** button in the bottom-left corner of the screen.

2. Add the frame as a step in the path by clicking on it. A small number indicating its location in the path should now appear to the left of the frame:

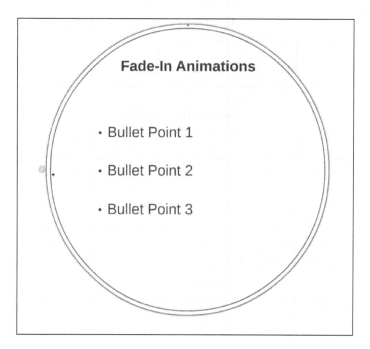

3. Once the frame has been added to the path, a small shooting star icon will appear next to the path number. Click this to enter animation mode:

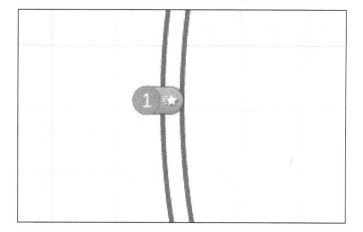

4. From here, you can click on each element in the order that you would like to fade them in. In this example, I'm going to click **Bullet Point 1** first, followed by **Bullet Point 2**, and then **Bullet Point 3**. As you add each animated point, you'll notice a green shooting star appear with a number in it. The number indicates the order in which that piece of content will fade in:

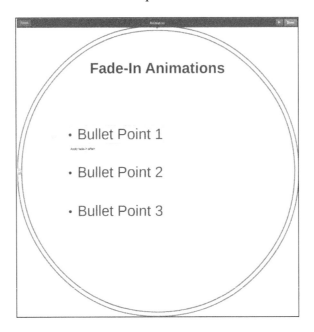

5. If you accidentally put something in the wrong order, you can easily remove that animation by hovering over the green star. A red "X" will appear, and clicking that will remove the animation. You can then go back and add the correct content:

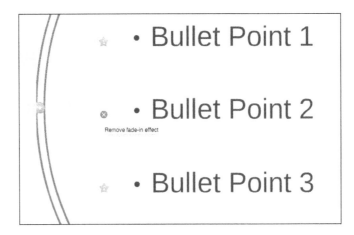

6. At any point during editing, you can click on the play button in the top-right corner of the animation window to get a preview of how the content will fade in:

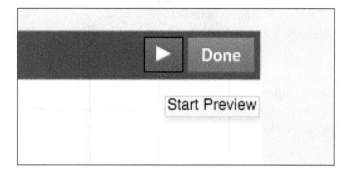

7. Once you've got all of the content added in the order you'd like, simply click on **Done**.

8. When you reach this frame during **Present** mode, clicking the same key that normally advances to the next point in the path will fade in each piece of content, one keystroke at a time.

Multi-fade and fade-out

If you'd like to fade in more than one piece of content at a time-for example, a bullet point and an image-you can group them together and fade in that entire group. You can refer to *Chapter 2, Hands-on with Prezi Mechanics* for a refresher on grouping. There's currently no natural feature in Prezi that lets you fade something out after it's been faded in. However, if you'd really like to utilize this functionality, there is a workaround. You could simply create a shape that is the same color as the background and have it fade in on top of the content you want to see fade out. When you're presenting, this will look exactly the same as fading out. You may need to edit the shape colors in the theme settings or CSS code to match your background. You can refer to *Chapter 3, Consistent Branding for Business* for a refresher on editing the themes.

Summary

Hopefully, you've found this chapter extremely useful and are well on your way to mastering the techniques described previously. We've looked at the differences between raster and vector imagery, where to find the best images, and also how to create your own that work in the best way possible for a Prezi presentation.

Raster images are simply made up of pixels, while vector images use lines or curves. This means that when you zoom in on a raster image, the image will appear blurry. A vector image, on the other hand, will look sharp no matter how closely you zoom in. When using a presentation tool such as Prezi, which focuses heavily on the use of zoom, it's important to make sure that your images look sharp!

Although it might be easier to only use vector images initially, sometimes all we have that will work is a raster image. In this case, we reviewed several ways that we can convert those raster images into vector images.

Remember, though, that business presentations need to deliver important messages on time and as effectively as possible. With this in mind, it's crucial that you decide just how much time you're going to spend on imagery when you also need to consider other important factors and probably juggle other projects. Give yourself enough time and do Prezi the justice it deserves to really make an impact in your business presentations. Don't rely on the fact that people will be wowed by the zooming and spinning if they haven't seen Prezi before. This won't last long and certainly won't deliver your message any more clearly. Make sure you project the right image.

Now that you've mastered imagery in Prezi, it's time to look at using sound as well. The skills you've learned in this chapter will help the visual learners in your audience understand your presentation, but what about the auditory learners in the crowd who need a little extra help?

In *Chapter 6, Using Audio,* we'll address the use of audio in Prezi. Whether you're standing in front of an audience and presenting or embedding your Prezi into a website for people to explore online and in their own time, sound can really help.

6
Using Audio

There's more to delivering a presentation than just making it look great with some snazzy imagery. Sure we can stimulate the audience visually to help them understand our message, but a lot of thought also needs to be given to what they hear. A lot of your audience may have a very auditory learning style, and so it's important that we try to factor this into our Prezi designs as well.

In this chapter, you'll learn how to add sound to your Prezi files and become aware of some important points to think about when in the design stage. Topics to be covered include:

- Where to find sounds
- Adding background music
- Using sound at specific points in your Prezi

Why use sound in Prezi?

Apart from the reasons mentioned previously, your Prezi will really benefit from having sound if you decide to embed it into a website or share it on the Prezi explore page (http://prezi.com/explore/). There's more detail on this in *Chapter 9, Prezi for Online Delivery*, but making Prezi files that people can explore on their own is a huge benefit to people who might not have had the time to be at your live presentation. Adding sound into these online Prezis will help the users exploring them to understand the content quicker and more clearly.

You might decide to have audio recorded from your live session and have it played at certain points in your Prezi. Or you might just want to create some kind of mood for the user that fits with your Prezi's message. For the latter, you can use a music track that loops continuously when your Prezi is viewed online.

Some other benefits that using sounds can bring are:

- Provides a bigger impact on auditory learners in your session

- Allows expert speakers to talk to your audience without even being there

- Gives people viewing the Prezi online a chance to feel like they were really there at your live event

- Online Prezis could offer translations into multiple languages to be selected and listened to at the user's discretion

- Generally makes a presentation more interesting, engaging, and memorable

 Unlike many of the features in Prezi, using sound is not easily achieved without using some third-party software. For that reason, we'll cover how to use some free software that can help.

How to find sound files

Knowing where to find great sounds from will save you lots of time, and just like with imagery, there are some great online libraries to choose from:

- `www.clipdealer.com`
- `www.sound-effects-library.com`
- `www.audionetwork.com`

Each of these online libraries offers thousands of sound effects and music tracks at very low prices. They all have very easy-to-use search facilities, and for those of you who are aspiring to become Prezi DJs, you can use Audio Network's beats per minute calculator in your search to help you find really fast-paced tracks or relaxing slow tracks.

Of course, you can also search for sound effects and music tracks that are free to download. In some instances, this will take a little longer but ultimately it means that you and your company aren't spending a penny and achieving some great results.

Here's the best of the free audio libraries:

- `http://www.freesound.org`
- `http://www.partnersinrhyme.com`
- `http://www.audiomicro.com`

 Just as we discussed with images, because of copyright restrictions, you can't simply use any music that you've purchased in iTunes or elsewhere. Those types of music purchases are for personal use only, and using it in a Prezi would constitute a public performance that requires a much heftier royalty fee.

Prezi currently supports these audio file formats: MP3, M4A, FLAC, WMA, WAV, OGG, AAC, MP4, and 3GP.

Creating your own sounds

You probably won't have time to sit there in the office and create your own sound effects of babies crying, dogs barking, or a T. Rex roaring. If you do, then please don't blame us when your boss calls you into their office because they think you're having a breakdown!

If you want to add narration to your Prezi or maybe have a subject matter expert speak to your audience without flying them in from halfway around the world, then you can use the following technique to record and edit your own sound files for free:

1. Go to `http://audacity.sourceforge.net` and download the free audio recording software.
2. Install the software onto your PC or laptop and then install the LAME encoder from `http://manual.audacityteam.org/help/manual/man/faq_installation_and_plug_ins.html#lame`. LAME is simply a plug-in that enables you to export your sounds in the MP3 format. Make sure you save it somewhere that you can remember easily, as you will need to tell Audacity where it is stored the first time you attempt to export as MP3.

3. Now open **Audacity**. When you first open the software, it will detect your machine's microphone. Results from the microphone that is built into most computers will provide decent results, but if you want top-notch professional results, it may be worthwhile to invest in a more expensive, professional microphone for recording. You will see the following screenshot when you open **Audacity**:

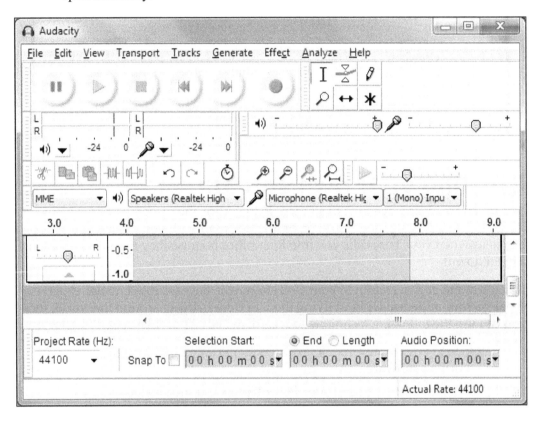

 Try not to be fazed by the number of buttons and functions in the software. For now, we'll just focus on the record button and export function.

4. Click on the record button (red circle) to start recording your audio, and click on the stop button (yellow square) when you're finished. You should see that your sound waves have been captured:

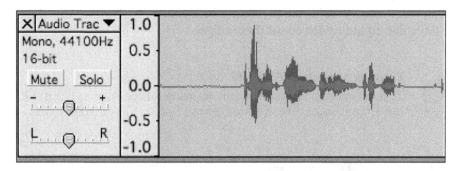

5. Click on the play button (green triangle) to review the sound. You can click the **x** on the audio track if you'd like to delete it and start over.

6. Once you're happy with your audio, click on **File** and then select **Export as WAV...** option. If you have installed the LAME plugin, you could alternatively select **Export as MP3** option. These files will typically be smaller than WAV files. The first time you choose to export a file as MP3, Audacity will ask you to select the location where you saved the LAME file. You won't have to do this again in the future:

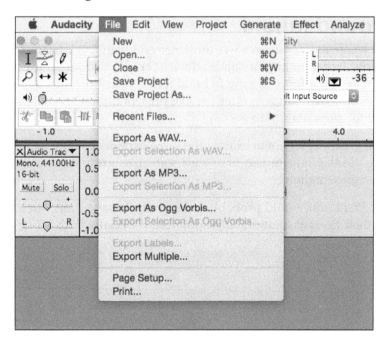

7. Open your exported WAV file to test it. Repeat steps 4-6 to create additional audio files.

If you do want colleagues or subject matter experts from overseas to speak in your Prezi, then you'll need to send the preceding instructions to them, unless they already have the capability to record their voices.

Learning more about Audacity

To learn more about Audacity and its many functions, go to `http://audacity.sourceforge.net/manual-1.2/tutorials.html`.

Adding audio in Prezi

There are two ways of using sound in your Prezi. You can have looping background music, or you can have sounds that just play once at certain path points in your Prezi, which is called voice-over. There are obvious benefits to using both of these different options, whether your Prezi is being shown online or in front of a live audience. By teaching you these techniques, it's our hope that you'll be able to come up with some really creative uses for sound that really take your Prezi skills to the next level.

Background music

Obviously, if you're delivering to a live audience and want background music, you can just use your laptop or another audio device separated from your Prezi. That will save you the time and effort of trying to build it into your Prezi file, and in business, time is money. But what happens after the live presentation when people ask you, "Can we have the presentation to review?"

Wouldn't it be great to give them exactly the same experience they had in the live session and to use the same music, or at least some background music, to help set the mood for your presentation?

Your average Prezi user would probably pass on this to save time. But a Prezi Master would make their Prezi as memorable as possible, especially if it's being viewed without them.

Here's how to insert the background music:

1. Click on **Insert** and then **Add Background Music...**:

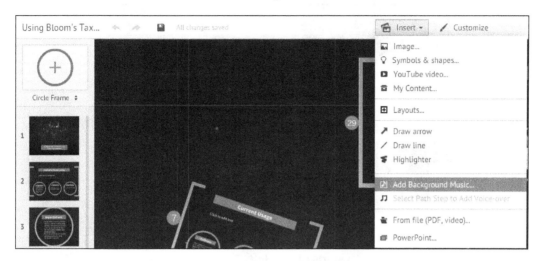

2. Select the file you would like to use and click on **Open**.
3. The file will begin uploading and you should see a progress bar:

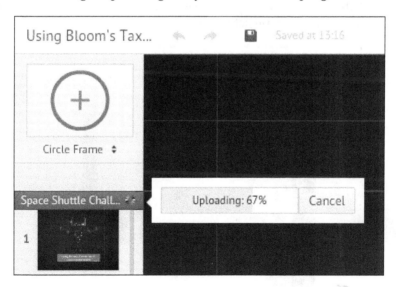

4. Once the upload is complete, you can click the play button to preview it, the trash button to delete it, or the **Done** button to finish the process:

5. Once you're done, you'll see the name of the background music track appear at the top of your path steps on the left.

6. If you decide to use something different for the background music, you'll notice the **Insert** menu has changed to read **Replace Background Music...**; selecting this will allow you to upload a new track that replaces the last one, as shown in the following screenshot:

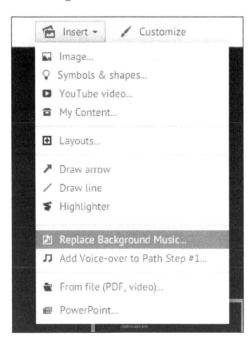

Voice-over

Adding a voice-over to any particular path point follows a process similar to that of adding background music, but it's based on each step in the path:

1. Click the point in the path on the left-hand side of your screen where you want to add the voice-over.

2. From the **Insert** menu, select **Add Voice-over to Path Step #2...**. You should see the path number that you've selected appear next to the number sign on the menu:

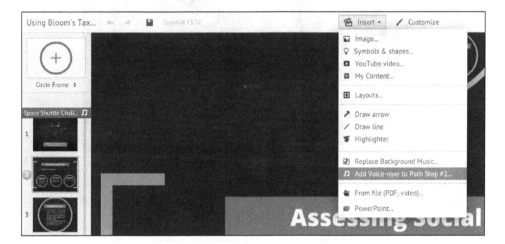

3. Wait for the upload to complete:

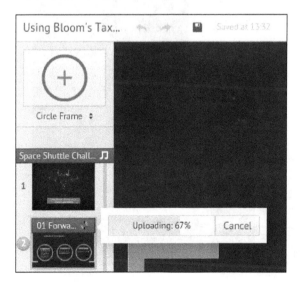

4. Once complete, you can preview the audio or delete it:

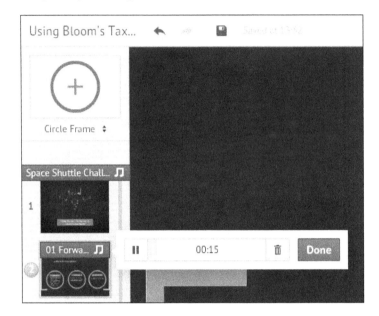

5. Finally, if you have uploaded the voice-over for the wrong path point, or simply want to make a change, you can right-click on the path thumbnail and select **Replace Voice-over on Path Step**:

Using the audio during presentation

Once you've added the proper audio, Prezi does a great job of automating the playback process for you. Once you're in presentation mode, the background music starts to play automatically. As soon as you navigate to a path point that has a voice-over associated with it, that voice-over will also play automatically.

 Prezi automatically lowers the volume of the background music once a voice-over starts playing. Make sure you preview your audio in presentation mode, not just editing mode, in order to make sure all of the audio works properly.

Once you've added audio to your Prezi, you'll see two new buttons in the bottom-left corner of your presentation mode screen. The play button allows the Prezi to automatically advance through the path voice-overs.

While you are in presentation mode, you can always click the pause button in the bottom-left corner of the screen in order to pause the background music, or you can mute it with the speaker button, as shown in the following screenshot:

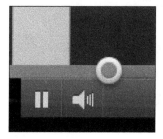

 Timing
If you have set up your presentation to advance from one path point to the next automatically, make it a point to watch through the entire presentation to ensure that all of the voice-overs play through to the end, or at least as far along as you need for the content.

Common problems

Although adding audio to your presentation can greatly enhance it, this also opens up the door to several new problems, for which you'll need to be on the lookout. We'll help you spot them ahead of time and show you how to overcome them.

Uneven volume levels

Depending on where you get your audio files, you might find that the volume levels are drastically different in each file, which can create a problem during your presentation. If you move from one path point where the audio is so loud that it hurts your ears to another that is so low that your audience can barely hear it, that will detract from your overall presentation and message. And it would be extremely inconvenient to have to adjust the system volume settings between each point, or to expect your online viewers to do so. Let's go back to Audacity for a better solution. You need to perform the following steps:

1. First, we're going to open our audio file in Audacity via **File | Open**. As you can see in the following screenshot, Audacity will allow you to open and edit a wide variety of files, including WAVs and MP3s:

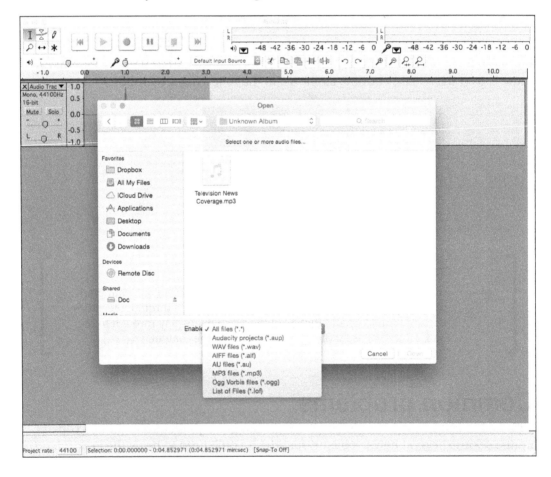

2. Next click on **Edit** | **Select** | **All** to select all of the audio. We have two potential options for how we want to proceed. If you have a wide variety of volumes all within a single file, then we can normalize the audio in that file to take care of the problem. **Normalizing** brings all of the audio within the same volume range, as shown in the following screenshot:

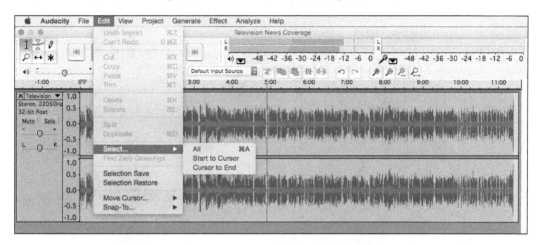

It's a good idea to normalize each of your audio files, anyway, especially if you have recorded them yourself.

3. From the **Effect** menu, select **Normalize** option.

4. You can leave both of the default boxes checked on this next options screen. Click on **OK** to complete the process:

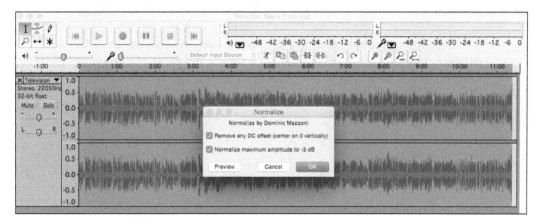

5. Next, we can increase or decrease the overall volume of the clip. There are lots of effects to choose from, but don't get overwhelmed! We'll just look at some of the basics to make sure our audio is in good playing condition. Make sure the entire clip is still selected and then click on **Effect | Amplify...** option:

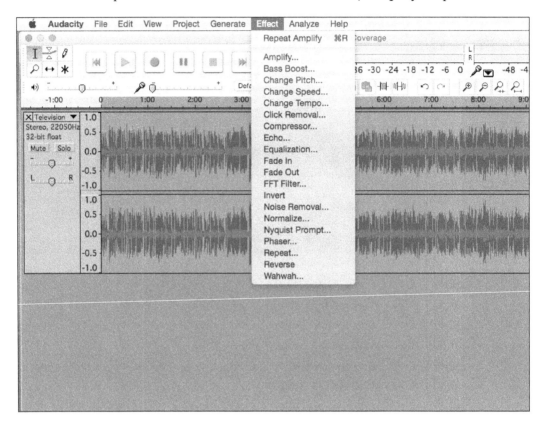

6. The default option here should offer to increase the volume by 3 dB. Try 3 dB first, and if needed, you can always repeat the process to increase the volume. If you're trying to decrease the volume, use the slider to adjust until you're at -3 dB, as shown in the following screenshot:

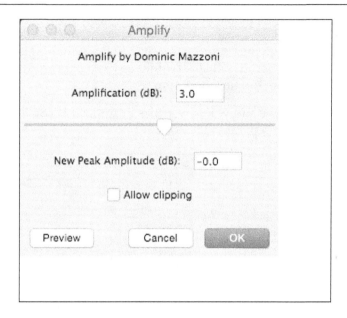

7. Save the file.

8. Upload the file into Prezi again, as we learned how to do earlier.

9. You'll need to repeat these steps for each of the audio clips that you're using in your Prezi and for which you want to adjust the volume.

Background music for only one path step

One common obstacle occurs when one wants to include background music only for one or a few steps in the path, rather than the entire Prezi. There are two different ways in which we can solve this obstacle, depending on exactly what we want to achieve.

Music only

If all you want to do is add some background music for one path step, the solution just requires a little thinking outside the box. Even though Prezi labels one feature background music and another voice-over, there's no reason that we can't use the voice-over feature to add some background music. When we upload music using the voice-over feature, it will function exactly the same as background music for one particular path step.

Music and voice

If you want to combine both music and voice-over in the same single path step, this is possible, but a little trickier. It will also require us to go back to Audacity to do a little more editing. Here are the steps to follow:

1. Open both the music and voice-over files in Audacity. You'll notice that it opens them in two separate windows:

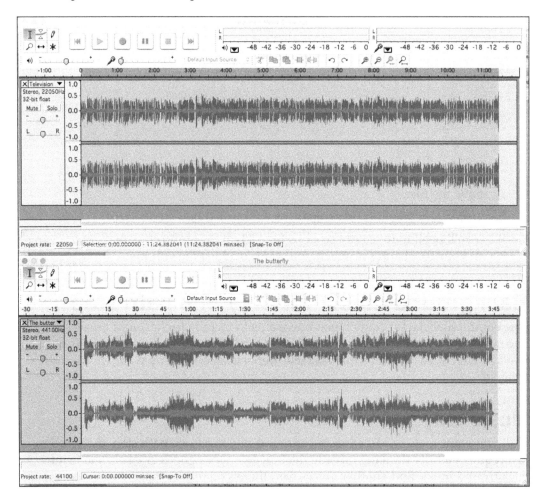

2. First, we need to combine these two files. Choose the second audio file to begin with, and use **Edit | Select | All** to select all of the audio in that file.

3. Next, click on **Edit**, followed by **Copy**.

4. Click back onto the first audio file.

5. From the **Project** menu, select **New Stereo Track**. This creates a new blank track under the original audio wave:

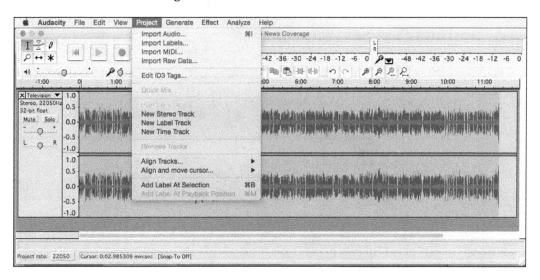

6. Use the mouse to left-click as close as possible to the **0** time mark on the left end of the track:

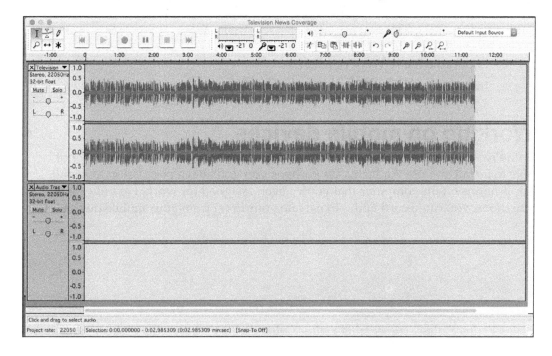

7. On the **Edit** menu, select **Paste**. You should now see both the music and voice-over tracks within the same Audacity window. You can press the play button to preview the new audio:

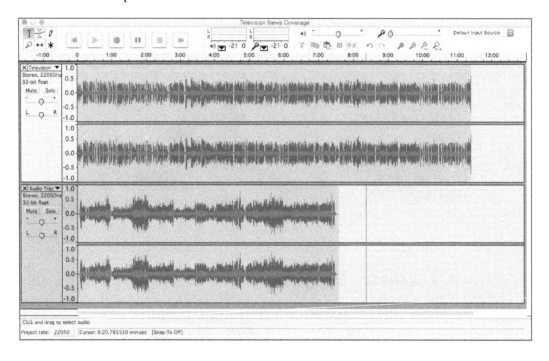

8. Export the file as WAV or MP3.

9. Insert it into Prezi as a new voice-over for the correct path step.

Working on mobile devices

If you're working on your Prezi with a mobile device like the iPad, you may not be able to install and use Audacity. Or perhaps you don't have permission to install applications on the computer that you've been assigned for work. For either of these situations, you can record audio to narrate your Prezi from your mobile device.

Android

There are several options for recording voice narration on Android. Two free apps that can be downloaded from the Play Store are:

- Smart Voice Recorder (`https://play.google.com/store/apps/details?id=com.andrwq.recorder`)
- Easy Voice Recorder (`https://play.google.com/store/apps/details?id=com.coffeebeanventures.easyvoicerecorder`)

Let's look at an example using Smart Voice Recorder:

1. After downloading the app, open it and hit the large red record button:

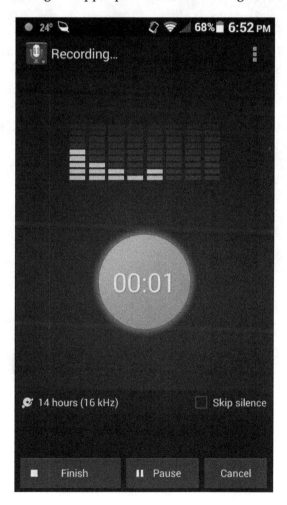

2. When done recording, you can click the **Finish** button. The app will then ask you to assign a name to the file:

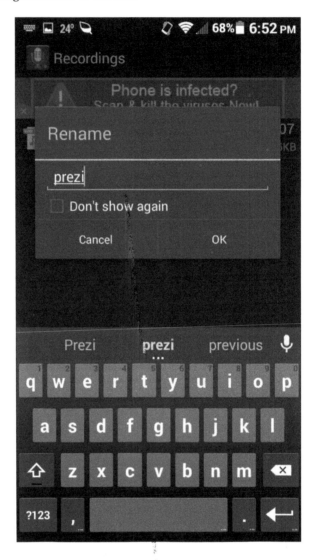

 In the preceding screenshot, you will notice one of the downsides of using free apps, the ads that appear in the background. If these bother you, it may be worth finding an application that you're willing to pay for.

3. Finally, you can click the drop-down arrow on the right, followed by **Share…**, to bring up a list of different ways you can export the file out of the app:

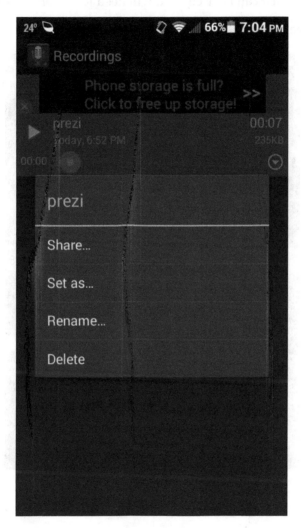

iPhone

The process for recording is similar on the iPhone; however, there is a built-in app called Voice Memos that can be used. You will need to perform the following steps:

1. Click on the red record button to begin recording:

2. Click **Done** to complete the recording process. The app will then prompt you to name the recording:

3. Click the iPhone share icon to export the audio out of Voice Memo and into the application of your choice:

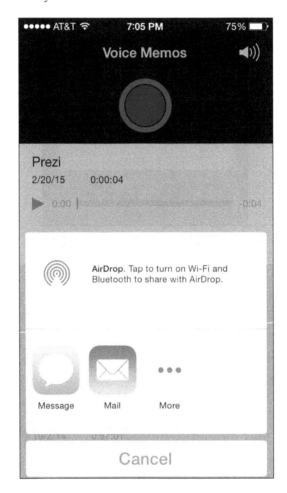

Getting the audio into Prezi

With both applications, if you export your file to e-mail, you can then send it to yourself and download the audio file to your desktop so that it can then be uploaded to Prezi, as we did with other audio files.

If you're using a Windows phone, a free app available for voice recording is Audio Recorder (http://www.windowsphone.com/en-us/store/app/audio-recorder/19d702eb-4847-4c24-ba71-7115ca0ad86b).

Example uses

Hopefully, by this stage, you will have a great understanding of how to get sound into your Prezi, and of course, what the limitations on the software might be. But how is this going to make your presentations better and more memorable? A few ways that sound can be used in your Prezi are discussed in this chapter.

Less text

One of the great benefits of using audio is that it simply frees you up to use less text on the screen. When sitting through a presentation, it's always a little disheartening to see a slide or path that is filled with text.

Now, instead of making sure everything you want to cover is written on the screen, you can add an audio element to your presentation that helps you to de-clutter the visual aspect of your presentation and appeals to the audio learners out there, as well!

Translation

If you are part of a large global organization or if you have an international customer base, you might decide to build a Prezi that can be embedded into your company website for colleagues and customers to explore.

The obvious way to use sound here would be to have some nice background music that plays throughout. Text could be displayed in one language, while a voice-over is narrated in a second language.

Narration

We've already mentioned having subject matter experts talk to your audience, but if your Prezi is part of a training program or a staff introduction, using narration at various points could be extremely powerful.

You might design a Prezi and deliver a presentation to colleagues yourself, but you could reinforce the message by using the same Prezi file and adding narration, then sending out the link for everyone to view it.

Or you might have a business critical process that needs explaining quickly to colleagues around the world. Create a Prezi with narration, share it online, and save yourself the airfare!

Using this technique, you could start to build an entire library of business processes, introductions, and training that your colleagues will be able to explore in their own time.

Creating an environment

When new members of staff join your business, they would normally spend a few days in a classroom environment receiving training. There's a projector and a whiteboard, and for the most part, they engage in good conversations with the trainer and each other, and learn a lot.

But then when they hit the retail shop floor or the sales floor of your busy call center, they feel slightly overwhelmed. This is mainly due to the fact that their training environment is very different from the real thing.

So why not use sound in your training Prezis in order to create the same kind of atmosphere? It doesn't have to be constant noise throughout, but by giving them a flavor of how their working environment will sound, you can help prepare them for the real thing.

If your training has lots of activities that involve the new staff thinking and working as a team under pressure, then giving them the same sounds that they'll hear every day will really help.

Customers

Along with introducing everyday background noise, why not give your audience sound clips of the types of customers they'll have to deal with. This is a great way to make role play much more engaging!

Testimonials

If you offer a product or service, let your customers speak for your brand. Include a picture or a brief snippet of a quote, and then let a recording of your customer gushing about your company play. This really reinforces the message.

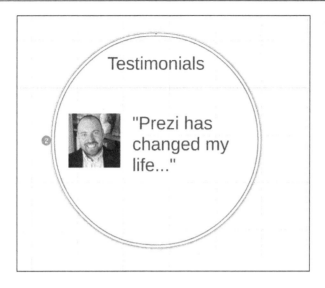

Example

Check out this example to see how powerful audio can be when you bundle it with an awesome Prezi:

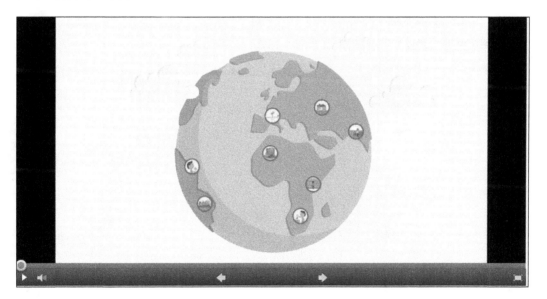

This Prezi, titled agriMORE, was designed by www.mrprezident.com and can be found at http://prezi.com/-kosjanxgdev.

The Prezi combines background music with voice-overs and a strong design to create a Prezi that was awarded the title of Best Overall Design in 2014, by the designers at Mr.Prezident.

Summary

At this point, we hope that you're itching to take what you've learned and find excuses to build it into your next Prezi.

By using the techniques in this chapter, you can help achieve two things: make yourself look like a true Master of Prezi, and make other Prezi users want to do the same.

You've also got a chance to do some basic audio editing. Once you feel comfortable, digging a little further into Audacity will really open some amazing editing opportunities that will allow you to create very polished audio that can be incorporated into your Prezi.

In the following chapter, it's time to take a look at how video can really make your Prezis shine and make them even more memorable.

If a picture says a thousand words, then moving pictures with sounds must speak volumes.

7
Inserting a Video

So far, we looked at using imagery and sound to grab our audience's attention. It stands to reason that a video is going to be even more engaging because it's a combination of these two elements.

Used correctly in Prezi, videos can give your audience the most engaging experience, and it can really help get your messages across in a memorable way.

There are lots of different approaches you can take to find, or even build, your own videos for Prezi. In this chapter, we will help you to understand those approaches and how they might fit into your business.

We'll cover the following:

- The technicalities of using videos in Prezi
- Searching for and using YouTube videos
- Creating your own YouTube account and editing videos
- Other sources of videos

The technical bit

As you may have already understood from the previous chapter, Prezi has its own built-in video player. Of course, the player sits behind the scenes of your Prezi canvas, so we never actually see it. What we do see are the videos playing beautifully in whichever format we've chosen to use. These might include the following movie file types:

- WMV*
- MOV*
- AVI*

- F4V
- FLV*
- MPG*
- MP4*
- M4V
- 3GP
- YouTube videos*

 Each of these formats differs, mostly in the way that they compresses the video that has been captured. For now, just know that the ones you'll probably come across the most are marked with an asterisk (*).

File size restrictions

If you are the proud owner of a **Pro** or **Edu Pro** license, then you'll be pleased to know that there are no file size restrictions at all placed upon your video files, except as limited by the total amount of storage allowed for your account.

 Remember, the bigger the Prezi file size, the harder it will be to carry on a memory stick and/or share with your colleagues. Try to keep file size down wherever you can.

However, if you use a **Public**, **Enjoy**, or **Edu Enjoy** license you will be restricted to inserting videos no larger than 50 megabytes. This is simply because these license types rely on using the online Prezi editor to build your Prezis, and this means that the file size has to be kept in check.

Online or offline?

There are a few things that you will need to know about your Prezi design before you decide on which video format is going to be best for you. These questions are very simple, but if they aren't given any thought at the very start, you can end up in all sorts of trouble!

Will your Prezi be viewed online?

If your Prezi can be viewed online, then you can really take advantage of the insert YouTube video option within the software. This means you'll be able to easily insert videos without having to worry about the huge file size, or having to wait forever for it to upload onto your canvas.

To take advantage of using YouTube for videos, you'll need to spend some time searching for the right clip or create your own YouTube account and upload your video to it. Both of these techniques are covered in more detail further in this chapter.

Will colleagues want a copy of your Prezi?

If you know that your colleagues will want a copy of your Prezi, and that they may even want to make changes to it, then you will need to keep a very close eye on the file size of your videos.

If your organization uses the Prezi Pro license and desktop application, then you'll have no restrictions on the video file size you can insert. However, no one wants to sit for ten minutes while the 4-gigabyte Prezi file copies to their desktop from the company's server, and you certainly won't be able to e-mail a file of that size.

Determining your design

Here is a quick summary of questions that you might want to consider before you begin your Prezi design. The *X* indicates the preferred option:

Questions	Your own offline video files	YouTube videos
You are the only person who will present your Prezi from the desktop player.	X	
You are presenting the Prezi, but others will need to view it online afterwards.		X
The Prezi is only for people to view online and in their own time.		X
The video used is sensitive and not for view by the general public.	X	

Playing videos

Before we look at the different ways of using a video, let's just cover the basics. Once a video is inserted into Prezi, you can decide how and when it plays.

Playing along a path

If you want the video to play automatically, then you'll need to add it to a path, just like we did with image files in *Chapter 5, Best Practices with Imagery*.

Once you are in the path editing mode, simply clicking on the video thumbnail on your Prezi canvas will add the video to your sequence of paths. This will mean that the video plays automatically, once this point is reached in your presentation.

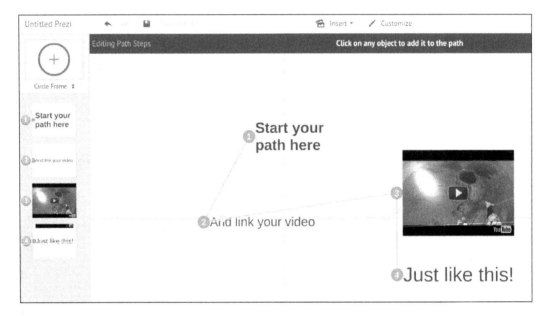

 Linking the path to a frame that surrounds your video will not make the video play. The path point must be attached to the actual video file or YouTube clip.

Letting the user play

You might decide early on that your Prezi isn't going to use a path, and instead the user can explore on their own and play the videos when they choose. If this is the case, then all you need to do is insert the video onto your canvas and ensure that the user will see it and know what to do with it.

You can use a simple arrow, as shown in the following screenshot, to point out where the play button is:

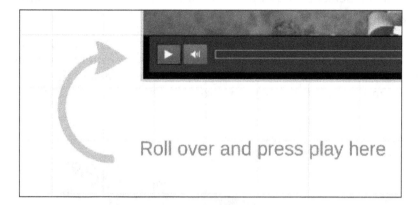

We'd also suggest giving the videos a heading by inserting a textbox with the title above the video, and a textbox with instructions below it, as shown in the following screenshot:

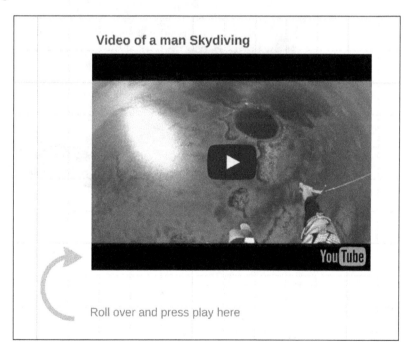

Positioning videos

As with any other elements you might insert into Prezi, the same rules apply when positioning your video file.

By simply selecting the video file, you can scale it up or down in size, spin it around at any angle, and even bring it forward to be above other elements or below them. This only changes the video in relation to your other content, and the video will not start playing until it is centered on your screen:

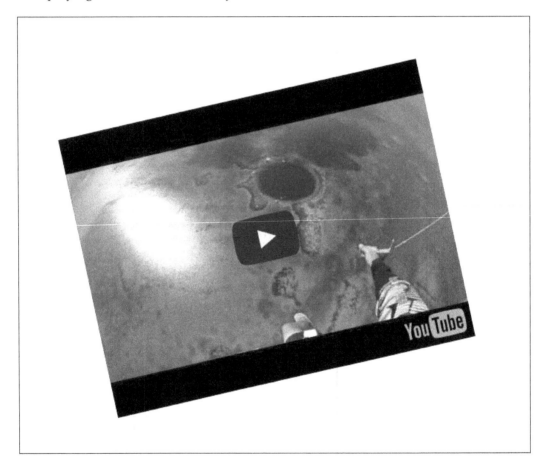

Now that the basics are covered, in the rest of this chapter we'll explore different methods for creating, editing, and inserting videos into Prezi.

Videos – the easy way with YouTube

There's no doubt that the easiest and quickest way to use videos in your Prezi is using the Insert YouTube option from the main menu. YouTube has millions of videos available and it takes much more time than you have available to watch every single video that's stored there.

With such an expansive free source of videos available, it's bound to be your first stop. We'll start from here and add more details as we go through the chapter.

Be a master

Make sure you explore everything in this chapter and go beyond simply inserting YouTube clips that already exist into your Prezi canvas. You picked up this book because you wanted to master Prezi and all of the elements it contains, so stick with it and give everything mentioned here a try.

Searching for the right clip

So you've come to a point in your Prezi where a video would be a really useful source of stimulation for your audience. But, how do you find the right clip and insert it into your Prezi canvas?

Let's pretend that we need a short clip of someone doing a parachute jump. The clip needs to be a couple of minutes long, and very high quality:

1. Go to www.youtube.com.

2. Enter a keyword or phrase into the search panel, for example, **parachute jump**.

3. Use the **Filters** option to find clips shorter than four minutes and in **HD** quality.

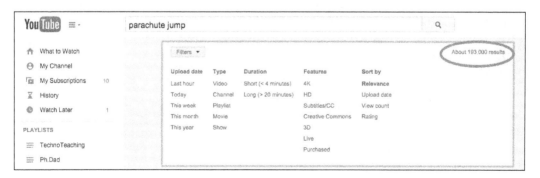

4. Using the filters will decrease the amount of videos available. This is circled in the upper-right corner of the preceding screenshot.

5. Click on a video that looks like a good match and watch it from start to finish, checking the quality.

6. Once you find the clip, copy the URL from the top of the web page.

7. Now, go into your Prezi canvas and click on **Insert** and **YouTube video...**. Then, paste the URL into the dialogue box provided and click on **Insert**:

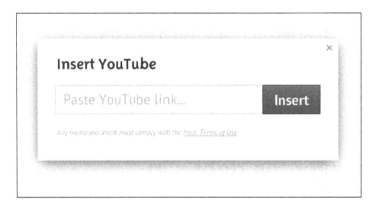

 To save a little time, you can skip step 6 and paste the URL of your YouTube clip into the Prezi as text directly onto your canvas. Prezi will do the rest for you.

It's definitely a good idea to use the filtering system on the YouTube website. By just selecting a couple of filters, you can reduce the number of videos in your search by a few thousand, or even more. This will save you a lot of time and help to give you exactly what you need.

 Using this method does not embed the YouTube clips into your Prezi, but simply creates a link to them. In order to use this method, you must be 100 percent certain that when you finally present your Prezi, there will be a reliable Internet connection available, and that the YouTube website is not blocked by your IT department.

Creating your own YouTube account

If you have your own videos that you'd like to use, and you know that there will be a reliable Internet connection when it comes to presenting and/or allowing people online to view your Prezi, then you can really take advantage of the Insert YouTube option and use your own videos.

Uploading your own videos to YouTube

It will definitely be beneficial for you to create your own YouTube account. If you already have a Google account, then you'll be able to use those details to access YouTube. If not, then just click on the **Create Account** button from the home page and enter your e-mail address and details. There are lots of benefits of having your own YouTube account, but the main one for you right now is the fact that you'll be able to upload your own video files and then link them to your Prezi canvas. This saves you the time required to insert large video files directly into your Prezi and increase the file size.

There are a number of ways to create your own video files, from using a smart phone that films in high definition to a digital camera or professional video camera. Whichever way you create your videos, you'll soon see that you can improve their quality a lot when you upload them to YouTube.

Once your account is created, follow these steps to upload your own videos:

1. Click on the Upload link located at the top of the screen.
2. Select the video file from your computer.
3. Give the video a title. Filling in the Description and Category fields are optional.
4. Select the privacy settings.

Ensure that you select the **Unlisted** option under the privacy settings if you want to allow Prezi to play the clip, but ensure that the video isn't viewable by the general public on YouTube.

5. Once the video is uploaded and processed, copy the link and insert the YouTube clip into your prezi.

Editing videos on YouTube

A great feature of YouTube is that you can edit videos once they've been uploaded and give them titles, captions, speech bubbles, and even special effects. This will really help give you that professional-looking edge and help give all of your videos a similar look and feel for use in your prezi. In order to edit videos on YouTube, follow the given steps:

1. Click on the **My Channel** tab on the left-hand side of the YouTube homepage:

2. Click on the **Video Manager** link that's now located just under the search box near the center of the page:

3. Then, click on the **Edit** button under the video you'd like to make changes to.

4. You'll then be taken to the **Info and Settings** page of your video. From here, you can access the editing features:

Enhancements

Accessing the enhancements area will automatically play two versions of your video. One is the original, while the other is a quick preview of how any changes that you've selected will look. In this area, you can improve the colors and brightness of your video. You can also trim any unnecessary delays from the start and end of the video, in order to make things very slick.

There are three subheadings within the enhancements area:

- Quick fixes
- Filters
- Special effects

Quick Fixes

The **Quick Fixes** menu allows you to very easily adjust the color settings of your video by adjusting the scales for **Fill Light**, **Contrast**, **Saturation**, and **Color Temperature**, as shown in the following screenshot:

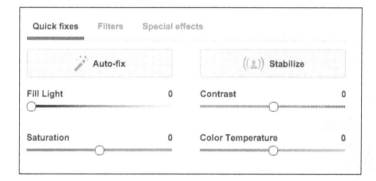

When you adjust any of these options, you will automatically see a preview of the changes, so you can decide whether they are of any benefit or not. The **Auto-fix** button will adjust all of the previously mentioned settings for you, based on what it thinks needs improving.

Also, in the enhancements area, you can use the **Trim** button to remove pauses at the start or end of your video. Rotate your video to the left or right depending on the camera angle it was shot at. Additionally, you can also use the **Stabilize** button to remove any jerky video and smooth things out. Finally, there is also the option to use **Slow Motion** on your video:

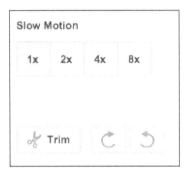

Filters

In this submenu, you can chose from a handful of effects that have been created for you. This could be useful if you wanted all your videos to match the same look and feel of other imagery in your Prezi.

In the following screenshot, you can see that the **Cartoon** effect has been applied, and the video on the right of the screen shows a preview of how this will look:

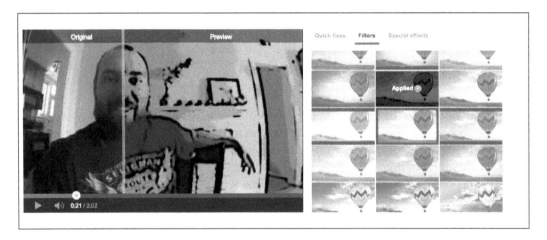

Special effects

In the special effects submenu, you can apply a filter that will blur all of the faces that can be automatically identified. Although this probably won't be a feature you use very often, it is very important if your video contains the faces of people who have not given you permission to use a video of them through a release form.

Audio

The Audio menu allows you to add music to your video that has already been licensed for YouTube, which means you won't have to worry about any copyright issues. A drop-down menu even lets you sort the music by genre, so you can quickly find the best match for your video:

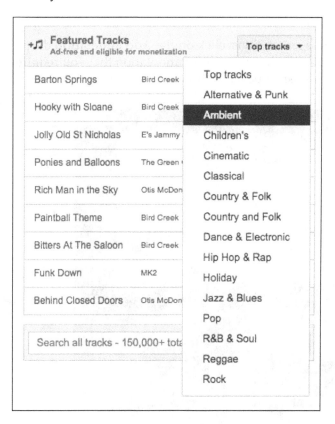

Annotations

By moving on to the Annotations menu, you now have the option to add **Speech Bubble**, **Note**, **Title**, **Spotlight**, and **Label** to your video:

To add any of these annotations, click on the **Add annotation** drop-down list on the right of the screen and select the type of annotation that you require. In the following screenshot, you can see a **Speech bubble** is selected:

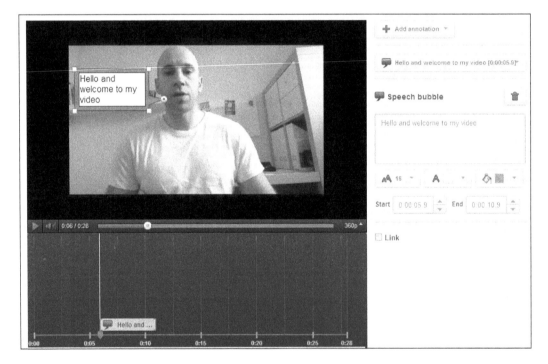

You will then see the **Speech bubble** settings and a textbox to enter the text you want to appear inside the bubble. You can select the color of the bubble and text and drag the corners of the bubble on screen to adjust its size and shape.

Ensure that you get the timings right in the **Start** and **End** options, so that your **Speech bubble** appears and disappears at the right time.

 Use the Title annotation at the start of your video to create a decent introduction, and again at the end for credits or instructions to the users on what to do next in the Prezi.

Captions

If you are part of a global organization and you'd like your colleagues overseas to understand your videos, then this section will allow you to add subtitles. This is obviously very useful for those that are hard of hearing, as well. YouTube will attempt to automatically add subtitles, but these can often be quite inaccurate. This method allows you to either add your own subtitles, or edit the automatic subtitles if they are available.

In order to add Captions, follow the given steps:

1. Click on the Subtitles and CC menu at the top of the screen. CC stands for closed captioning.

2. You will be prompted to select the language spoken most in the video. You will probably set this to **English**:

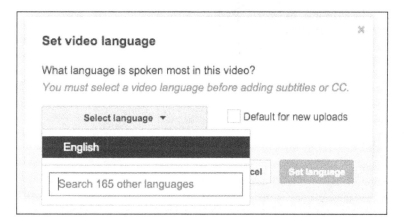

3. If YouTube has automatically subtitled your video, you'll see the subtitles, denoted here by **(Automatic)** next to the language:

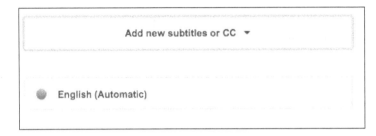

4. If this option is available, you can click on **English (Automatic)** in order to access a screen where you can edit these subtitles easily:

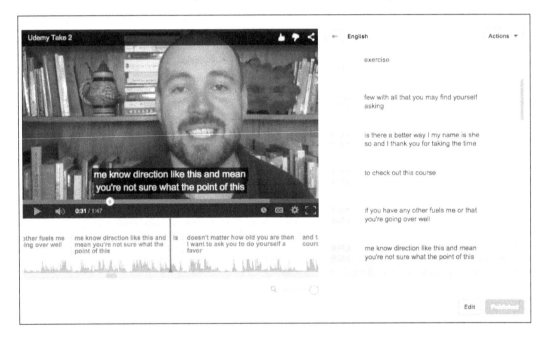

5. After clicking on the **Edit** button, you can click on each subtitle to edit it, and it will automatically advance you to that point in the video so you can listen to the audio in order to make corrections:

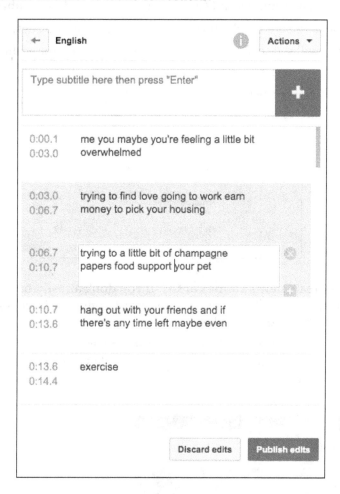

6. Once you've finished editing, simply click on **Publish edits** to save your changes.

If YouTube has not automatically added subtitles, you can easily add them yourself by following the given steps:

1. From the main Subtitles and CC screen, click on **Add new subtitles or CC**.

2. Select the language in which you'd like to create the subtitles.

3. Here, you will see several different options presented for adding subtitles:

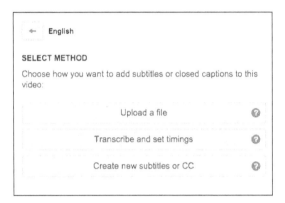

4. Click on **Create new subtitles or CC**. If you don't already have a written script, using this will probably be the easiest option, as it works similar to the editing method we saw earlier.

5. As you play the video on the left, you can type in the subtitles on the right. There's even an option to pause the video while you're typing, so that you don't fall behind:

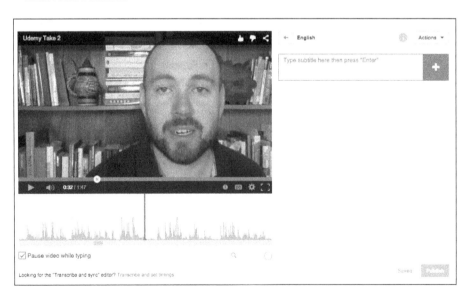

6. After you've added all of your subtitles, simply click on the **Publish** button to save them.

Other sources for videos

Hopefully by now, you fully understand the benefits of using such a great video resource to enhance your Prezis. The fact is that YouTube will continue to grow at an incredible rate, and there's no doubt at all that the features mentioned previously will only get better with time.

Unfortunately, many large businesses choose to remove access to YouTube for fear of employees wasting time watching the Ninja Cat, or other such videos. This, of course, will have a huge impact on your Prezi designs, and may even mean that YouTube just isn't an option for you.

If you're lucky, though, you should be able to convince those important people in your IT departments that when used correctly in Prezi, YouTube can become an extremely powerful business tool.

Also, don't forget to remind them that any videos you upload can only be viewed by those who see your Prezi because of the privacy settings that we mentioned earlier.

Vimeo

Sometimes, even when YouTube is blocked, other video sites such as Vimeo are available for use. These sites offer even more sources for videos. Usually, you can insert a video from Vimeo in exactly the same way as you would from YouTube. Either paste the URL into the canvas as a link, or use the Insert and YouTube video menu options. Even though you're using Vimeo rather than YouTube, this will still import the video exactly as it would from YouTube.

Using Windows Live Movie Maker or iMovie

When everything else fails though, fear not. You can always use software such as Windows Movie Maker or iMovie to create your own videos. Although video editing in these programs is beyond the scope of this book, there are plenty of help guides available online. For example, Microsoft offers the following **Move Maker** guide, which is available at `http://windows.microsoft.com/en-US/Windows-Live/movie-maker`. Once you've created your video in that software, you simply need to click on Insert and From file (PDF, video)... from the main Prezi menu, and then select your file to be uploaded.

Remember, these direct uploads will take up much more space than videos inserted from YouTube!

Fun with videos in Prezi

So now that you know how to create great looking videos and insert them into Prezi, you might be wondering how you can actually use them in your presentation. Here are just a few suggestions to get you started, but try to think beyond simply inserting a video into a presentation. Try and make the use of videos fun and engaging for your audience.

Check out this example of how **RedBull** used a video in their Prezi to help promote the free fall by Felix Baumgartner:

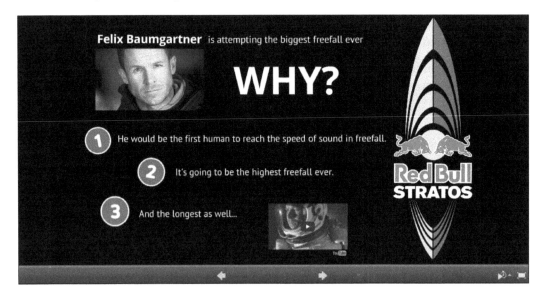

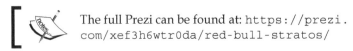 The full Prezi can be found at: https://prezi.com/xef3h6wtr0da/red-bull-stratos/

Many of the creative uses of videos using Prezi are created by companies that use them externally and do not share them via the Web. However, to get your creativity flowing, we have some ideas and suggestions in the next section that we've seen used.

Questions

In most presentations you deliver, there will be some element of quizzing the audience. This should happen throughout, so that you can check the audience's understanding of your subject.

Why not use a video clip of a subject matter expert or another colleague other than yourself asking the question, pausing, and then giving a full explanation of the answer.

This will be more visually engaging and will add a really nice touch to your presentation.

Experts

In *Chapter 6, Using Audio*, we mentioned using subject matter experts to provide audio content for your Prezi. Of course, this goes one step further by using a video of them discussing a certain subject.

If they have a good webcam, they can easily record a short clip that can be sent to you for editing, either in software or directly YouTube.

Hearing information from experts will be a massive benefit for your audience.

Customer scenarios

Most of us have had to be part of some embarrassing role-play game during a training session, but a fun way of delivering customer service or soft skills training would be to have a video clip of the customer inserted into your Prezi.

The customer could ask your audience a product-related question, or make a complaint of some kind. Then, someone from your audience could deliver a response.

To make it even more fun, why not have two alternative videos following on from that—one where the customer is happy with your response and the other where they become slightly more annoyed. Based on the response given from your audience, you can then decide where the Prezi goes next.

Summary

Whichever way you decide to use videos in your Prezi, ensure that you use the information in this chapter to make your videos look great. As we mentioned at the very beginning of this chapter, a true Prezi Master wouldn't just find a YouTube clip and insert it; they would take some extra time and care to ensure that the video at least has a heading. A Prezi Master would also be able to use their own video files and make them look as professional as possible.

Make sure that you are also aware of the potential pitfalls of both methods. To avoid these, you need to know exactly how your Prezi is going to be delivered before you start building it.

In *Chapter 8, Using Projectors with Prezi*, we will consider the first method of presenting your Prezi to an audience in more detail.

Using Projectors with Prezi

8

This chapter looks at some technical aspects that you should be aware of when using a projector to show off your Prezi. Although a very simple subject, there are some things to point out that are important to know for your design process.

We'll also introduce you to an exciting new concept that, with a small amount of time and investment, is sure to wow your audience and really open your eyes to a new way of delivering.

We will cover the following topics in this chapter:

- Advantages of Prezi
- Planning your Prezi
- Aspect ratios
- Sharing Prezis for others to present
- The blackout screen
- Creating an interactive whiteboard

Advantages of Prezi

One of the main advantages of using Prezi is that it automatically adapts to unusual presenting situations. For example, my university's library features several innovative technology spaces that, among other things, allow for a full wall projection:

Presentation at SpeedCon in Raleigh, NC, 2014.

As you can see in the preceding image, the full wall produces a projection area that is much wider than its length. Without major modifications, most PowerPoint files would simply project a smaller slide in the middle of the wall, or two of the same slide side-by-side.

Prezi automatically adapted to this full wall projection setup and filled up the entire wall. This created a dramatic effect, especially coming after several PowerPoint presentations.

These advantages stem from the ability to relatively easily adjust Prezi's aspect ratio. The best presentations will plan ahead, but even without planning, Prezi can make you look awesome. As part of this chapter, we'll delve into aspect ratios.

Planning your Prezi

In the previous chapters, we talked about getting into the Prezi frame of mind and how to add several different types of media. Hopefully, by now you realize the importance of planning your Prezi. If you don't, then stop right here and go back to *Chapter 1, Understanding the Prezi Frame of Mind.*

One of the questions you needed to know the answer to in the planning stage was: Will my Prezi be presenter led, or will people access it online?

We'll cover the approach needed when designing Prezis for online use in the next chapter; for now, let's imagine your Prezi is going to be presenter led. The chances are that this will be true for the vast majority of Prezis within your business anyway, so it makes sense to tackle this subject first.

Beware of overlapping content

Before we go into any real detail on the subject of projectors, it's important that we explain a simple concept that most of us struggle with initially in Prezi. Thankfully, there's a simple solution as well, so read on.

Let's imagine that we have just designed the Prezi shown in the following screenshot:

We want to introduce our audience to the three characters, one at a time. We've linked the frames containing each character with a path and we want each frame to fill the screen that we are projecting onto.

What do you think will happen when we go into show mode and click through the paths? Let's take a look at the following observations when overlapping occurs:

1. **PathPoint 1**: What's that orange blob on the right?

2. **PathPoint 2**: This looks okay, but there's a lot of empty space above and below the frame.

3. **PathPoint 3**: Whose arm is that in my view?

You can see in the preceding screenshots that as we move to each frame in the path, we can see parts of the other frames around them. PathPoint 3 is the best example to demonstrate this, as you can see the arm of the purple character creeping into the left of the screen. This can cause a lot of frustration, and if there are even more objects in your design, it can be very distracting for the audience. Some will lose focus, and others may sit there thinking, "What is that on the side of the screen?", while you're trying to deliver an important message!

So what's happening here? Hopefully, the Prezi Master in you spotted the cause of all this trouble. If not, then take another look at the screenshot, which shows all of the frames together.

Figured it out yet? Okay, we'll put you out of your misery. The size and placement of the frames are so close to each other that when they are centered on a rectangular screen, the content next to them is also displayed. The wider the screen, the more surrounding content will be visible.

If we're telling our Prezi's path to link to a frame, then that's what it will do. It will place this frame in the center of your rectangular screen or wherever you're projecting. It therefore stands to reason that anything else around the frame is going to show up around the edges.

Changing the aspect ratio

A very useful, but not well known, shortcut that helps when designing for use on projectors is to hold down the *Ctrl + Shift + M* (*command + Shift + M* for Mac) keys on your keyboard. You can also change this setting by clicking on the gear icon near the top-right corner of the Prezi screen:

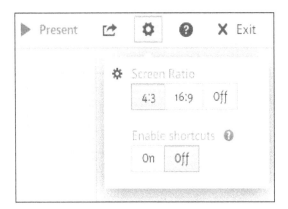

Doing this will allow you to change the aspect ratio of the preview thumbnails in your path steps. There, you can more easily tell what will appear on screen and what will not. You'll see the change displayed in the center of the screen:

Most importantly, you'll notice the changes in your thumbnail previews, as you can see here:

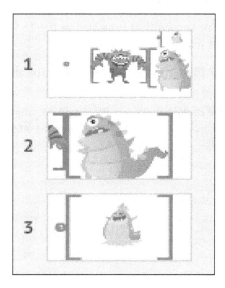

The previous image shows the thumbnails in the 16:9 ratio. The following images are the same thumbnails displayed in the 4:3 ratio:

You can see from these screenshots that the 16:9 ratio shows a little more of the surrounding content than the 4:3 ratio.

If you're using a projector or screen that operates at the 16:9 ratio, then your frames and content will need to fit inside the grid.

Pressing the *Ctrl* + *Shift* + *M* keys again will switch to the next aspect ratio.

 If you're certain that your Prezi will be projected, then use the *Ctrl* + *Shift* + *M* shortcut as soon as you create the new Prezi file.

Why do you need to know about ratios?

Nowadays, most PCs and Laptops are widescreen. However, the majority of projectors on the market have an aspect ratio of 4:3. The term aspect ratio refers to the ratio of a picture's width to its height. If the aspect ratio of a picture were 1:1, the width and height would be the same, and you'd have a perfect square.

The aspect ratio of 4:3 means for every four units of width, the picture will be three units high, as shown in the following screenshot:

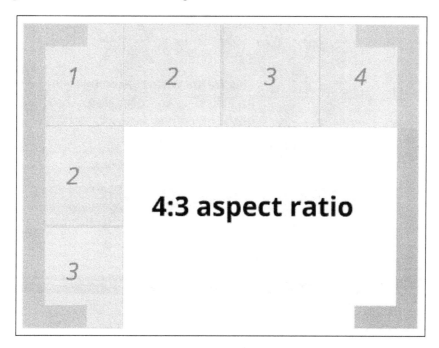

What this means for your Prezi?

Essentially, what's happening here is that most of us are designing our Prezis on a screen that is much wider than the projector being used during the actual presentation. What happens, then, is that our Prezis end up with lots of empty space in each frame, or elements from other frames creep into view because the frame isn't spaced correctly.

The following screenshot is an example of a Prezi being designed on a widescreen laptop. It's a very common mistake to try and fill the screen with content and then insert a frame around everything that fills the screen:

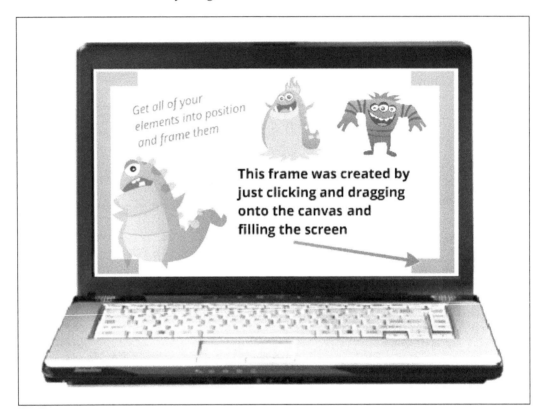

This may look fine when on a laptop screen, but when projecting at a ratio of 4:3, as shown in the following screenshot, you can see that the frame does not fill the screen and there is a lot of space wasted in the preceding and the following screenshot:

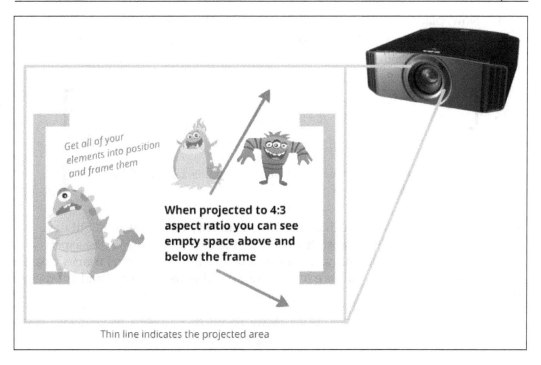

Get all of your elements into position and frame them

When projected to 4:3 aspect ratio you can see empty space above and below the frame

Thin line indicates the projected area

As we saw earlier in this chapter, a major cause of annoyance might be that the space around your frame contains other elements that shouldn't be in this view. This will be very distracting to your audience, and if you're trying to use the BIG picture method, it could actually give the game away too early.

Building your Prezi at the correct ratio

As we explained earlier, to make your Prezi look exactly the same on your laptop as it would look when projected, design it in the 4:3 aspect ratio, unless you know that the projector you will be using will have a different aspect ratio. You should attempt to determine this ahead of time, if possible.

Prezi uses a 4:3 ratio bracket frame by default so that you won't be disappointed by things looking different when projected. Follow these steps, and projectors won't trouble you anymore:

1. Decide where your frame should go and move to that area of the canvas.
2. Click on Frames and select any of the frame types you would like to use.
3. Click on the frame to add it to the canvas.

4. Now, place your content inside the frame and continue with your design.

5. Check the path preview thumbnail to ensure that your frame is going to be displayed exactly as you would like it.

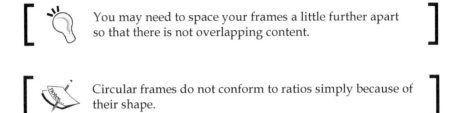

You may need to space your frames a little further apart so that there is not overlapping content.

Circular frames do not conform to ratios simply because of their shape.

Hopefully, now you have a much clearer idea as to why this problem might have crept into your designs in the past. It's important to create the Prezi in the aspect ratio in which you'll be presenting, because it creates different bracket frames based on this aspect ratio. Here, you'll see one frame created in the 16:9 ratio and another in the 4:3 ratio:

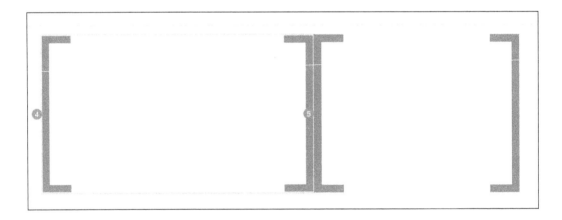

Sharing your Prezi

If you're building a Prezi for someone else in your organization, it might be safer (for you and them) to export your design in a way that does not allow them to edit. There are two options that will allow you to share in this way. You can either share an online link or create a portable Prezi. The advantage of a portable Prezi is that all of its content is saved locally, and the presenter will not need an active Internet connection in order to present.

Remember, if you include embedded videos from a source such as YouTube or Vimeo, you'll need an active Internet connection for the presentation, no matter which method you choose.

The advantage of sharing a link to the online version of the Prezi is that it is a bit easier to use and requires much less file space, so it's easier to send.

 It's always a good idea to have a backup plan. You may want to share the easier online version and the portable version so that the presenter has a backup option in case there are problems accessing the Internet during the presentation.

Sharing the online link

To share the online link for your Prezi, follow these steps:

1. Click on the export button near the top-right corner of the Prezi screen:

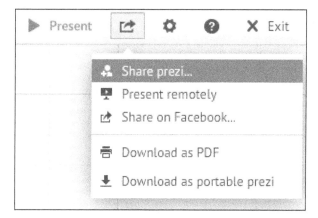

2. Click on **Share prezi...**.

3. From the new sharing settings dialogue box, you can choose either the **Copy link** or **Add people** option to share the presentation:

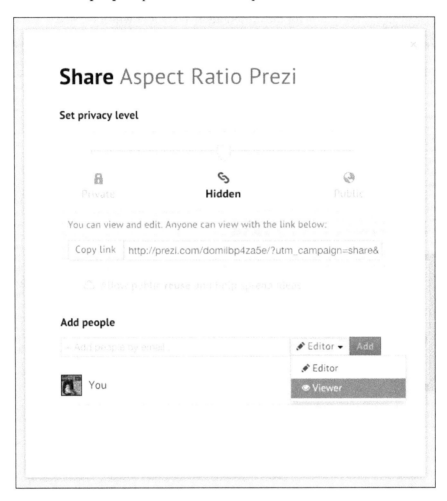

4. If you choose to copy the link, you can then paste this into an e-mail or another delivery method, and simply send it to your colleague.

5. If you choose to add the person, you will need to type their e-mail address directly into the sharing settings box on Prezi. Also, ensure that you click on the drop-down box next to their name and select **Viewer**. This will prevent them from making any changes.

6. Once you're done, you can click on the **X** button in the corner to leave the sharing settings.

Sharing portable Prezis

The following steps will allow you to share a portable Prezi that can be presented offline:

1. Click on the **Export** button near the top-right corner of the Prezi screen.

2. Wait while Prezi prepares the portable version:

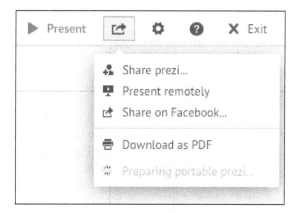

3. When finished, a compressed (zipped) folder containing your files will automatically be downloaded.

4. You can share this zipped file with your colleague. It will likely be too large to attach it directly to an e-mail, but you can share it through a service such as Google Drive or Dropbox.

When the compressed folder is opened, you'll see a folder and two executable files, as shown here:

The **Prezi** file will open the Prezi on a Mac, while the **Prezi.exe** file will open it in Windows. The **content** folder must be kept with the Prezi file as it contains content items that the file needs in order to function properly. It's definitely worth dropping a note to whoever will be presenting the prezi that it must not be removed from the main project folder.

Screen blackout

The **screen blackout** is a simple trick, which can be extremely effective. Sometimes the content on the screen can be a distraction from what the presenter is actually saying. This can be especially true if you've created a Prezi that looks stunning. Of course, you want your audience to see your masterwork, but you also want to ensure that they hear what you have to say.

In these situations, you can simply press the *B* key to black out the screen temporarily. This puts all of the focus back on you, the presenter. The act of clicking on the mouse or any other key will bring back the normal screen and allow you to continue normally. You should also ensure that your projection method has sound, because there's no sense in having a soundtrack if no one can hear it!

Interactive Prezis

In the previous chapter, we talked about how Prezi presentations can be nonlinear, and how the information and order in which you present can be led by the audience, rather than following a rigid script. Well, what if we could take that concept one step further and actually put the presentation into the hands of our audience for them to explore?

What if we created a presentation that the audience could explore on an **Interactive Whiteboard (IWB)** that is being projected on a wall or desk in front of them? You, as the presenter, could simply facilitate their exploration, show them how to use the tools, and of course, help them out if they get stuck. Wouldn't that increase the engagement levels even more?

If you like the sound of that, but are thinking, "Wait, there's no way I can get signed off to buy an IWB!", don't panic because there is a way to create your own IWB that you can carry around in your bag, which costs less than $200 and works great with Prezi.

All you need are the following items to get you started:

- A standard projector.
- A Smoothboard IWB software installed on your PC or MAC. This can be purchased from `http://www.smoothboard.net` for less than $30.
- An infrared pen.
- A Nintendo Wii remote.
- A USB Bluetooth module to link the Wii remote to your PC. (If your PC has built-in Bluetooth, you won't need to purchase this.)

How it works

The full user guide for the Smoothboard IWB software can be found at `http://www.smoothboard.org/manual`, where detailed information on the software is available. We aim to give you a simple explanation of how it works, and, of course, we'll give you some ideas on how it might be used to create some exciting Prezis.

Once the Smoothboard software is installed on your PC, you can access a feature called **SmoothConnect**. This feature will automatically detect any Wii remotes that are turned on nearby.

 You will need a Bluetooth-enabled PC or a USB Bluetooth module in order to connect the Wii remote to your PC via SmoothConnect.

Once the Wii remote is connected to Smoothboard, you can position it on your desk so that it faces toward the same area that you are projecting your Prezi canvas to.

The infrared pens transmit a signal whenever they are pressed. If the Wii remote picks up an infrared signal in the area being projected, it will behave the same as it would if you were clicking on the Prezi canvas. This means you can click and drag the canvas in any direction, or click on frames to zoom in on certain details and objects.

 The Wii remote can be placed anywhere in the room, but must be pointed at the projected area in order to create the IWB effect.

The following image shows how all of the different items work together to create the IWB:

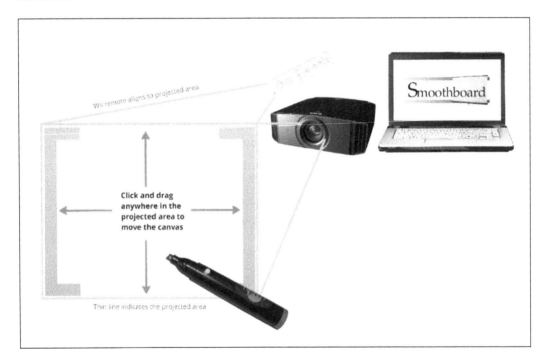

How will you use it?

You might not want to use this method for all your presentations, but it can certainly add more interaction than the standard way we deliver information. We hope that you can come up with some really creative uses for Prezis being displayed with an IWB, but here are some tips to help you make the most of it.

- **Give instructions**:
  - Some people fear technology. To ensure that your session is highly interactive, start explaining how the system works within five minutes or so. You don't want to scare people off before you even get started, so let everyone have a chance to use the pens and drag the canvas around.
  - It might be a good idea to create an individual Prezi that has instructions all over it for people to follow. Once you and your audience feel confident enough, and then get started.

- **Carry a spare battery:**
  - If you're planning on using this system for a whole day, then ensure that you have some spare batteries for your Wii remote and infrared pens. Nothing is more annoying than when you have told everyone to expect something amazing, and then it doesn't work.

- **Try using more pens:**
  - You don't just have to use one pen in your presentation. You might want to split the audience into groups and give them a pen each. Then, when it's their turn to interact with the canvas, they can take control.

 Note that using two pens does not give you the pinch and zoom effect that we're all so used to on smart phones and tablets.

- **Project onto a desk**:
  - If you want to get a little more creative and really make your presentation a memorable one, then why not try projecting on something other than a wall or white screen. If you have a boardroom with a decent-sized desk, then you could project onto that and create an interactive surface there instead.

- You need to ensure that you can place your projector and Wii remote high above the desk so that your Prezi fills the available area. You can do this safely using a projector stand, extending it as high as it will go, and pointing it down at the desk.

- You may need to adjust the keystone settings on your projector so that you get the same rectangular shape as the desk. Accessing these settings will be different on every projector, but normally accessed via the menu button on the projector itself.

- **Use the space**:

  - You want to make this as engaging as possible for people, so use a lot more space in between the frames and areas of content than you would normally use. This means that the audience will have to physically drag the canvas a lot more to find different areas of your design. People learn from experiences more than anything else, so make it fun and ensure that they are all on their feet, exploring the canvas.

Summary

As you can see from the topics covered in this chapter, the way in which you project your Prezi can add so much more to the impact of your presentation. It's an area that is often overlooked and not given much thought to because we've become so used to just plugging projectors into our laptops and using the cleanest wall space available.

Ensure that you give this area some thought in the planning stage of your Prezi. If you know which projector is to be used in your organization, then check whether it uses a 4:3 ratio. If your Prezi is going to get passed around and used on multiple projectors and screens, then stick to the 4:3 ratio in your design to be safe.

For those truly dedicated to becoming a Prezi master, invest some time (and a little money) in setting up your own IWB. Design a Prezi that allows your audience to explore and interact with your Prezi. Sit back and revel in your greatness.

In the next chapter, we will look at designing a Prezi that will be accessed by people online. You'll need to take a slightly different approach and think about your audience a lot more. People have a very short attention span when working online, so this chapter will help you engage with them and keep them focused by using some added extras in your design.

9
Prezi for Online Delivery

When you first discovered Prezi, you probably spent a long time on the Explore page, available at www.prezi.com, looking at other people's designs. Most of the Prezis you'll come across on the Explore page are designed for delivery by a presenter, so they don't make sense sometimes, or there just isn't enough text or video to understand the points trying to be made.

One of the amazing things about Prezi is that it's very easy to share your presentations with colleagues in your organization and even with the rest of the world, if you choose to. However, what's the point of doing this if your Prezi hasn't been designed with online viewing in mind? Will your colleagues be amazed by the spinning and zooming, but not realize the message that you're trying to get across?

There are a number of business reasons why designing a Prezi for people to explore online is more beneficial than delivering it face to face. This chapter sheds some light on how best to approach the design of Prezis for online delivery and covers the following topics:

- Your Prezis
    - Privacy settings
    - Sharing a Prezi
    - Search engines

- Embedding a Prezi into your website
- Approaching your design
- Designing tips for online Prezis

Your Prezis

If you are building Prezis for your business, there are some very important things to be aware of. From the Prezi website, you can access the **Your Prezis** tab to edit, delete, or share a Prezi that you have designed:

 If you are using the Prezi desktop application, you will need to upload your Prezi to www.prezi.com before you can share it with anyone.

Private Prezis

We obviously don't want to make our business presentations public, so uploading a Prezi from the desktop application will automatically make it private. This means that no one will be able to find your Prezi on the Explore tab by using the search box. Phew!

If for some reason, you do want to make your presentation accessible to Prezi public and searchable from the Explore tab, you can change the type of access with the following steps:

1. From the Your Prezis tab, click on the Prezi you'd like to share.

2. On the next screen, click on the **Private** button in the lower right corner just below the Prezi you're viewing.

3. You can then change the access rights to **Private**, **Hidden**, **Public** or **Public & reusable**, as shown in the following screenshot. You can also share your presentation with specific individuals via their e-mail address.

 Only Prezi users with a paid or education license will be able to change privacy settings.

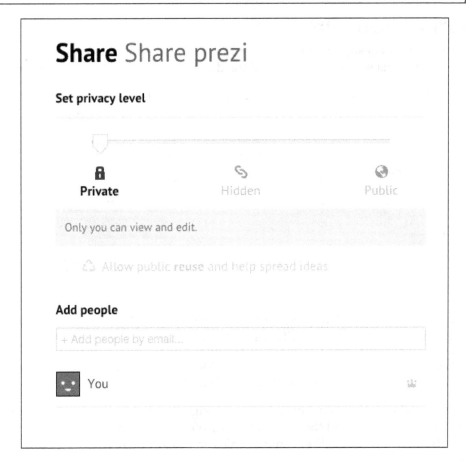

The four options shown in the preceding screenshot are as follows:

- **Private**: Under this option, only you can view and edit the Prezi from your own account.

- **Hidden**: Under this option, only you can view and edit the Prezi, but anyone you share the link with can also view your Prezi. It cannot be found through a search on the Prezi website.

- **Public**: Under this option, anyone can view your Prezi on the Explore page, but they won't be able to make a copy for themselves.

- **Public & reusable**: If you set the presentation to public, you can additionally check the box for public reuse, which means that anyone can view your Prezi on the Explore page of `www.prezi.com` and create a copy to modify it themselves.

Sharing your Prezi

Before we get into designing a Prezi for online use, it's important you know how to share your designs with colleagues, and the different ways in which this can be done.

From the same menu where you set the various privacy levels, you can also choose to share your Prezi with particular individuals. To begin, you can simply type their e-mail address into the box:

Once you enter the e-mail address, click on the drop-down box and select whether you want that person to be an **Editor** or a **Viewer**.

A **Viewer** will only be able to view the Prezi from www.prezi.com. This is helpful if you want to share a **Hidden** presentation with someone else.

If you are working with someone on a Prezi design and would like them to make some changes, you can add them as an **Editor**. Whoever receives the link will be given full access to edit the Prezi online. This can be extremely useful when working across geographies.

Any time you enter the privacy settings menu, you will be able to see each person who has access, and whether they can edit or only view the Prezi. Clicking the drop-down menu at the right of their name will allow you to change the levels of access between **Editor** and **Viewer** and remove their access completely.

It's also worth knowing that by clicking on the envelope button on the Share screen, you can send the links to view or edit your Prezi without the need to use Microsoft Outlook or another piece of e-mail software.

Search engines

If you do decide to publish your company's Prezi to the Explore tab of www.prezi.com, then we're guessing it's because you do actually want people to find it and look through the information it presents regardless of who they are and what business they belong to.

It's important to point out that the name and description you give to your Prezis can be found by search engines. If you are really keen on people finding your design, then you might want to add your company name to these areas.

To change your Prezi's name and description, follow these steps:

1. From the Your Prezis tab, click on the Prezi you'd like to edit.

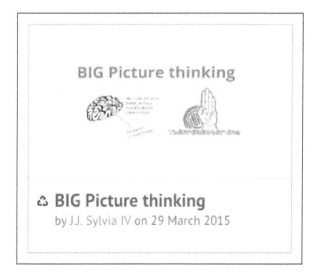

2. Click on the title or description to enable the editing option.

3. Type in a new title or description that contains your company name or relevant text for search engines to find.

4. Click on **Save**.

Embedding your Prezi

On the same share screen that we've been looking at, you can also click on the **Embed** button that will enable you to embed your Prezi into a company website for all to see. This method of sharing a Prezi can give your design a lot more exposure when posted to company blogs, intranets, and your website. Depending on your level of knowledge and access to the areas above it can take a little longer to set up. Here, we'll explain the fine details of how to embed your Prezi.

First of all, from the share page, click on the Embed link, as shown in the following screenshot:

Sizing your Prezi

You can adjust the width and height of your Prezi by typing a value of pixels into the spaces provided. We recommend that you keep as close to the default measurements as possible, and definitely do not go any larger than a width of 800 pixels and a height of 600 pixels.

User experience

Once you are happy with your Prezi's dimensions, you can then decide how your Prezi will work once embedded into a web page. The two options available to you on the embed screen are:

- **Let viewers pan & zoom freely**
- **Constrain to simple back and forward steps**

The option you chose will define the online user's experience. If you simply want to deliver a message, then keeping the Prezi constrained to back and forward steps will help. Letting users pan and zoom freely can make the Prezi very interactive if designed correctly, but it can also mean that your online users get lost in the canvas and quickly lose interest. Unless you design the Prezi really well, they might also miss important bits of content on your canvas.

 Later in this chapter, we'll look at how to approach a Prezi design that allows the user to explore on their own.

Embedding the code

The scary looking code on the embed screen is what you need to embed your Prezi into a web page. The code is written in **HyperText Markup Language (HTML)**, which is the standard programming language for web pages.

You don't need to understand this code or be a programmer to embed your Prezi into a website, but if you have an in-house IT expert, it's worth being nice to them just for one day!

If you have access to your company's website and want to embed the Prezi into a web page, follow the simple steps given here:

1. Copy the code from the Prezi share screen.
2. Open the web page you want to insert your Prezi into.
3. Get into the **HTML** mode and paste the code in the page.
4. Ensure that you preview the page before you publish it to the Web. The following screenshot is the WordPress web page in HTML mode.

If you do decide to make changes to the dimensions of your Prezi, go back to the share screen and make adjustments there. As soon as you type in new dimensions, the HTML code will update itself. Paste this new code in your web page. Once successful, the embedded Prezi should look like this:

It's also important to note that when you embed a Prezi into a web page, you are simply creating a link between the website and your Prezi design on www.prezi. com. Should you change any content at all on your Prezi, it will automatically be visible through the web page with the embedded code in it. You won't have to go through this entire process again once the Prezi is embedded.

You don't need to be a web guru to embed your Prezi, and this is a great way to share ideas and company messages with your colleagues.

 If your organization has a web developer who controls all the company's web pages, then ensure that you're always nice to them. You never know how many times you might want to embed a Prezi and will need their help!

The online design approach

Designing a Prezi for online delivery needs a very different approach than designing for a face-to-face presentation. As viewers will be viewing your Prezi online, and in their own time, you should assume that their attention span will be very limited. Most people viewing content online only have about eight seconds before they become uninterested and move on to something else.

You should also assume that people might not know what Prezi is or how it works. This could send the technophobes in your office running straightaway.

In the rest of this chapter, we'll look at how to design your online Prezi with these things in mind.

The three Prezi design steps

The three design steps you learned in *Chapter 1, Understanding the Prezi Frame of Mind* still apply:

1. Plan your Prezi.
2. Get the flavor right.
3. Build in layers.

In step 1, you need to ensure that you don't get too carried away with your ideas and stick to a very simple approach. No one is going to click through a Prezi that takes an hour to complete online, so try and make your content as simple as it can be. A no-frills approach is a good idea for online Prezis. You can still use step 2 to get a nice flavor and design.

Giving instructions

Throughout your Prezi design, you should always give the user instructions on how to navigate through the canvas. If people can't quickly grasp what they need to do, then they might give up after only a few seconds. Instruct the users on exactly how to use it, and help guide them along the way.

A simple example of a Prezi using good instructions in the opening frame is shown in the following screenshot:

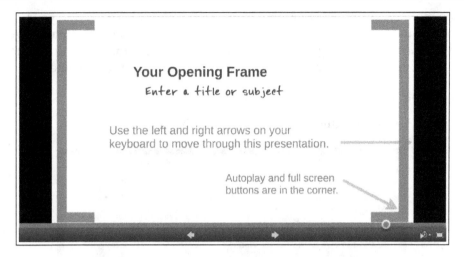

Even if the user hasn't used Prezi before, they should instantly know how to move through the Prezi.

Ensure that your instructions are not too detailed, can be read in a few seconds, and stand out from other text that might be on the canvas. Use the arrow shapes from the bubble menu to point out certain areas to the user.

If your Prezi has been designed for the user to explore, then you will need to explain how they can move through the canvas. An example of this is shown in the following screenshot:

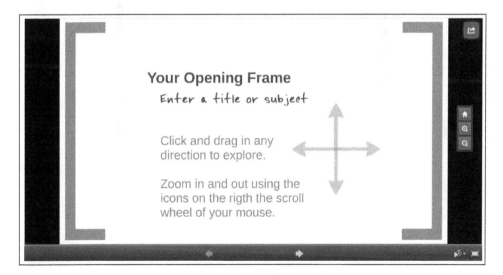

An even more powerful way of giving instructions while also engaging your audience would be to use a video in your very first frame. Using the knowledge you gained in *Chapter 7, Inserting a Video*, you can create a video that nicely introduces your subject, and also tells the user how to use the Prezi at the same time.

You can create a video and upload it to YouTube. In order to do this:

1. The Prezi is introduced and explained to the user.

2. The video finishes with instructions on screen as well.

Click the right arrow to
continue or just go and explore

Adding instructions can really help improve the success of your Prezi. Remember that you don't have the advantage of being there with the person viewing it.

Narration

In *Chapter 6, Using Audio*, you learned how to insert audio into your Prezi. Mastering this skill can be extremely useful when designing for online use. The beauty is that your user will feel as though they are being presented to, and therefore, will be engaged from the start.

In your opening frame, add some narration to introduce the subject and also explain how the Prezi works.

Instructions

If you do use audio, ensure that you have an instruction at the start that tells the user to turn up their speakers!

Highlighting

If you designed a Prezi that's completely nonlinear and that users can explore on their own, then good for you. Ensure that your users don't get completely lost in the canvas though; otherwise, they will switch off very quickly.

Aim to strike a balance between allowing them total freedom, and gently directing them to certain areas. You can do this using simple markers to highlight important information.

Highlighting with frames

The simplest way of doing this is using bracket frames to clearly highlight where a user can zoom in to view the content. The following image shows a full Prezi canvas that a user can explore. Although the user can zoom anywhere they want to, you can clearly see where content is on the canvas:

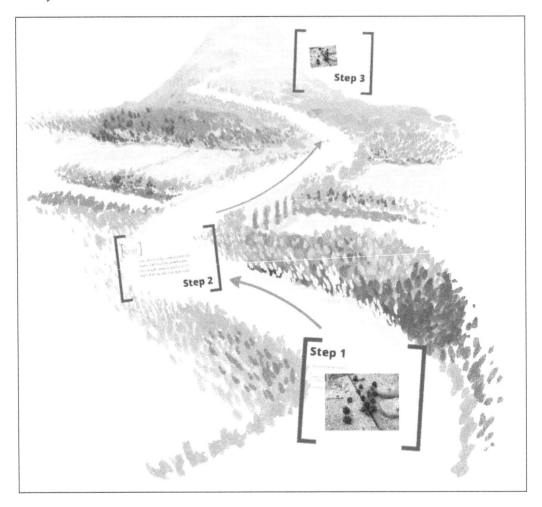

You can also add further details within frames as shown in the following image. There is no limit on how many levels of information you can add, but using bracket frames is a clear indicator that there is something here that needs to be viewed.

Add levels of content hidden within frames

Highlighting with color

If you're creating your own imagery, then you might want to be clever with your design and use color to highlight key areas. A good example of this is available at http://prezi.com/jukqtsincrom/the-destruction-of-linear-learning. In this Prezi, the users are encouraged to explore. Some clear instructions are given explaining how to do this, and the areas of important content are in a much brighter color than the rest of the imagery being used. There are no visible frames on the canvas at all.

The following screenshot shows clear instruction and good use of color to highlight key areas:

Invisible frames have been inserted around the highlighted areas to make it easier for the user to zoom in with just one click. You can see from this example that it also has another level of content within the frame. If the user spots it and wants to zoom in, they can do so with just one click.

The good thing about using invisible frames is that they won't distract the viewer from any nice imagery you have. On the flip side, it can mean that the viewer misses important information. Using color, arrows, or even icons to highlight key areas is a must for any online Prezi design.

 Whichever technique you decide to use, always think about the user and try to strike the balance between giving them freedom and guiding them to content areas.

Timing

How is your attention span when viewing content online? Like the rest of us, it's probably very low, and only a fraction of your real world attention span. If you use the techniques explained in this chapter so far, you'll be on track to create a very engaging online presentation. What we don't want to do is ruin any initial engagement by creating a Prezi that takes 30 minutes to view from start to finish.

If your Prezi is nonlinear and asks the user to explore on their own, then they'll probably complete it fairly quickly and leave it once they have the content they need.

If your Prezi follows a path, we strongly recommend that you try and design it to be no more than ten minutes long at the absolute maximum. Also, if you do build it to be delivered in over ten minutes, we suggest that you divulge the time it will take in your very first frame.

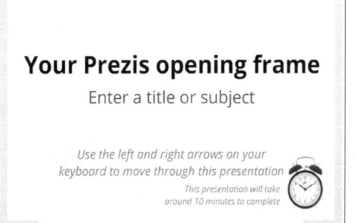

 Think about what your key message is and try and deliver it as quickly and as simply as you can. Do not try to deliver an hour-long training session through an online Prezi.

The BIG picture hook

In *Chapter 1, Understanding the Prezi Frame of Mind*, we explained to you how the BIG picture technique works. If you use this technique very early in an online Prezi, it will grab the user's attention and engage them from the start. Put differently, it's best to work from the general to the specific levels.

Try to use the following structure when putting your online Prezi together with a path:

1. Give users an opening frame with instructions as explained earlier.

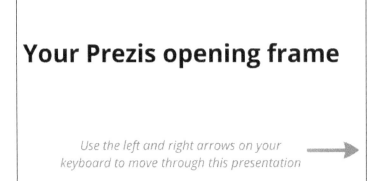

2. On the next transition, zoom out to show users the whole canvas (the BIG Picture).

3. Now, zoom back in to the details and deliver the content.

First detail

Add your content here

4. Zoom back out at the end to reveal the BIG Picture again.

By doing this, you give the user an idea of the path they are about to follow. It will grab their attention and keep them engaged.

Imagery

Ensure that you use some exciting imagery when revealing the whole canvas in step 2. The more visually stimulating you make your design, the more likely it is to be viewed right to the end.

Summary

Being able to share your Prezis so easily is a brilliant feature of the software. However, if you do not take into account the simple points raised in this chapter, your design is likely to fail. It probably won't engage your audience as you'd hoped it would, and this can mean you've wasted an awful lot of time designing it in the first place. Be realistic when you plan your online Prezi. People are extremely busy these days and normally have e-mail, web pages, Skype, and other distractions coming through their computer screens at them all day long.

If you want your Prezi's message to hit home and engage, then make it clear from the start what the user has to do, design your Prezi to look and sound great, and above all keep it short and to the point.

In the next chapter, we will look at creating custom interactions, such as menus, for your Prezi. We'll discuss why this can be an especially helpful tool for business presentations that are created for online viewing.

10
Customized Interactions

In the previous chapter, we discussed some of the ways in which your Prezi can be customized for online delivery and presentation. In this chapter, we will explore a way to make the online presentation interactive and even more useful for online viewers by creating an interactive table of contents.

Fair warning: This will be the most technical chapter in this book, and we will have to dig into a little bit of code to get this feature working. Even if you've never coded before, don't worry! We'll walk you through exactly what you need to do in order to get Prezi menus working. If you already know that coding is simply not for you, you can skip this chapter completely or consider bringing in your company's IT person for additional help.

Learning how to work with the API, which is the specific kind of coding you will do here, will result in an even more engaging and interactive Prezi for your business! Here's what we'll be exploring in this chapter:

- Benefits of interactive Prezis
- The Prezi API
    - Preparation
    - Basic operations
- Creating menus
    - Creating submenus

Benefits of interactive Prezis

Although users can autoplay or click through each path point of a Prezi, it's possible to give them even more control by enabling navigation through a menu or table of contents.

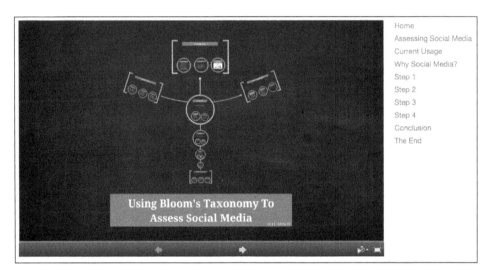

In the preceding example, *Using Bloom's Taxonomy To Assess Social Media* by *J.J. Sylvia IV*, I used a Prezi that I created for an academic conference. It was originally designed for presentation in person. However, adding the menu and making a few other tweaks can modify it to work well for online delivery once the conference is over. In the preceding example, you can see the clickable menu on the right. For example, clicking on **Why Social Media?** will zoom in to that section of the Prezi:

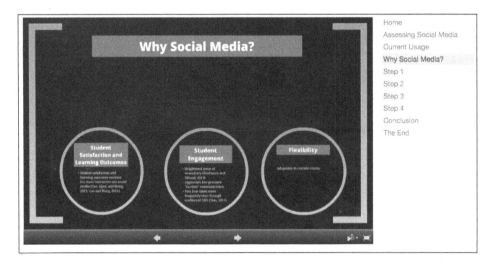

Let's think about an example where this functionality might be helpful.

If I decide to open a consultation business that focuses on training teachers to integrate and assess social media assignments, this Prezi might be a great sales tool. Although many teachers are excited about social media, there are some teachers who still aren't convinced about the use of social media in the classroom at all. If one of these teachers is viewing this Prezi, they can easily see on the menu that there is a section of the Prezi devoted to explaining why social media should be used. Instead of clicking through every preceding path point to get to that section, this teacher can click on the menu and jump straight to that section first. This reduces the chance that they will navigate away because of either their skepticism about social media or the number of clicks required to get to that section.

In addition to the creation of the menu that we will cover in this chapter, the Prezi API web page gives the following suggestions for potential uses of the API:

- Nonlinear storytelling
- Games
- Quizzes
- A chat room
- Syncing a Prezi with a video
- Controlling the Prezi by using gestures or even sounds.

All of these offer exciting possibilities that can be worked into a business Prezi with a little creativity!

The Prezi API

You may be asking yourself what exactly an API is at this point. It stands for Application Programming Interface. Many websites such as Prezi, Twitter, Wordpress, and Facebook, open up their programming interface to allow third-party developers access to the functionality of the site, so that they can integrate and further develop specific functionalities from the host site on their own site. For example, if you've ever been to a website that allowed you to comment using your Facebook account, the developers of that site were making use of Facebook's API.

 More information, documentation, and the latest updates about Prezi's API can be found at `http://prezi.github.io/prezi-player/`

Note of caution

Note the warning from the Prezi API Page: "The status of the API is alpha, currently we are looking for feedback. We are dedicated to support it, but we may be slow to fix bugs or implement new features. Also, your code may clash with an upgrade." This means that the API could change in the future, so you'll want to check your creations every so often to ensure that they are still functioning correctly.

Preparation

You'll need to ensure that you have the following in order to make use of the information presented in this chapter:

- A modern web browser (Firefox, Chrome, Safari, Opera, or Internet Explorer 8 and above will all work just fine)
- Your own web server that will host the page with the Prezi and table of contents
- Basic JavaScript knowledge (we'll walk you through this)
- An HTML editor

Web servers

Unlike most of the work we've done with Prezi, in order to make use of the API, you must have a place to host files that you'll be creating. This cannot be done exclusively through the Prezi website.

Many organizations will already have a website hosted on a server. If that's the case, you may need to work with the IT department to establish a procedure that will enable you to upload your own files, or that will allow you to submit files for uploading.

Practicing with the Prezi API

If you'd like to practice with the tools that we're discussing in this chapter, but you aren't ready for this to be live on your organization's website, you can consider creating a free Google Sites account, which will allow you to easily create your own content and can be set to private. Visit https://sites.google.com/ for more information.

The HTML editor

HyperText Markup Language (**HTML**) is the default language of the World Wide Web and it makes up the core of most web pages you'll visit. HTML uses tags that almost always come in pairs. These tags tell your web browser exactly how to display the information that is contained within them. Consider the following example:

```
<html>
<head>
<title>Example Page</title>
</head>
<body>
<h1>Example Heading</h1>
This is text that appears underneath the example heading.
</body>
</html>
```

In this example, we can see that all of the tags have both an opening and closing. For example, <h1> opens the heading and </h1> closes it. Notice that the difference between these two is the forward slash in the second tag. Everything contained between those two tags will be displayed as *Heading 1*, which is the largest heading option available. If I were to open a file with these contents inside a browser, it would display something like the following:

Example Heading

This is text that appears underneath the example heading.

There are a wide variety of options available for HTML editors, and at a wide variety of prices as well. Many of them will offer very advanced features, and also allow you to design sites through a graphic interface rather than through code. Many allow switching between both. **Adobe Dreamweaver** is a popular option. If you already have some software that allows you to edit code, you can definitely use that. However, for our purposes, we only need very basic software.

Most operating systems will also come with some built-in software that will work just fine for creating and editing HTML. If you use Windows, the Notepad application will work. Mac and Linux have several editors that are available from the command line (via the Terminal application on Mac).

From the Mac terminal, you can type **nano** to open a basic text editing program:

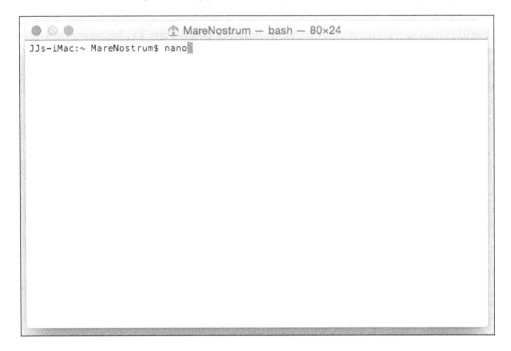

This will open up a basic editor that allows you to input HTML code:

Another free option that will work for Windows or Mac is Brackets. This software is useful because it automatically color codes the code you're typing to make it more readable, and it creates a closing tag automatically for you when you insert an opening tag.

In the preceding example, you can see that the HTML tags have automatically been colored blue, making them stand out from the content of the page.

Alternatively, if you've decided to use Google Sites, you can type the code directly into their web interface, rather than using an HTML editor.

Basic operations

In order to get the API working on your own site, there are a few steps you'll need to take, which are as follows:

1. Loading the JavaScript code from the Prezi API.
2. Loading the Prezi Player onto your site.
3. Connecting the Prezi Player to your Prezi.
4. Using the API code to create new functions.

We'll cover each of these steps in detail, but first, we thought we would offer a basic idea of the types of things the API can do:

- Querying information about the Prezi, such as the title
- Querying information about the current state of the Prezi, such as the current step number or object identity

- Monitoring changes in the above information (that is, if the viewer clicks to move to a new path point)

- Navigating to a specific step or object

Creating menus

In this section, we'll start to put together all of the things you learned in the preparation section to actually create the menu that you saw for the Prezi about Bloom's Taxonomy.

Coding shortcut

If you don't want to type the code yourself, refer to the example hosted at `http://jjsylvia.com/blooms.html`. You can visit the site and view the source, where you can then copy and paste the code for your own use and adaptation.

The base HTML file

Go to the text editor that you've chosen to use on your own computer, and create a new blank HTML file similar to the one we saw earlier, but this time with only a title and no heading or content:

```
<html>
<head>
<title>Using Bloom's Taxonomy to Assess Social Media</title>
</head>
<body>
</body>
</html>
```

HTML makes up the core content of your page, while we will use CSS, similar to what we covered in *Chapter 3, Consistent Branding for Business*, to change the style of the page.

You can save your file as `blooms.html`.

JavaScript implementation

The next step is to use JavaScript, a web-based programming language, to access and load the Prezi Player from the Prezi API site. This step allows you to embed the player into your own site. The most convenient way to do this is to load the Player directly from the Prezi API site, which can be accomplished with just a couple of lines of code.

Looking at the HTML code you've already created, simply insert the following code between the <body> and </body> tags:

```
<script src="http://prezi.github.io/prezi-player/lib/PreziPlayer/
prezi_player.js"></script>
```

This code loads the actual player from prezi.github.io. Next, we'll use this newly loaded code to embed the Prezi Player into our page. Add the following code immediately after the previous code, before your </head> tag:

```
<script type="text/javascript">
var player = new PreziPlayer('prezi-player', {
  preziId: "sk845xdbl9dn",
  width: 640,
  height: 480,
  controls: true,
  explorable: true
});
</script>
```

Let's look a little closer at what each piece of this code does, and how you can change it to meet your own needs.

The first thing that you'll notice is that some of the lines are indented and included on their own separate line. If you close the line breaks, the code will not run correctly. These lines are indented as a visual cue to allow us to easily see that we are operating inside the {} symbols.

The first two lines tell the browser that it will be processing JavaScript code and loading the PreziPlayer. The variables between the two {} symbols are the options that will be set when opening the Player.

`preziId` is probably the most important variable here, as it tells the player exactly which presentation from Prezi it should open. This must be a Prezi that has been saved onto the Prezi site, and not just locally on your computer or tablet. Additionally, the Prezi must be set to the public privacy setting.

In order to find the `preziId` for any Prezi, you simply need to look at the URL. For example, the URL for my Prezi about Bloom's Taxonomy is: `https://prezi.com/sk845xdbl9dn/using-blooms-taxonomy-to-assess-social-media/`. The string of letters and numbers that appears after `prezi.com/` is the `preziId`, which, in this case is `sk845xdbl9dn`.

If you're creating your own embedded example, you simply need to insert your own `preziId` in the preceding code.

The next two variables, `width` and `height`, tell the Prezi Player how large the Prezi should appear on the screen. The value is measured in pixels, and defaults to `640` wide by `480` high. However, you can set this to any number that you'd like. The trick is that it should be large enough for the viewers to see and interact with the Prezi, but small enough to fit the entire Prezi on the screen.

Average screen size

If you visit `http://www.w3schools.com/browsers/browsers_display.asp`, you can browse the statistics of the average screen resolution, in pixels, of most Internet users. Although there is a wide range of sizes in use, over 99 percent of users have a resolution greater than 800 x 600, so you should be able to safely make your Prezi that large without it making it too big to fit the screens of most viewers.

Here's an example of what it might look like if the size of the Prezi is set to be larger than the user's screen size:

As you can see, it's hard to use the menu and see the Prezi.

The controls variable determines whether or not the built-in Prezi controls are displayed on screen. These would include elements such as the next and previous path point buttons and the progress bar. In our example, this is set to true, which means that these controls will be visible. If you change the setting to false instead, the controls will not be visible.

Finally, the `explorable` variable is also set to `true`. This will enable users to manually click and drag around your Prezi canvas using their mouse. In other words, they can deviate from the predetermined path points if they desire. You can prevent this exploration by changing this value to `false`.

In order to actually make the Prezi Player visible, we need to insert one more bit of HTML, this time just after the opening `<head>` tag and before the JavaScript we just added:

```
<div id="prezi-player" class="player"></div>
```

 The `<div>` tag is used both to divide web pages into sections and to apply styles using CSS. We'll add some style to our page using CSS a little later.

If you've been following the instructions, your full code should now look like this:

```
<html>
<head>
  <title>Using Bloom's Taxonomy to Assess Social Media</title>
</head>
<body>
  <div id="prezi-player" class="player"></div>
<script src="http://prezi.github.io/prezi-player/lib/PreziPlayer/
prezi_player.js"></script>
<script type="text/javascript">
var player = new PreziPlayer('prezi-player', {
  preziId: "sk845xdbl9dn",
  width: 640,
  height: 480,
  controls: true,
  explorable: true
});
</script>
</body>
</html>
```

Save this file and then load it in your browser using the File… Open File command from your browser. You should see the Prezi, as in the following screenshot:

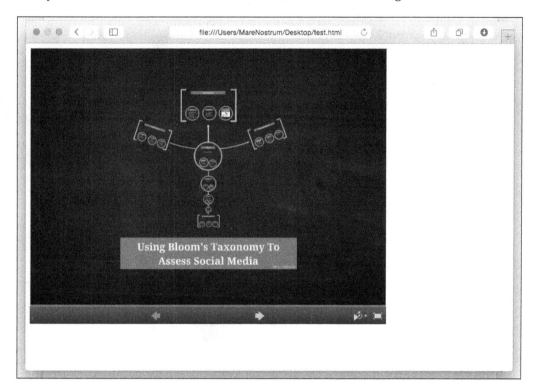

 You might have noticed in the preceding image that I've opened this file locally on my own computer rather than through a page saved on the Internet via my webhosting service. Although the Prezi API documentation says that it will not work locally, this is only true if you are using callbacks, which are special parts of the code that interact with the Prezi website. We're not using these in our example.

Coding the menu

Now that we've got the player itself loading on our website, we can move on to create the actual menu that will accompany it. This is where we really move into the functionality of the API in order to do something that's not possible on the `prezi.com` website.

We will add the code for the menu after the `<div>` tag, which we created at the end of the last section. Let's take a look at the full code for the menu, and then break down what it means and what each section does:

```
<div id="menu">
<ul id="nav">
<li><a href="javascript:player.flyToStep(0)">Home</a></li>
  <li><a href="javascript:player.flyToStep(1)">Assessing Social
Media</a></li>
  <li><a href="javascript:player.flyToStep(6)">Current Usage</a></li>
  <li><a href="javascript:player.flyToStep(10)">Why Social Media?</
a></li>
  <li><a href="javascript:player.flyToStep(15)">Step 1</a></li>
  <li><a href="javascript:player.flyToStep(18)">Step 2</a></li>
  <li><a href="javascript:player.flyToStep(22)">Step 3</a></li>
  <li><a href="javascript:player.flyToStep(25)">Step 4</a></li>
  <li><a href="javascript:player.flyToStep(28)">Conclusion</a></li>
  <li><a href="javascript:player.flyToStep(33)">The End</a></li>
  </ul>
</div>
```

The `<div id="menu">` code creates a new section of the website, which we identify as the menu. We do this so that we can apply CSS styles to our menu later on.

The `<ul id="nav">` code is an HTML command that creates a new unordered list (`ul`), or in other words, a bulleted list. We will identify this list as `nav`. Each new `<li>` (**list**) tag creates a new bullet point in our list.

After each bullet point, we create a link that, when clicked, will cause the Prezi to navigate to a specific step in the path. Normally, an HTML link would look something like `<a href="http://www.prezi.com">Prezi</a>`. This HTML would display the word `Prezi` as a link, that when clicked on, would load the `prezi.com` website.

Our links will work a little differently than this because we aren't linking to another website. Instead, we're going to use JavaScript to move to a specific point in our Prezi. Rather than the URL, we're using the code from the Prezi API, `javascript:player.flyToStep(0)`. This code tells the player to move to `0` in the Prezi.

Learn to count

Although we typically start counting with the number 1, most programming languages actually start with the number 0. In the preceding example, you can see that our first `flyToStep` code is for step 0. This is actually the first path point we have created for our Prezi. This can be a little confusing because when you're editing your Prezi, it labels the path points starting with 1. Just remember that when you're coding the path point you want to move to, always subtract 1 from the number that's displayed in the path preview in the Prezi Editor!

Finally, we put in the text that we want to display for the actual clickable link, and then we close our link and our bullet point with the `</a>` and `</li>` tags. Once we've created all of our bullet points, we can close the entire list with the `</ul>` tag.

In this example, I've used each of the major headings in my presentation to create a menu item. For example, the second path step, `flyToStep(1)`, is the entire section for **Assessing Social Media**:

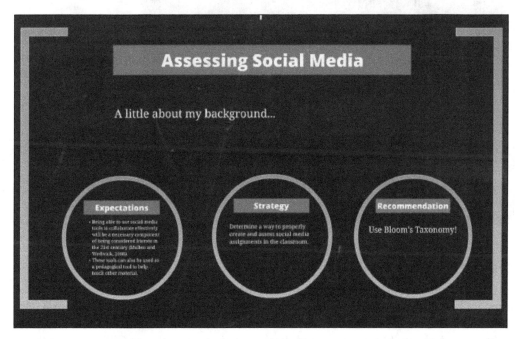

If you save your file and reload the page in your browser, you will now see the newly created menu:

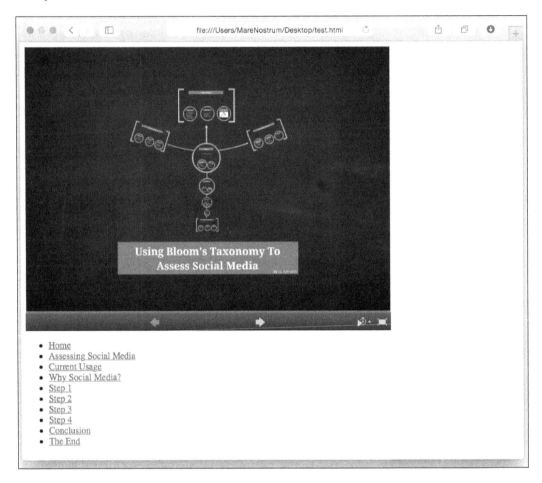

Styling the menu

In the previous screenshot, you might have noticed that the menu we created appears below the Prezi Player by default. Although this will function just fine, it may be off the visible screen for many users and they will have to scroll to use the links. Also, it doesn't look very good. In this section, we will use CSS to move the menu to the right of our Prezi and add some additional style elements to make it look even better.

In order to insert the CSS code, we're going to add a `<style></style>` tag set to the `<head>` section of our document, just after the `</title>` tag.

Just as we did earlier, let's look at all of the code we will insert first, and then break down what each piece means:

```
<style>
#prezi-player {
  width: 640px;
  float: left;
  margin-left: 20px;
}
#menu {
  width: 250px;
  margin-left: 640px;
  font-family: "Helvetica Neue", Helvetica, Arial, sans-serif;
}
#nav {
  list-style-type: none;
}
#nav li a {
  display: block;
  color: #0645AD;
  padding: 3px;
  margin-bottom: 3px;
  text-decoration: none;
}
#nav li a:hover {
  background-color: #d6d6d6;
  color: #003e5c;
}
</style>
```

The `<style>` tag alerts the browser that the content between it and the `</style>` tag will contain CSS code.

If you've been paying close attention to the `<div>` tags that we created as we constructed this document, you'll notice that the IDs that we associated with those tags are listed here after the hashtag sign in each section. So for example, where we had `<div id="prezi-player">` as an HTML tag, we now have `#prezi-player {` as CSS code. This naming scheme tells the browser that the style for `#prezi-player` should be applied to the content within the `<div id="prezi-player">` tags.

The { opens up the settings for each section and allows us to set values using variables, much like we did with the JavaScript code when we were loading the Prezi Player earlier.

The `width` variable sets how large this section of the page should be. In this case, we want to match the width of the page with the width of the player we embedded earlier. Recall that we set it to the default 640 pixels. Here, `width: 640px`; designates this in the CSS code. This decision is based on our earlier discussion of the ideal screen size.

`float: left`; means that the section will float outside the normal flow of HTML content, and in this case, we want to align it to the left-hand side of the page. We're asking that appear 20 pixels away from the very left edge of the browser with the code `margin-left: 20px`;.

More about CSS

Although we're explaining what each bit of CSS code actually does in our example, we're not elaborating on all of the possible ways in which we can change the CSS code to make the menu display differently. If you're interested in experimenting with different settings, you can visit `http://www.w3schools.com/cssref/` to see a list of the variable settings available in CSS along with a description of how each setting will modify the appearance of your web page.

We see some similar variables for our `#menu` settings as well. You'll notice that we are making our menu 250 pixels wide, and giving it a margin of 640 pixels. Why are we using this margin? As our previous section was 640 pixels wide, this margin will ensure that this section for the menu appears just to the right of the previous Prezi Player section.

Additionally, using the `font-family` variable, we're telling the browser what fonts we would like used for the text in our menu.

Fonts are stored locally on each user's computer rather than on the Internet. Although many fonts are standard across different operating systems, there are many fonts that some users may have and others won't. For this reason, we can list several fonts in our style settings. The browser will try the first one, and if it's not available, move on to the next until it finds a match. You can define a particular font using quotation marks, or a font family without the quotation marks.

It's fine to customize your menu with a font that you like, but ensure that you select fonts that your viewers are likely to have on their own computers! A great resource for this is `https://www.google.com/fonts`.

When we coded our menu, we used the HTML for the unordered list to create bullet points for each menu item. However, the menu actually looks much better without the bullet points. Luckily, we can use CSS to hide these, which is exactly what we will do with the `list-style-type: none;` code in the `#nav` section. This tells the browser not to use any marker for our unordered list.

Within the `#nav` section, we can also define the style of particular HTML elements. For example, `#nav li a {` allows us to change the settings for all of the links (a) that are part of lists (`li`) in our `<div id="nav">` section.

`display: block;` tells the browser to display each element as its own paragraph.

`color: #0645AD` sets the color of the text. The `#0645AD` text is a color represented in hexadecimal. Don't panic if you don't know anything about hexadecimal. There are plenty of free tools available that allow you to select a color and then report the hexadecimal value to use.

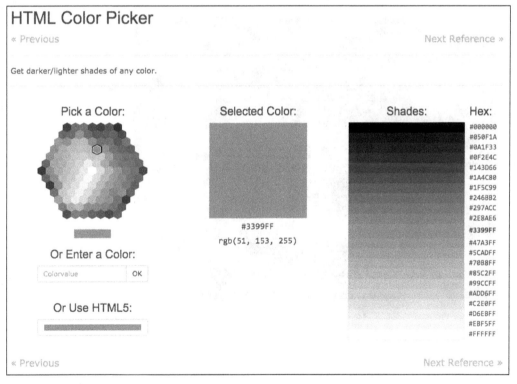

This color picker is available at `http://www.w3schools.com/tags/ref_colorpicker.asp`

The padding setting clears an area around the content. You can set how large you would like this cleared area to be in pixels. In our example, we set a 3px padding area.

`text-decoration: none;` removes any added decoration to the text. We use this setting because browsers usually underline all links by default. Using this code, we can remove the underline from our menu links.

The `#nav li a:hover {` section defines settings for what should happen while the mouse is hovering over the links that are part of the list. In our example, we're changing both the background color and color of the text, again using hexadecimal color settings.

If you save your file and reload it in the browser, you should now see an updated and much more aesthetically pleasing menu:

Additionally, you can see that when the mouse hovers over one of the menu items, it gets highlighted due to the hover CSS code that we added:

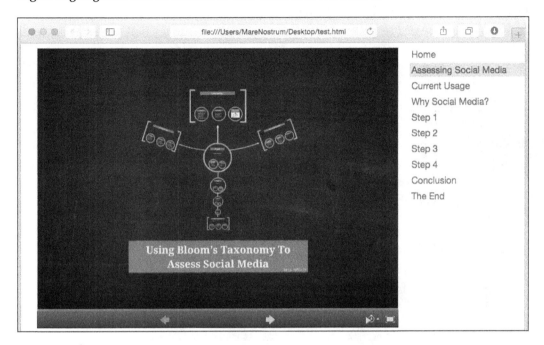

Creating submenus

Finally, let's add some submenus to our current menu. The easiest way to do this is to create what's called nested lists. This means we have lists inside our other lists. For this example, let's say I want to add in each path step contained within my "Why Social Media?" section. This will not only allow users to jump directly to that section, but it will also give them a preview of what's in that section.

This code can be inserted under the `<li></li>` tags for "Why Social Media?":

```
<ul>
    <li><a href="javascript:player.flyToStep(11)">Student
Satisfaction and Learning Outcomes</a></li>
    <li><a href="javascript:player.flyToStep(12)">Student
Engagement</a></li>
    <li><a href="javascript:player.flyToStep(13)">Flexibility</
a></li>
</ul>
```

We can continue to add these submenus to each of our points on the list if we desire. Remember that you want to use each of the subheadings in your presentation to create these menu items. Let's see what this looks like:

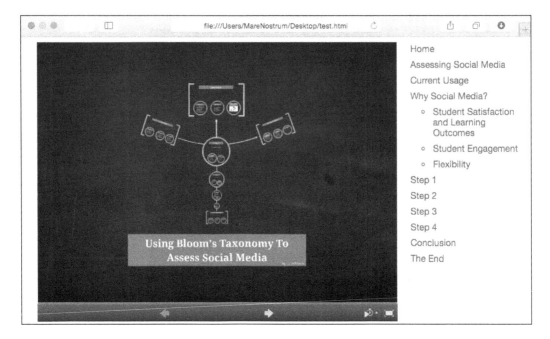

Immediately, you'll notice that our new list has bullet points again! This is because our CSS code only applies to our main list, and not our nested list. To correct this, we can add the following CSS code:

```
#nav li {
    list-style-type: none;
}
```

This affects the second level of `li` in the `nav` section.

I'm also going to shorten the rather long Student Satisfaction and Learning Outcomes to simply **Student Satisfaction** to improve the way it looks. Now, our menu looks like this:

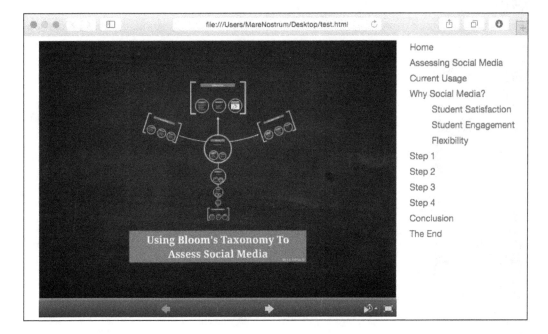

And with this, we have a fully working and interactive menu for our Prezi!

The full code should look like this:

```
1  <html>
2  <head>
3      <title>Using Bloom's Taxonomy to Assess Social Media</title>
4          <style>
5  #prezi-player {
6      width: 640px;
7      float: left;
8      margin-left: 20px;
9  }
10 #menu {
11     width: 250px;
12     margin-left: 645px;
13     font-family: "Helvetica Neue", Helvetica, Arial, sans-serif;
14
15 }
16 #nav {
17     list-style-type: none;
18 }
19 #nav li a {
20     display: block;
21     color: #0645AD;
22     padding: 3px;
23     margin-bottom: 5px;
24     text-decoration: none;
25 }
26
27 #nav li a:hover {
28     background-color: #0D9D66;
29     color: #001e5c;
30 }
31
32 #nav li {
33     list-style-type: none;
34 }
35
36 </style>
37 </head>
38 <body>
39     <div id="prezi-player" class="player"></div>
40     <div id="menu">
41     <ul id="nav">
42     <!-- programmers start counting with 0 -->
43     <li><a href="javascript:player.flyToStep(0)">Home</a></li>
44     <li><a href="javascript:player.flyToStep(1)">Assessing Social Media</a></li>
45     <li><a href="javascript:player.flyToStep(6)">Current Usage</a></li>
46     <li><a href="javascript:player.flyToStep(10)">Why Social Media?</a></li>
47         <ul>
48         <li><a href="javascript:player.flyToStep(11)">Student Satisfaction</a></li>
49         <li><a href="javascript:player.flyToStep(12)">Student Engagement</a></li>
50         <li><a href="javascript:player.flyToStep(13)">Flexibility</a></li>
51         </ul>
52     <li><a href="javascript:player.flyToStep(14)">Step 1</a></li>
53     <li><a href="javascript:player.flyToStep(18)">Step 2</a></li>
54     <li><a href="javascript:player.flyToStep(21)">Step 3</a></li>
55     <li><a href="javascript:player.flyToStep(25)">Step 4</a></li>
56     <li><a href="javascript:player.flyToStep(26)">Conclusion</a></li>
57     <li><a href="javascript:player.flyToStep(33)">The End</a></li>
58     </ul>
59     </div>
60 </div>
61 <script src="http://prezi.github.io/prezi-player/lib/PreziPlayer/prezi_player.js"></script>
62 <script type="text/javascript">
63 var player = new PreziPlayer("prezi-player", {
64     preziId: "5kd45vdbisdb",
65     width: 640,
66     height: 480,
67     controls: true,
68     explorable: true
69 });
70     player.on(PreziPlayer.EVENT_CURRENT_STEP, function(e) {
71     oldLink.removeClass('active');
72     var stepId = e.value;
73     $('select your link based on stepId').addClass('active');
74     });
75 </script>
76     </body>
77 </html>
78
```

Summary

In this chapter, you learned how to use some of the basic functionalities of the Prezi API in a file that we host on our own website. Along the way, you learned to use and manipulate some HTML, CSS, and JavaScript code! We've also brainstormed some ways that these features can benefit our business presentations.

The ability to access the API really opens up a lot of creative potential. If you're interested in exploring further, ensure that you check out the full list of API functions, available at `http://prezi.github.io/prezi-player/lib/PreziPlayer/`.

In the next chapter, we will look at how Prezi works on tablets and phones, and how that might benefit our business presentations.

11
Prezi for Tablets and Phones

Have you noticed the increasing number of people in meetings with iPads or other tablet devices lately? Tablets are becoming extremely useful business tools for recording and sharing ideas. The market for these devices is becoming fiercely competitive but there is still one clear winner (in terms of sales)—the Apple iPad. A very close second are devices that run Google's Android platform.

In this chapter, we will explain how Prezi can be used on either of these platforms, the benefits and downfalls of each, and also how you can make an impact by presenting a Prezi from a tablet device.

We'll cover the following topics:

- The Prezi iPad app
- Prezi for iPhone and Android
- Accessing your Prezi files
- True nonlinear delivery from your device
- Connecting to a projector
- Using remote desktop apps

The Prezi iPad application

At the time of writing this chapter, the Prezi viewer application is at version 3.5.4, and it's fair to say that the application has come a long way since its first release in 2011:

Opening the Safari browser on your iPad, browsing to `www.prezi.com`, and clicking on one of your Prezis will direct you to the App Store where you can download the Prezi viewer application. You won't be able to view your Prezis through the Safari browser on iPad because Apple devices do not support Flash content. This is one reason why a Prezi iPad application was needed in the first place:

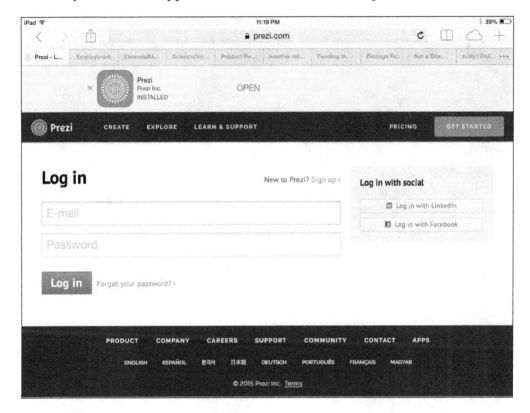

In this screenshot, you can see that Safari automatically recognizes that we have the Prezi application installed and suggests that we open that instead of using the web interface.

Using the Prezi viewer

A quick search in the App Store for Prezi and you will find the Prezi viewer application, which is free to download. Follow the given steps after Prezi is installed:

1. Once installed, you can open the application and log in to your Prezi account using the fields shown in the following screenshot:

2. Once your account details are entered, you will be taken to the Prezi viewer where you can see all of your Prezis that are stored on www.prezi.com and also a selection of Prezis that have been specially selected by Prezi.

3. If you are using the Prezi desktop on your PC or Mac and want to view your Prezis through the iPad application, you must upload them to www.prezi.com first. Once uploaded to www.prezi.com, your Prezi will automatically be set to private and won't be visible to other Prezi users.

There are three main areas in the Prezi viewer application. The default area is all of the Prezis you have available online:

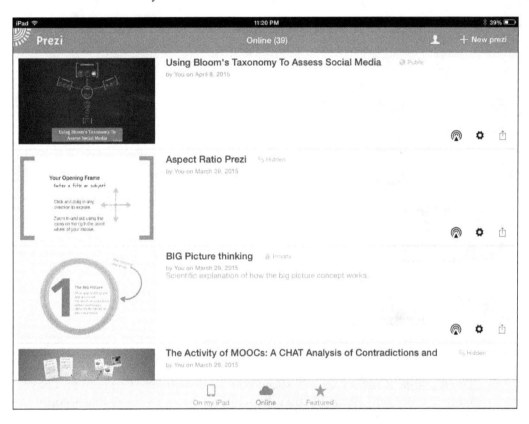

4. At the bottom of the screen, you can see the other two options, which include **Featured** and **On my iPad**. Selecting **Featured** will allow you to browse, but not search, the currently featured Prezis:

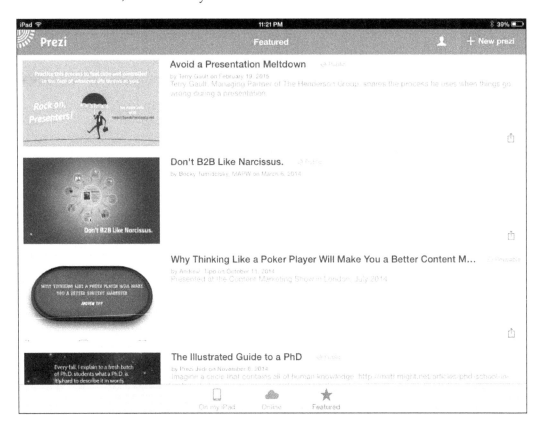

5. The top area of the screen will show you the downloaded content you have, while the bottom area will either display Prezis from your online account or the Prezi designs selected by Prezi.

6. You can switch between these views by clicking on the **Your Prezis** or **Prezis we like** button on the right-hand side of the screen.

I

To add a Prezi to your downloaded content, do the following:

1. Click on the **Your Prezis** button on the right to see a list of your Prezis from www.prezi.com.

2. Scroll through the list of Prezis and click on the one you want to download.

3. You'll see the Prezi downloading and once it's ready the application will open with the Prezi on your iPad:

4. When you have a Prezi downloaded onto your iPad, you can view it offline. This makes it a brilliant business tool to share ideas with colleagues in meetings or just on the fly at coffee breaks and so on. It's definitely an impressive way to give your CEO an elevator pitch on your new business idea.

 If your Prezi uses YouTube clips, you must have a Wi-Fi connection for them to work on your iPad.

Edit mode

When you open a Prezi in the viewer, you'll automatically enter the Prezi viewer's edit mode:

1. In the center of the screen you will see an instruction to **Tap and hold any object to edit**.

2. Clicking on the **Question mark icon** in the top-left corner of the screen will give you a clue to some of the gestures you can use to edit your Prezi in the iPad viewer.

3. To move any object, simply **Tap and hold** it on the canvas.

4. You'll then be given the options **Edit** or **Delete**. If the object you're selecting is text, the iPad's keyboard will appear. If the object you've selected is an image, you will then need to use two fingers to either scale or rotate it however you like.

Editing your Prezi in the viewer takes a little time to get used to. Like anything though, it'll soon become second nature to you if used enough. It's an incredibly powerful feature for making those last minute changes that you think of on the way to a meeting—especially if you spot an embarrassing spelling mistake just in time!

Once you download a Prezi to the viewer on your iPad, you can make changes to it without the need for an Internet connection.

As this can be a little more difficult than using a mouse, those clever people at Prezi have put in a much needed **Cancel** button in the top-left corner. This will only appear once you've made a change to the Prezi. Follow the given steps to move back to the Prezi's main menu:

1. Once you have finished editing a Prezi and want to move back to the main menu, you can simply click on the **My Prezis** button in the top-left corner.

2. After doing this, you will be asked if you'd like to save the changes you made.

 Any changes you make to a Prezi on your iPad will not link to the same Prezi in your account on www.prezi.com. We suggest that you only use the edit mode in the Prezi viewer app for light retouches and editing text. Any major design work should be done in the original Prezi from your online account. Changes made there will feed through to your iPad as long as you have an Internet connection.

Show mode

Although you enter a Prezi in the **Edit** mode, there is a **Show** mode button located in the top-right of the screen at all times. This is the equivalent of the **Play** mode online. Clicking on this button will put the Prezi into fullscreen view so that all buttons disappear. To leave the **Show** mode, click on the very subtle grey square in the top-right corner. This will return you to the **Edit** mode.

Touching the right or left sides of your iPad screen will move you backward and forward through any path that you may have added. However, if your Prezi doesn't use a path and is intended to be nonlinear, you can move through it using the touch gestures that we all know and love on the iPad. This can really add a different dimension to your Prezi, especially if you are putting it in the hands of your boss or a colleague to explore.

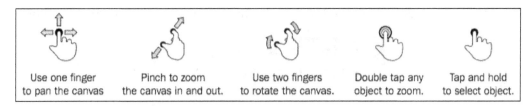

The preceding diagram shows you the different gestures available for use when viewing a Prezi. By now, we are all familiar with these but it's important to think about how they might have an effect on your Prezi design. For instance, do you need to add a frame if someone is going to pinch and zoom into your Prezi to look at the details?

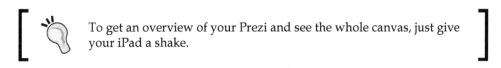

> To get an overview of your Prezi and see the whole canvas, just give your iPad a shake.

Prezi for iPhone and Android

Prezi applications for both iPhone and Android function very similarly. We'll cover the Android version here since we looked at the iPad version previously.

The most important thing to note is that these applications do not allow editing on your phone (or Android tablets). The application description pitches it as a companion application for Prezi users. Pitch, practice, and present, anytime, anywhere. Many of the reviews of these applications complain about the lack of an editing feature, but it's important to realize that Prezi made a considered decision to leave this feature out of the application, largely because of the difficulty of editing on such a small screen.

The first step is to download the Prezi application from either the Google Play Store:

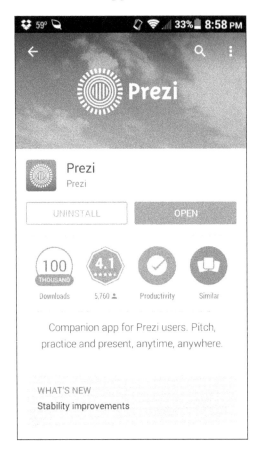

When you first open the application, the default view will be a list of your own Prezis:

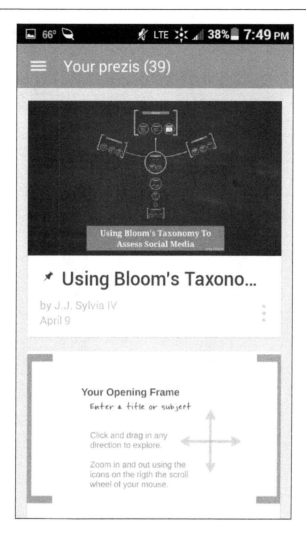

We'll explore what we can do with these momentarily, but first, if you're interested in browsing Prezis created by others, you can use the **Explore** mode in the application:

1. Start by clicking on the icon with the three horizontal lines in the upper-left corner of the application:

2. From here, you can select to view **Your prezis** which is where we get started, or you can select **Explore.** You can leave **Feedback**. If you tap **Explore**, you'll be taken to a list of interesting Prezis that you can browse:

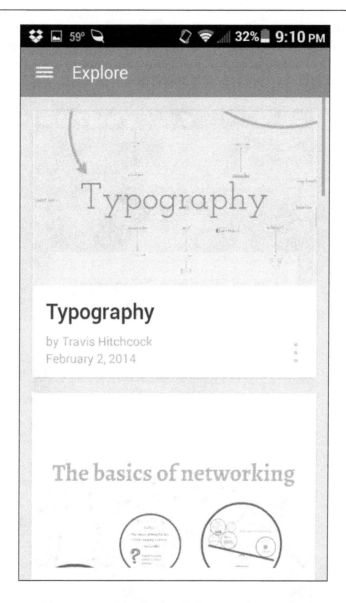

At this time, it's not possible to search for specific Prezis in the application.

3. Navigating back to the **Your prezis** section, we can see that we have a few
   options for the Prezis that we created here as well. First, if you select the
   three vertical dots that appear just below the name of your Prezi, you will be
   presented with two options as shown here:

4. The **SHARE PREZI** option will allow you to send a link to anyone which
   allows them to view the Prezi. However, they will not be able to edit it. We
   will cover the option to **PRESENT REMOTELY** in more detail in *Chapter 12,
   Online Collaboration*.

5. Finally, selecting the Prezi itself will load it for the viewing mode:

6. Once you have loaded the presentation, you'll see a message that notifies you that this Prezi has been downloaded to your phone and can be accessed without any wireless Internet or data access. If you're going to use your phone or Android tablet for a presentation, ensure that you have loaded it and saved for offline viewing first, as you never know when you'll run into Internet connectivity problems! Don't forget that if your presentation includes YouTube clips, these will still not play without an active Internet connection.

 The application saves the previous 10 Prezis that you have accessed on your phone for offline viewing. This includes both your own Prezis and those created by others.

Once you've loaded a Prezi, the application disables the automatic screen timeout that most cellphones and tablets have. This means your screen will stay on and active until you purposefully turn it off. This can be a large drain on your battery, so ensure that you either turn off the screen or back out of the Prezi as soon as you're done with it.

There are two ways to use the application for viewing your Prezi:

- First you can tap the left and right sides of the screen. This will help you advance forward or backward through the path steps that you have already set.

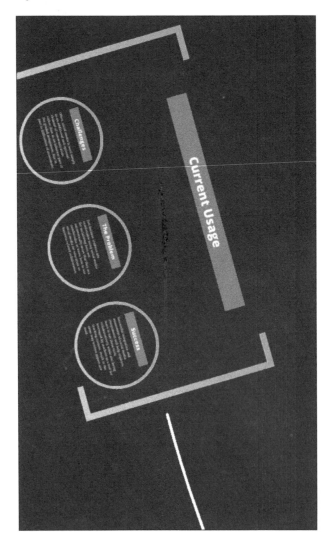

- Alternatively, you can use your fingers to navigate through the Prezi in an open, nonlinear way - scrolling, twisting, and rotating without regard for any path, as seen previously.

Presenting with a tablet

Being able to present your Prezi via a tablet opens up a whole new dimension for sharing ideas with your colleagues. Let's say that you have an amazing new business idea that you want to pitch to your boss. If you know that she/he prefers to see a visual presentation but is too busy to sit down in a boardroom and wait while you fire up the projector, then using a tablet is perfect.

Open the Prezi on your tablet and put it into the **Show** mode, then simply put it in the hands of your boss and let them click through it while you stride along next to them on their way to their next important business lunch. If anything, they'll love the fact you're being innovative with how you present ideas to them. Ensure that you get the tablet back though.

Don't assume that your boss or colleague will know how to navigate through the Prezi. Tell them how to click through it, but let them do all the work so that they are fully engaged in your presentation.

Brainstorming sessions are also a great place for you to use a tablet and run Prezi. You can place it in the center of a desk or allow people to pass it around as they have an open discussion. You may also want to show off (which we totally condone by the way) and connect your tablet to a projector.

However and wherever you decide to present a Prezi with a tablet, ensure that you let people hold it and play with it themselves. This makes for a much more engaging experience and one that hopefully they'll remember more of.

Using a tablet to project your Prezi

If you have an iPad 2 or a new iPad, you can link it to a projector using the Apple VGA adapter cable that can be purchased from any Apple store. You can also do the same with Android tablets. However, there are so many different devices that run the Android platform that we would advise you look into this before setting your heart on one particular product.

Using a tablet and projecting your Prezi can be a great experience for you and your audience, especially if you've designed your Prezi to be completely nonlinear.

First, it will make navigating around your Prezi very easy for you because you're holding it in your hands. If someone in the audience wants to focus in on point C, you can simply touch that part of your Prezi to zoom in. Once done there, you can give the Prezi a shake (a lovely feature) to return to the overview. If you were using a laptop, you'd have to use a mouse and click on the screen. You'd either have to sit down or hunch over the laptop, so this makes for a much more natural experience.

If your room is set up well enough, you might even be able to pass the tablet around to the audience and let individuals zoom in and share their ideas on various points. By doing this, you're turning your audience into presenters and letting them know that their views are important. If you're not sure about how the equipment in your room is set up and whether or not this is possible, it is a good practice to touch base with the IT person or department in charge of the room for advice on getting it connected properly.

This is a really exciting way to present and it definitely makes for a much more interesting session.

 Don't be afraid to let your audience hold the tablet and zoom around. If you really are a Prezi master, you might even want to hide snippets of information on the canvas for people to find as they start using the Prezi presentation you have made on your tablet.

Another benefit of using an iPad to present your Prezi is that you remove the need for a mouse to scroll and zoom around. This helps your Prezi look even better and means that your audience won't be distracted by seeing an arrow cursor on the screen.

A bit of fun

You may have seen some Prezis on the **Explore** page of www.prezi.com titled *Prezi + iPad =*. These were all entries for a competition that Prezi held in 2011. To stand the chance of winning an iPad 2, Prezi users had to create a Prezi explaining the benefits of the Prezi iPad application.

The winning entry can be seen at http://blog.prezi.com/latest/2011/3/1/ prezi-ipad-contest-we-have-a-winner.html.

If you want to see a more comical Prezi that was one of the runners up, then go to http://prezi.com/yl9_u5si57pp/prezi-ipad-freedom.

There were hundreds of entries for this competition and they all gave a great explanation of how beneficial the iPad application is. Other awesome entries can be seen at http://blog.prezi.com/latest/2011/2/24/awesome-submissions- from-the-ipad-contest.html.

Summary

Hopefully, in this chapter you made some decisions about whether or not using tablets to present Prezis is going to work in your business and if so, which tablet you'd be best off using. Sure the iPad is a great device; it wouldn't sell millions and millions each year if it weren't. Would the fact that Android devices don't have a Prezi application really stop you from buying one? We don't think so, but ultimately it's about you and how you work in your business that matters.

Whatever device you decide to buy (or already own), we only wish for one thing — that you try to be as creative as you can with your Prezi design. Also, it's equally important that you give lots of consideration as to how you present it. Don't just let people see the screen without touching it themselves to have a play.

In the next chapter, we'll look at how you can use Prezi to collaborate with colleagues and present remotely.

12
Online Collaboration

Prezi offers several different ways in which you can collaborate or interact with colleagues and others online. As businesses continue to expand globally, this ability to work from a distance becomes more necessary than ever. With Prezi, you can create together, present remotely, and share your work across an organization.

In this chapter, we will explain how Prezi can be used to collaborate and present online, and offer some tips on how to make all of this work smoothly.

We'll cover the following topics:

- Shared folders
- Cocreating Prezis
- Avatars
- Presenting remotely
- Tips for presenting remotely
- Creating and sharing videos based on presentations

Shared folders

At their most basic, Prezi folders represent an organizational strategy similar to the traditional file management system that you're used to on your computer You can create and name any number of folders to hold and organize the Prezi's that you create. To see how this works, let's try to create one to get started.

 If you've been added to a multi-license group, you'll already be part of, and have access to, a shared folder with the name of the company.

Creating a folder

In the **Your Prezis** section of http://www.prezi.com, you'll see the **New folder...** option in the menu on the left:

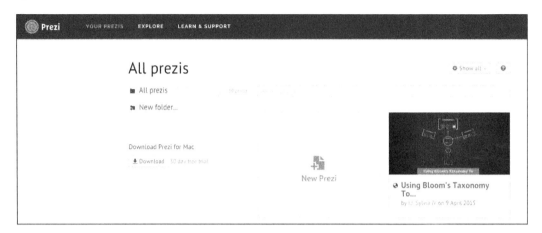

From there, you will see you can now rename your new folder, which will be called **Untitled folder** by default:

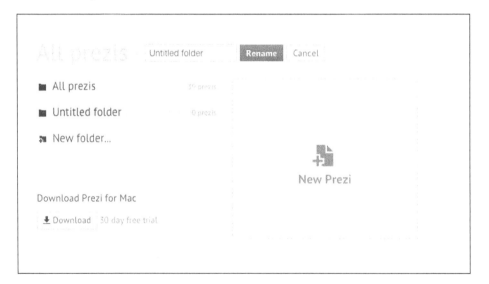

We'll name ours as **Collaborations** to get started. You'll see this name change reflected on the left-hand side of the screen. If you ever want to change it, just hover over the name of the folder at the top and then click on the pencil icon to edit:

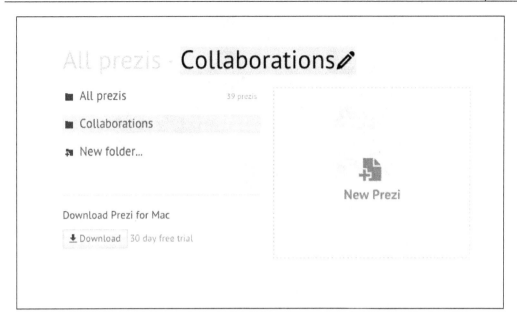

Now that we have created a folder, there are two different ways we can add Prezis.

First, we can simply drag and drop a Prezi by left-clicking and holding that click while we move the Prezi on top of the folder we'd like to move it to. Releasing the mouse button will then drop it into the folder:

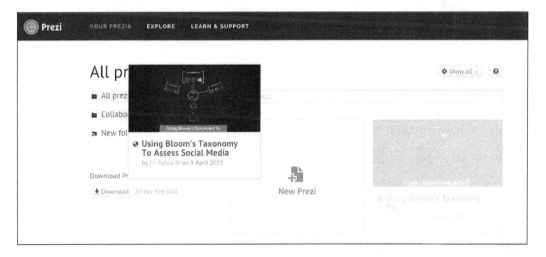

Second, click on the folder icon on any of your Prezis. A drop-down menu will appear that allows you to select the folder that you'd like to move this Prezi to:

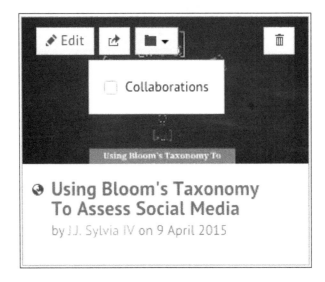

 You can add any Prezi to a folder, it doesn't have to be the one that you created. However, you should be aware that when you add a Prezi, everyone else who has access to that folder will receive an e-mail notification and gain access to the Prezi, even if it was previously marked as private! If you're worried about the privacy settings of your Prezis, you'll want to be particularly careful working with folders.

Managing folders

Once you've created folders, you can then choose to share access to those folders with others. This makes it easy to create folders for many different areas and keep things easily organized. For example, you might create folders for:

- A sales team to create sales pitch presentations
- Sales reports created for the management team
- Public Prezis created by the communication team

Adding viewers

If you want to add a viewer, you'll first need to navigate to the folder you'd like to share. Then, you'll look for the **Add viewer** button near the top-right corner of the screen.

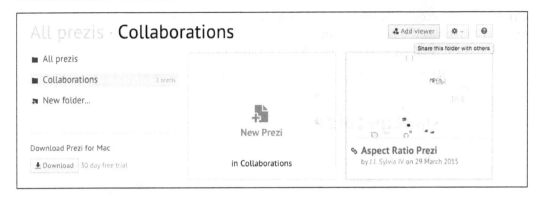

This will bring up the **Manage folder** dialogue box where you can add other viewers by entering their e-mail addresses:

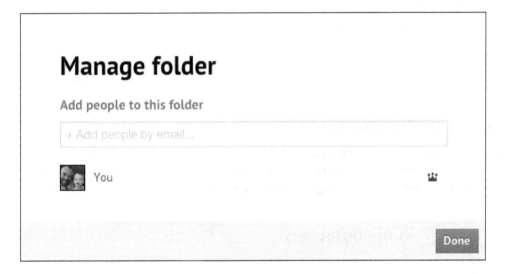

Once you've typed in the e-mail address, click on **Add**; you can continue adding as many viewers as you would like. Once you're finished, click on the **Done** button.

> You will not be able to add someone as a viewer if they have not already created an account on Prezi with that e-mail address. They will not need to have a business account, as any type of Prezi account will work.

Once you've successfully added someone, you'll see an **e-mail sent** notification appear, as well as the person's name below yours in the list of people who have access to the folder, as seen in the following screenshot:

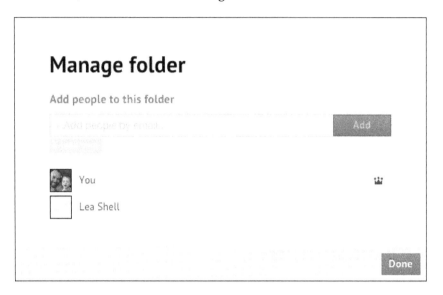

Removing viewers

Removing someone's view permission from a folder is also easy. Once you share the folder with someone, the previous **Add viewer** button will read **Shared with 1 viewers**. Clicking on this will again bring up the **Manage folder** dialogue box:

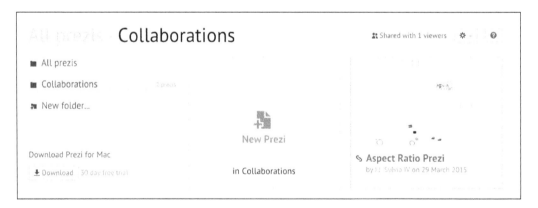

If you hover over any of the viewers, a small trash can will appear to the right. Clicking on this trash can will remove them from the shared folder.

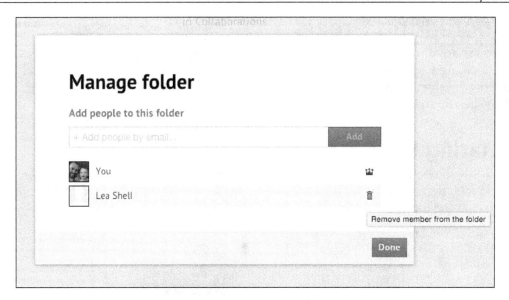

 If you are added to a folder that someone else owns, you can remove yourself from the folder by following this method.

Deleting a folder

From the main folder page, click on the gear icon that appears at the top right of the screen. From this drop-down menu, click on **Delete folder…** and remove the entire folder. The Prezis that were part of the folder will still exist, but no longer remain organized in the folder.

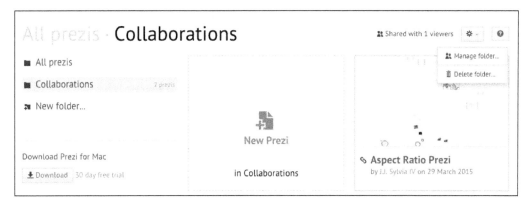

Cocreating Prezis

If you're anything like me, you probably don't like anyone leaning over your shoulder and making suggestions as you're working on a creative project. Thankfully, Prezi offers a solution to this problem that will also let you collaborate with co-workers anywhere in the world. Now, you can co-edit with other Prezi users!

Sharing the Prezi

To allow someone to edit with you simultaneously, you'll first need to share your Prezi with them while you are in editing mode. To do this, simply click on the share icon near the top-right corner of the screen, and then select **Share prezi...**.

This will bring up the **Share** dialogue box:

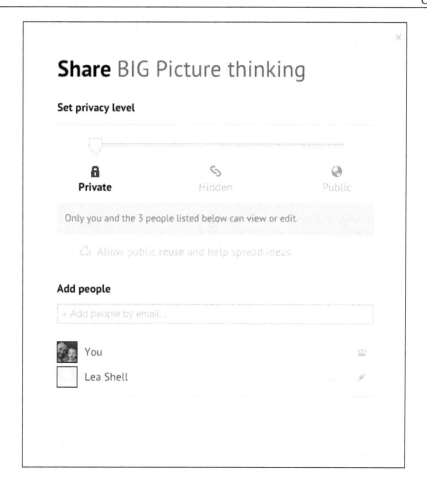

If you have an Education, Enjoy, or Pro plan for your account, you can set the Prezi to any level of privacy that you'd like here.

The first thing you'll notice is that if you have this Prezi in a folder, anyone you've shared the folder with is already on the list of people with whom this Prezi is shared. You can also add additional people to the Prezi in the same way we added them to the folder earlier.

One thing you should notice is that if your privacy level is set to **Hidden** or **Public**, then you can use a **Copy link** button.

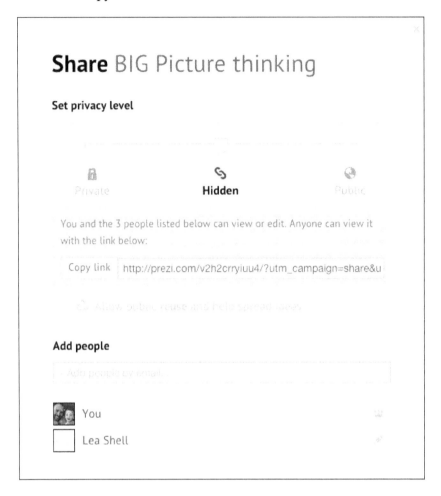

However, using this link will only allow people to view the Prezi, and they will not automatically have the permission to edit it. Once you add people, however, you can specify whether you'd like them to be editors or viewers by clicking on the pencil icon that appears to the right of their name when you hover over it, as seen here:

 You can edit simultaneously with up to 10 other Prezi users.

Avatars

Once someone else joins the Prezi and begins editing, you'll notice that their avatars appear on your screen. Avatars are the small pictures that represent someone else's account profile picture. It's possible to upload a picture, as I have with my account. However, if no picture is set, you'll see a colored smiley face as shown here:

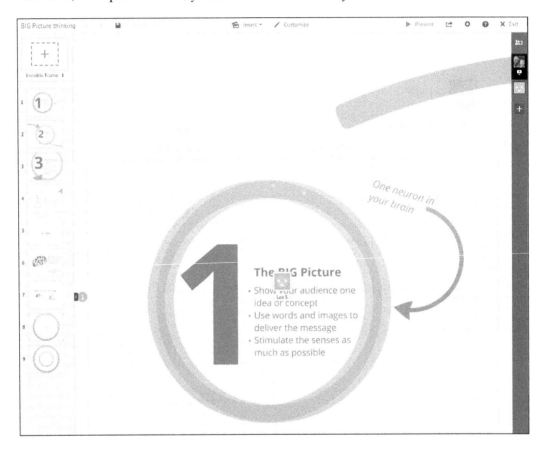

As you can see in the preceding screenshot, the avatar appears both in the right column of the Prezi window and on the canvas itself to represent where the other person who is editing is focusing their efforts. Above the avatars on the right, you'll also see the total number of people who are currently editing, as shown in the previous image.

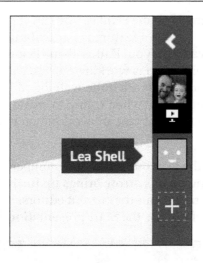

If the other editors don't have avatars with pictures that easily identify them, you can always hover over the avatar to see their name, as shown in the preceding screenshot.

If you click on the avatar that's on the canvas, you can click to either **Zoom to position** or **Open profile**. The zoom feature is particularly helpful if they are editing a different part of the canvas than you. Rather than clicking, dragging, and zooming to get to the section another person is working on, you can simply zoom straight there. These online collaborations work quite well for adding content, though they can become somewhat chaotic when trying to create paths. Communicating with your collaborators about what you are working on is an important part of the process.

Finally, if you hover over the icon that shows the number of people editing, it will turn into an arrow. Clicking on this arrow brings up further options that allow you to either get more information about the current editors, invite additional editors, or start the presentation. We'll discuss the **Start presentation** feature in the next section.

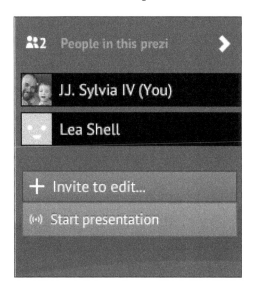

Presenting remotely

In previous chapters, we discussed ways in which you can set up your Prezi so that others can lead themselves through it while viewing it online, and this is probably the method used to view Prezis most frequently. However, it is also possible to lead a live presentation.

In many ways, this mirrors the process of presenting your Prezi using a projector, but in this case, your audience can be widely dispersed. For example, you will control the pace of the movement through the Prezi. The viewers will not be able to move through the Prezi on their own, nor will they be able to edit it. However, there are some important differences that you should keep in mind.

First, the audience will not be able to see or hear you. They only see the Prezi. This means you're losing a lot of important communication cues such as gestures, facial expressions, and tone of voice. Just like when you're writing an e-mail, it can sometimes be harder to convey humor or other emotions without these additional communication cues. We will discuss some options for dealing with these communication issues later.

Additionally, you won't be able to see your audience and the feedback cues that their actions can give you. This means you won't know if you've lost their interest and they are actually browsing another website in a different tab, for example. For this reason, you'll want to work extra hard to ensure that your presentation is engaging!

 You can present to up to 30 people at once using the remote presentation. Unlike with editing, remote presentation viewers do not need a Prezi account.

The remote presentation setup

Let's look at how to get started with remote presentations:

1. From the editing mode, you can click on the share icon and then select **Present remotely**:

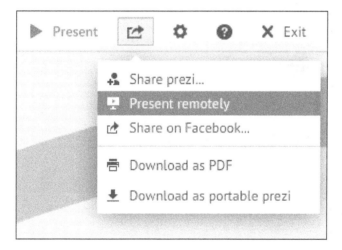

2. You'll also see the same option in the **View** mode just below the Prezi:

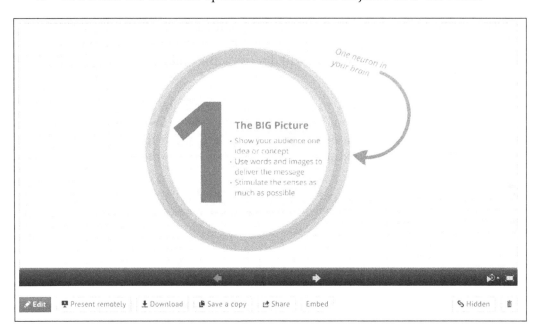

3. Clicking on this will bring up the **Present remotely** dialogue box:

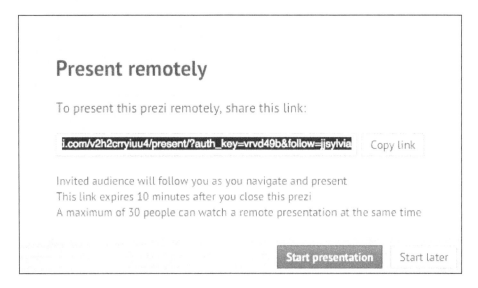

4. As this dialogue explains, you can only present to a maximum of 30 people at a time, and the link will no longer be valid after you have left your presentation unattended for 10 minutes.

5. In order to get started, you need to share the link, which is presented by this dialogue, with your viewers. It can be shared easily via e-mail for a more limited audience, or social networking sites such as Facebook and Twitter, if you're looking to invite a broader, more public, audience.

6. If you do share this link on social media and have a large following, you might want to note that only the first 30 who join will be able to view the presentation. This can also be used as a way to add a sense of excitement around the exclusivity of your brand — especially if you're presenting something new!

7. Clicking on the **Start later** option will exit this dialogue box and bring you back to the edit screen. Once you're ready to start, you can click on the **Start presentation** button.

If anyone enters the presentation using the link you shared before, click on the **Start presentation** button; they'll see the following message until you choose to begin:

Please wait, the presentation hasn't started yet

As soon as the presentation starts, you will automatically follow the presenter.

The presentation

Once the presentation starts, every movement you make within the Prezi canvas, whether it's clicking and dragging or zooming in or out, will be reflected on the screen of all of the viewers in real time. Both the presenter and all of the viewers will appear in the bar on the right-hand side of the screen. You'll notice that the person who is presenting—that is the person who has control of moving the Prezi canvas—has a small presentation icon under their avatar.

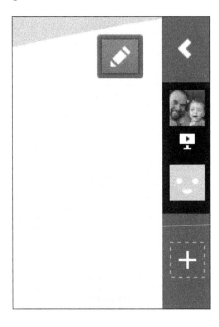

If you're in the middle of the presentation and realize that something isn't quite right—don't worry! Prezi makes this change extremely easy! Simply click on the pencil icon that appears when you hover over the right menu bar, as seen in the preceding screenshot.

This brings you back into the editing mode. Although all of the viewers will still be able to see wherever you move on the Prezi canvas itself, they will not see any of the editing tools or be able to make any edits themselves.

However, unlike normal editing mode, the collaboration bar on the right-hand side of the screen remains in place, and the Prezi canvas displays a message to remind you that you're still editing. It also gives you the option to end the presentation, if needed:

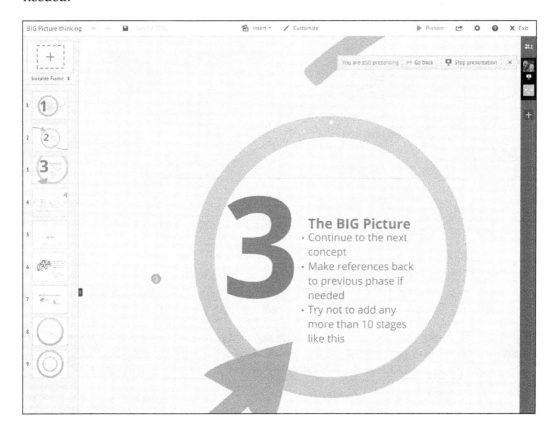

For example, let's imagine that we really meant for the third bullet point in this path step to say that you should not try more than 5 stages. Once I'm in the edit mode, I can click on the textbox and start editing, just as I normally would:

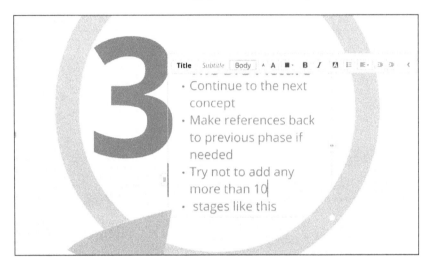

Your audience will not see every text edit that you make live. Once you click off the textbox to stop editing, all of the changes you've made will instantly be updated on your viewers' screens.

Another unique feature to the Prezi remote presentation software is that you can hand over the presentation to another viewer at any time by clicking on their avatar in the right-hand side bar, and then selecting **Hand over presentation**:

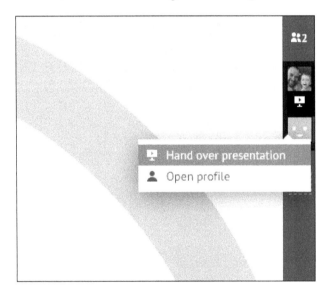

The viewer who is handed the presentation will see a message informing them of the handover:

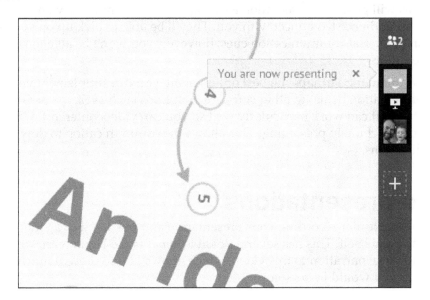

The viewer can also hand the presentation back to you or to other viewers at any time. If that viewer happens to leave the presentation while they are the presenter, the presentation will revert to your control.

 Transferring control of the presentation can be a very useful feature when you're working with known colleagues, but it can be a bit of a gamble if you've invited the public via social media. You can never be quite sure that the person will hand control back over!

Tips to present remotely

Due to the communication limitations of presenting remotely that we considered earlier, you may want to think about a few options to supplement your presentation. Consider some of the following options:

- **Extra text**: Although it's normally a good idea to keep the amount of text on the screen to a minimum, you may want to add some extra textual cues to your presentation if you're presenting remotely. These can orient the viewers and take the place of what you would normally be saying in person.

- **YouTube videos**: If you have enough time to plan ahead, create YouTube videos of yourself talking and sprinkle these throughout the presentation. This will give the presentation a stronger sense of immediacy and allow your audience to connect with you. They'll be able to pick up on your verbal and physical communication cues; however, you won't be able to read their reactions.

- **Supplement**: Perhaps the best option of all, you can supplement your presentation by using other software. Solutions such as Skype or Google Hangout can work particularly well so you can videoconference while you're remotely presenting! This allows the communication to flow in both directions.

Video presentations

You can also consider recording your presentation and posting it as a video rather than as the Prezi itself. This has several possible benefits. To begin with, you'll be able to add voice narration to this video, which allows you to present much more naturally as you would in person.

Additionally, it means that you can reuse the same presentation, so you don't have to do it over and over again for many different audiences. Finally, if you post it online to a social networking site such as YouTube or Vimeo, you can potentially take advantage of a wider audience.

You'll need the **screen capture software** to be able to record your presentation.

You can use `http://www.screenr.com` to create up to 5 minutes of screen capture for free on any operating system. There is also an additional software that can be purchased, notably **Camtasia**, available at `https://www.techsmith.com/camtasia.html`.

If you're using a Mac, the system comes with built-in software that works quite well for this. To begin, open QuickTime Player and follow these steps:

1. From the **File** menu within **QuickTime Player**, select **New Screen Recording**.

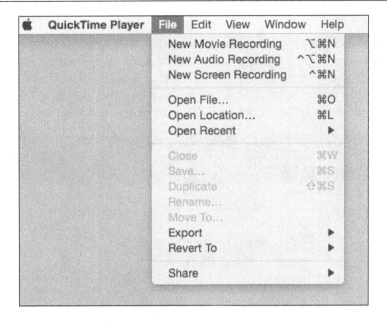

2. A new window will open that has a record button. Before you click on record, click on the down arrow next to the button and ensure that you have selected the correct microphone that you'll be using so that the recording picks up your narration.

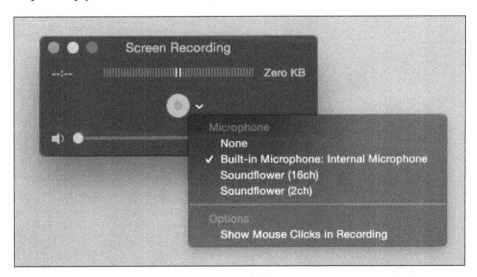

3. Click on record.

4. You'll see a message that tells you to either click to record the full screen or to drag to record part of the screen. For the most effective recording, you'll want to select only the portion of the screen that actually displays your Prezi. In the following screenshot, you can see that I've only selected the inner portion of my browser window, so only that will be recorded as part of the video:

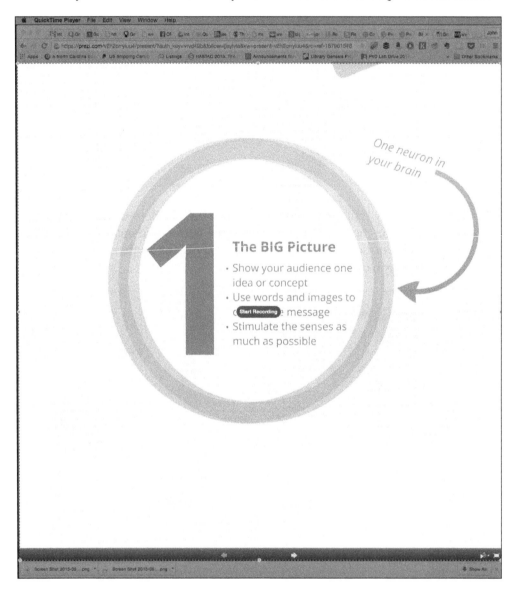

5. Navigate through your Prezi and also narrate it as you move through it.

6. Once you finish, click on the **Stop** button in the menu bar, which is the icon on the far left, as shown in the following image:

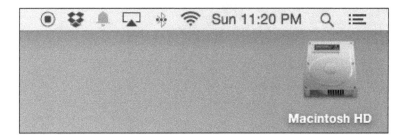

7. Finally, use the **File** menu to save the recording.

 If you use Windows or Linux, you can use a web-based screen capture platform such as the one available at http://www.screenr.com. This uses Java to record your screen, and functions much like the QuickTime example we just saw. It will even automatically convert and upload your video to YouTube!

After your video is saved, you can simply follow the same steps we covered in *Chapter 7, Inserting a Video,* to upload your own video content to YouTube!

Summary

In this chapter, we looked at some of the innovative Prezi tools that allow online collaboration, and explained ways in which they can be used to benefit your business along the way.

These collaboration tools allow you to edit with co-workers, present to others, and even record your presentations for easy distribution and reuse. However, if you decide to use these tools, you'll want to practise using them before attempting to engage either customers or your boss with them. Get a feel for how they work and then you'll start to understand how to incorporate them into the Prezi frame of mind that we've discussed.

In the next chapter, we will look at some specific case studies that explore the ways in which Prezi has been used by businesses!

13
Case Studies

In this chapter, we'll explore the various ways in which Prezi has been utilized by other businesses, and in this way stimulate our own thinking about how to use Prezi. After briefly discussing some of the strategies that can be used to implement Prezi, we'll look at some real-world implementation examples.

We'll cover the following topics:

- Collaboration and brainstorming
- Marketing and web presence
- Sales
- Case studies

Collaboration and brainstorming

In the previous chapter, we learned about the various ways in which Prezi facilitates online collaboration. Now let's think about how we can put that functionality to use for our business. Using Prezi as a whiteboard is one of the best ways to increase productivity and creativity when you're brainstorming new business ideas. Let's look at some of the ways Prezi can be useful as a whiteboard-brainstorming tool.

Getting visual

Prezi makes it easy to add visuals to your ideas; best of all, it doesn't require any special art skills with a dry erase marker. For those of you like me, who are artistically impaired, the built-in graphics in Prezi make it easy to add visual flair to the ideas we're developing. This can be done through the basic graphics (such as arrows and frames) that are included to help organize our ideas, or by adding images from a Google image search.

Why does this matter? Graphics can almost immediately affect us both emotionally and cognitively in ways that words alone simply cannot. Prezi makes it easy to break out of our reliance on bullet points and words, and demonstrate an idea in a way that is memorable and visually appealing.

The perks of digital presence

Prezi's online collaboration tools also allow you to work with others who may not be in the same building as you are. The ability to see their avatars and where they are working on the Prezi canvas makes it feel like they're right there in the room with you.

On the other hand, for those of us who might be introverts, this also has the added benefit of not allowing people to get too close to us, as they lean over our shoulders to see what we're doing. In this way, it can offer the best of both worlds—¾ social collaboration without any of the potential drawbacks of a physical presence.

Easy sharing

Once your idea has been through its initial development, it's easy to share it with a wider audience. You can include more team members in the shared folder that you've created for it or even make the Prezi public and push it out via social media. The great part is that the amount of sharing you want to do is completely up to you.

Marketing and web presence

Outstanding Prezi design can create a wow factor with your audience that leaves them talking about and sharing your brand message. We'll consider some of the unique features of Prezi that can help you achieve that wow factor.

Prezume

First, we want to mention that are two different ways to think about branding— there's your business brand, which represents the company you own or for which you work, but there's also your own professional brand. One genre of Prezis, known as the Prezume, allows you to create your own online brand by turning your résumé into a Prezi, and it can be a creative way to boost your own web presence.

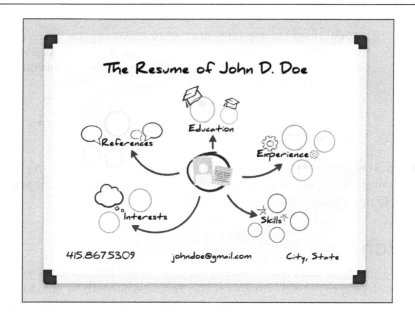

 Full Prezi available at: `https://prezi.com/lcigxq_fsccw/whiteboard-prezume-template/`

The preceding is an example of one template that someone has created to make it easy for you to plug in your own information and quickly and easily build a Prezume. But remember, if you really want to stand out, you'll be creating your own custom Prezume!

Storytelling

The thing that Prezi can do better than other presentation software is help you craft a story around your business or brand. The ability to use visually illuminating narratives can help your business really stand out and get its message across clearly.

Easy incorporation

One of the best things about using Prezi for your web presence is that you can easily incorporate it into other content that you've created, such as a blog or company webpage.

An embedded Prezi is not optimized for search engines. If you'd like to make sure that your content shows up in searches, you'll need to include other content on the page in which it is embedded. This content can then be optimized for search engines.

Sales

One of the most straightforward ways to think about including Prezi in your business is using it to generate sales leads. A Prezi can serve as another avenue to reach out to new customers.

The pitch

This style of Prezi will tell viewers about you, your business, and what you do, in the process of trying to get new business. The Prezi master will be able to leverage the unique features of Prezi to keep viewers engaged and hopefully lead to them contacting your business after viewing the Prezi. These types of presentations can be hosted on Prezi but also incorporated into your own sites and shared via social media.

In the field

I first started using this method when I worked for a nonprofit organization that had me traveling to many different school districts, but it can also translate very well into business uses.

Because I was constantly meeting new teachers and administrators who wanted to know exactly what my organization did and how it could help them, I created a Prezi that gave an overview of the organization and examples of the impact that it made in several different areas, both economically and geographically. I could then hand them my iPad with a copy of this Prezi loaded, and they could make their way through it with me there to answer any questions as they went along.

This addition of the Prezi on the iPad created a strong and compelling vision of the organization that a simple verbal explanation could not do entirely on its own. It also saved me from having to repeat the same information over and over again!

Think about the ways that you could use a similar Prezi on your iPad if you're making sales in the field. You can pitch your services, show examples of your work and its impact, and show products or statistics that pop in ways you could never achieve just through talking with a potential customer. Allowing a customer to hold a demonstration such as that in their own hands can be powerful sales tool!

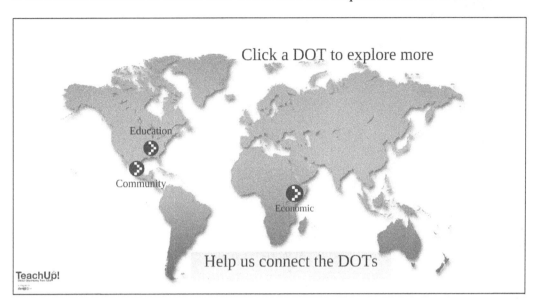

Example case studies

If we're going to look at examples of ways in which businesses have used Prezis, then perhaps the best place to start is with a Prezi advertising a business that creates outstanding Prezis for other businesses. If a company is going to create great content for you, it only makes sense that they utilize their skills to create content for themselves.

The sales pitch

That's exactly what the company Mr. Prezident has done.

The Prezi starts with a voiceover and a shot of the team's office, making a clear and humorous reference to the presidential association that their company name plays on by calling it their (not so) oval office.

 Full Prezi available at: `https://prezi.com/xgsht4javy4n/mrprezident/`

Next, the Prezi zooms in to the interior of the office where the team comes to life, fading in from outlines to an actual photo of them at work. The voiceover describes a group of people who are young and passionate about their work.

After this general introduction, we get to meet each of the main team members individually, getting a little bit of background on their lives and experiences that brought them to the company. This particular tactic really humanizes the company and makes a very effective use of the power of storytelling—you really feel like you get to know the team that is behind Mr. Prezident.

Next, the Prezi discusses some of the projects and brands that the team has already worked with, which helps to build their ethos and credibility. The logos of these major brands are displayed in frames on the wall to reinforce the message. After this brief discussion, the next step in the path zooms to the computer monitor where we are shown their work in motion while an integrated video plays music and demonstrates samples of their work.

Finally, the Prezi gives a demonstration of what it would be like to work with the team and an overview of their process of creating Prezis for clients.

So what's the point of this particular case study? It's not meant to be a referral to this company by any means. You've purchased this book because you want to create masterful Prezis, right?

The important thing to take away from this presentation is the sales pitch that's hidden in the larger narrative of the company. The Prezi introduces you to the team, gets you to relate to them through their personal stories, and shows you a portfolio of work. Walking you through the process of working with them follows this. The only thing it leaves you to do at the end is to contact them, and the Prezi ends with exactly that—details on how to get in touch. It's a well-crafted sales pitch wrapped in the team story.

Let's take a look at another awesome Prezi crafted to work as a sales pitch. This hand-drawn Prezi ultimately pitches a service that helps train change managers, who are depicted as superheroes attending school.

After seeing the disgruntled team, we see the school where they will be training.

The use of zoom with this feature is particularly effective. The Prezi zooms into various windows to make it feel as if you're actually entering the school. You can see this transition in progress here:

And once you're inside, you're in a training room with Professor Change, where you can see his super powers.

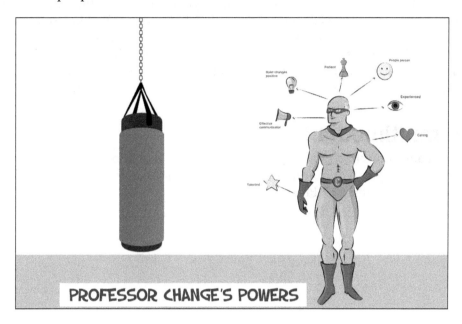

After training, we see the battered superhero now completely refreshed and ready to help facilitate change. And the Prezi leaves us with a pitch, letting us know what's next if we choose to work with this organization.

And the Prezi concludes with contact information on the very last screen.

Hopefully, through these two examples, you've gotten an idea of the way that Prezis can be used to engage users through a sales pitch but in a way that keeps them engaged along the way. This is similar to what commercials using video have long done but the Prezi tools offer some unique differences, including the fact that your viewers will be actively choosing to participate by moving to each new point in the path. This subtle detail increases the psychological buy-in of the viewer.

The multimedia tie-in

Larger organizations have also begun to incorporate Prezi into their larger advertising strategies. For example, CBS in the Netherlands created a CBS Outdoor campaign through Prezi:

 Full Prezi available at: https://prezi.com/dipjmhydzm-a/cbs-outdoor/

This Prezi prominently featured the CBS branding, and upon zooming in on the city, featured extra information on the outdoor billboards that were part of the city streetscape.

Perhaps most interestingly, this campaign was used on actual outdoor billboards. The cross-platform connections, along with the orange that makes this Prezi pop, stands out as a strong example of how to make a Prezi really communicate the message of your brand.

Visual appeal

Another way to make use of Prezi's unique appeal is to lean heavily on stunning visuals. These will come across especially vibrantly if the Prezi is viewed in fullscreen mode.

 If your presentation is strong on visuals, include a message at the beginning suggesting that the viewer enter fullscreen mode.

The following Prezi uses powerful imagery to promote **Rio de Janeiro**:

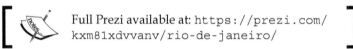

Full Prezi available at: `https://prezi.com/kxm81xdvvanv/rio-de-janeiro/`

In this Prezi, the scenery of **Rio de Janeiro** really pops. In addition, the famous Christ the Redeemer statue is a separate layer, so it moves at a different speed than the 3D background, creating increased visual interest. Finally, the hang glider in this image actually moves across the screen via an animation in the Prezi, really bring the scene to life.

Moving through the path in the Prezi highlights several attractions and interesting locations along the way. But another spot for potentially strong business appeal is a calendar of events as part of the Prezi.

Although the events on this calendar are somewhat generic (in that they don't match up with an actual calendar) it would be very easy for a business to include an actual calendar with updated events for the current month! Further details for each of the events could only be a short zoom away.

Full Prezi available here: `https://prezi.com/edmaw41a5s9i/pillowmints/`

PillowMINTS used a Prezi that makes great use of the combined power of hand-drawn graphics with powerful photographic images. It opens with an intriguingly drawn quote from the book *Oh, the Places You'll Go!* by *Dr. Seuss*, as seen in the preceding screenshot. After explaining the gist of the business, this quote is later completed with a map that pinpoints all of the possible places one could travel to.

Here again you can see the consistently themed color, tied to a particularly powerful and memorable quote. In addition to that, the user can then zoom through these locations to see larger and equally powerful photographic images of each of these locations.

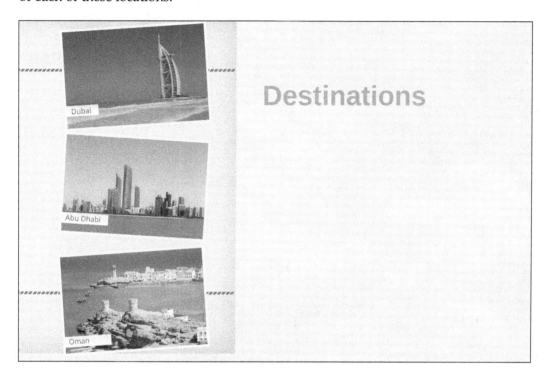

These examples show how graphics, both hand-drawn and photo-generated, can really help your Prezi stand out and draw in your viewers.

Summary

In this chapter, we've considered different ways that Prezis can be used in a business and seen some real-world examples of companies that have used Prezis in these ways. Hopefully, seeing these examples has inspired you and allowed you to start thinking about how you want to implement Prezi into your own business.

In the next chapter, we're going discuss some ideas for how to introduce Prezi into your own business, especially if those you work with seem to be stuck on using PowerPoint.

14
Getting Prezi through the Door

We felt that it wouldn't be right to finish this book without spending some time on the hardest task you're likely to face as a Prezi master. That task is getting Prezi through the door of your business, adopted and loved by all your colleagues.

The very fact that you've purchased this book shows how much you appreciate Prezi. However, this isn't going to be the case for everyone in your business. With the constant grind of day-to-day tasks, it's difficult for workers to commit to learning new things. Prezi is not just a new piece of software but a whole new way of thinking and presenting.

To help you get Prezi through the door of your business, we'll look at the following:

- PowerPoint's grip on business
- Opportunities to zoom
- Using PowerPoint to introduce Prezi
- Educating your business

PowerPoint's grip on business

Although we sing the praises of Prezi's non-linear format and want everyone to use it to create beautiful presentations, there's a lot to be said for a piece of software that's stuck around as long as PowerPoint has.

PowerPoint gave everyone in business the chance to be heard. Anybody could create a slideshow and make their message one hundred times louder than just saying the words. It added a visual element to important business messages, it was fairly easy to use, and it has now become a standard piece of kit that you'd expect to see in any organization. Giving credit where credit is due, those trusty old linear slides have helped most of us in business to create some decent enough presentations in our time.

But this is a different time and the people joining today's workforce are very different thinkers from those of the good old days!

PowerPoint was created in a different decade when people wore different types of suits to work, bread and milk were cheaper, there was no Facebook or Twitter, companies didn't have to think outside the box much to survive, and a presentation had to have beginning and end points. Ah, the good old days!

Nowadays, companies will/should do all they can to look different from their competition, innovation is desperately sought after and creativity is encouraged wherever possible. There's a constant wave of new organizations springing up shouting about how they think bigger and better than the next guys and how innovative they are. How many of those companies' sales people have you let through the door and then have had to sit through a hundred tired old PowerPoint slides that have been passed down from one sales guy to the next. Innovative? Come on, really!

This sales scenario is a perfect example of how tight a grip PowerPoint has on business presentations. We happily admit that it is a great tool and it's changed the face of business presentations forever. But surely, it has to be time for a change, right? Unfortunately, there are many people in business who truly believe that PowerPoint is the only medium they have to present their ideas with or who simply use whatever software is already used at their place of business. Until you show them otherwise, the world's workforce will spend thousands of man-hours each week sitting through slide after slide after slide. Prezi can add some much appreciated relief to this monotony.

The hard truth

Being a Prezi advocate, as we're sure you are by now, this news is going to be hard to deal with: PowerPoint is going to be around in your business for a long, long time.

Many people are resistant to change and proper use of Prezi takes some practice. So it would be difficult to introduce Prezi to your business on Monday and have everyone hang up their PowerPoint boots by Friday to fully adopt Prezi as the new presentation tool of choice.

We really want to help you be as realistic as we think you should be. Yes, your business may adopt Prezi but we doubt very much that they'll totally ditch PowerPoint. If you can live with that fact, then you'll save yourself a lot of stress and sleepless nights wondering why no-one else gets it but you.

Fingers can remain crossed that in 25 years from now Prezi will be the number one presentation tool for business, but look at it this way: If some of your colleagues won't adopt Prezi and decide to stick with PowerPoint, whose presentations are going to have more impact?

Pssst, it's "yours", dummy!

The first hurdle

Before we look at some techniques for getting Prezi into your business, we'll look at some of the questions you are bound to be asked when you first introduce it. Be ready for some very frosty stares from your colleagues!

- Why should I use Prezi?

  Because it will really help our presentations stand head and shoulders above competitors. Plus it has some really nifty features for helping us collaborate online and share ideas.

- Can't I just import my PowerPoint slides?

  Yes you can, but we would then spend some time prezifying them to get the most out of the software. Tell me the key points of slide 2 and I'll show you how to zoom in and focus on them.

- It's just a fancier version of PowerPoint, isn't it?

  Actually, no. It's a completely different way of presenting that allows you to spread out your ideas on one canvas and see everything, rather than just move from slide to slide in one direction. PowerPoint imposes a hierarchy on your information, but Prezi allows you put your information into the hierarchy that suits you.

- I've seen a prezi before and it made me feel seasick!

  That's the fault of the presenter, not the software. We'll create your Prezi so that the audience feels engaged, not ill.

- Can I use animations and have things fading in and out or flying all over the place?

  Prezi doesn't have many animation features because it simply doesn't need them. The way you can move around the canvas is enough to grab your audience's attention. You can use a fade in effect, however.

- So I can only use Prezi online?

  Not at all. If we get you a Pro license, you'll be able to use a desktop application and keep all your Prezis on your computer.

- What's the pricing model?

  To see the latest information on pricing, you can visit `https://prezi.com/upgrade/`. In general, Prezi offers a free account for individual users that places limits on the amount of storage available and the ability to edit offline, among other features. These can be upgraded for a monthly fee. Large organizations need to contact Prezi to request volume-based pricing.

- What will have to change in our IT suite to incorporate it?

  Because Prezi is web based, there should not be any significant IT changes. If users decide to purchase and use the offline editing edition, IT will need to make sure that applications can be installed on the computers or include it in the set of preinstalled software.

- Will this integrate with our clients' software?

  Because the Prezis can be shared via the Internet, they will work well with any computer system that is able to view web content.

- Apart from being new and visually appealing, what's the use of it?

  Prezi is able to convey ideas in a more flexible manner that can better make connections between material, adding a third dimension to the presentation that helps make the bigger picture clearer.

Opportunities to zoom

If by now you're trying to hatch plans that will see Prezi being used in your company, let us help you out. It's important you look for as many opportunities as possible to show off Prezi and get it in front of your colleagues so that they start to ask, "Oooo, how did you zoom in like that?"

You should be on the lookout for opportunities such as these:

- Company events
- Training days
- Sales presentations

And it is also recommended that you start to build a list of colleagues that make presentations as part of their job. They might be in sales, training, or business development, for example. Try to find out who hates presenting, and tell them you can turn their slides into a rock concert that no one will forget!

Be prepared

An opportunity to show off Prezi could come along at any time. You need to be prepared to act fast so there's no time wasted at all. In *Chapter 9, Prezi for Online Delivery*, we showed you how to brand your Prezis in order to make sure the corporate colors and logo were always present in your designs. With this in mind, it's crucial that you create a branded Prezi template that can be used at any time. Your company is bound to have a standard PowerPoint template that people use, so create a company Prezi template and make sure it's always there when an opportunity arises.

Using Theme Wizard

Follow these steps to create a standard company Prezi template:

1. Open **Colors & Fonts** | **Theme Wizard**.

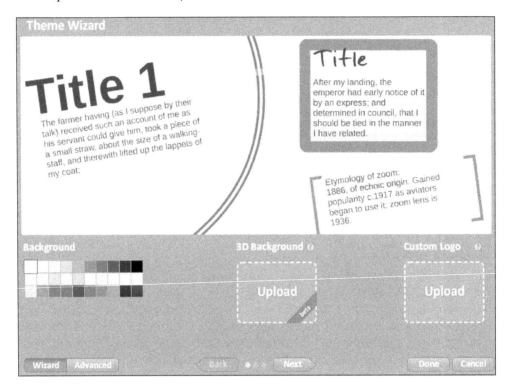

2. On the very first screen of the wizard, click on the **Custom Logo** button to add your company logo. The logo must be a .jpeg file and no larger than 250 pixels in width and 100 pixels in height. Clicking on this button will allow you to search for your logo, which will then be placed in the lower-left corner of your Prezi every time.

3. On the next screen of the wizard, we recommend that you switch to **Advanced** mode by clicking on **Advanced** in the lower-left corner. On this screen, you can select the fonts to use in your Prezi.

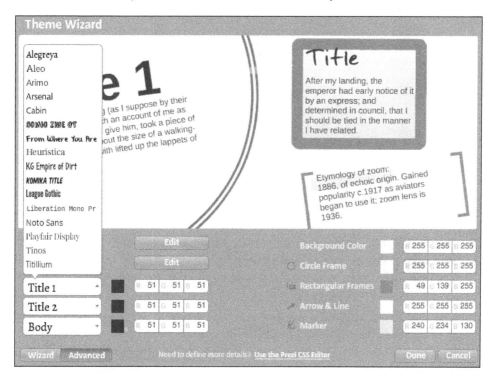

The reason we suggest switching to Advanced mode is because you'll be able to enter the RGB values for your corporate colors.

 You'll need to know the RGB color values specified in your corporate branding. If you don't know where to find them, speak to a marketing person or someone in design. Definitely don't guess!

Frame templates

Early in the book, we explained that it's a good idea to create frame templates that keep your Prezi's style consistent. We'd definitely recommend you create these as part of your company Prezi template.

1. Go to a blank space on your canvas and place a frame there.

2. Enter some text inside the frame and call it **Templates** so you don't forget what it's for.

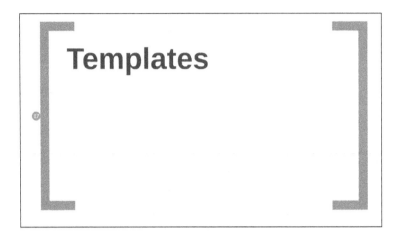

3. Inside this new frame, create the frame templates to use throughout your Prezi. They can be as detailed or as simple as you like. And remember: because Prezi zooms, you will be able to place these templates inside one another in your design.

4. Use Prezi's rectangle shapes tool to indicate where images should be positioned and simple text fields where information can be entered. The examples in the following screenshot are very simple but hopefully give you the right idea:

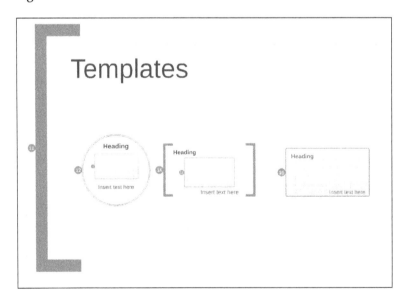

Once you have these frame templates in place, you can move to this area of your canvas at any time to copy one of them and then paste it into the position that is required in your design. You can also add them to your favorites.

Backing it up

Once you have your company's Prezi template, make sure you save it and back it up on a separate memory stick or somewhere on the company server. If you do this in addition to saving the frames as favorites, you'll be able to share them more easily with others. When you're trying to win Prezi allies in your business, this file will give you a huge advantage and enable you to act fast when you get the chance to Prezify a colleague's presentation for them. We'd also suggest you share this file and make its presence known to everyone in the business that has an interest in Prezi and builds presentations as part of their job.

Using PowerPoint to introduce Prezi

One of the best ways to win your colleagues over with Prezi is to fly under the radar and apply a very subtle approach. They'll all be used to seeing PowerPoint slides, so why not let them think that's what they're looking at and then WHAM! Hit them with a nice bit of Prezi zooming.

There are a couple of ways in which you can do this, so we'll start with the simplest one first. Rest assured though, that if you try this trick you are bound to have people asking about it after your presentation, and it's that level of curiosity that we really need to get us started.

Inserting PowerPoint slides

In *Chapter 4*, *Importing Slides into Prezi*, we saw how to insert PowerPoint slides into Prezi. A part of that chapter advised you to spread the slides out so they aren't as linear.

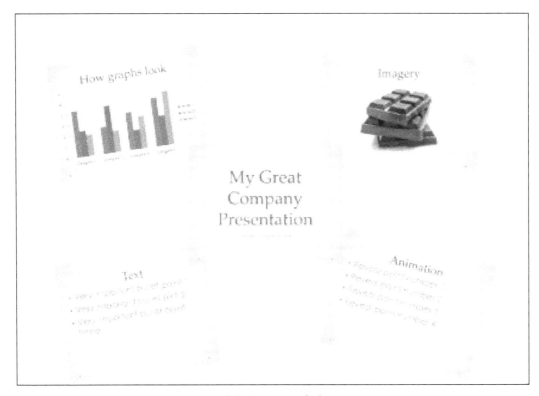

Slides being prezified

If you're prezifying some PowerPoint slides, then we still recommend you spread the slides out. However, if you're trying to give Prezi a low profile so that it subtly grabs attention, insert your slides and line them up next to one another in a linear format.

"What? This is madness!", we hear you Prezi masters saying, but trust us for a second. Follow these steps:

1.   Insert your slides and line them up, as shown in the following screenshot:

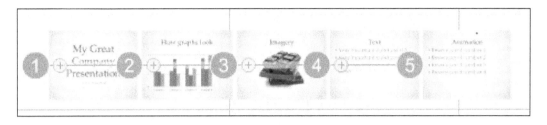

2.   Link them together in order with a path.

3.   Insert frames around the key bits of information that will be talked about in the presentation.

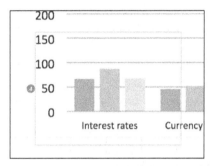

Graphs are perfect for zooming in on details

4.   Link these key areas to your path so that you zoom into them during the presentation.

 When you use the zoom feature, don't make a big deal out of it. Just casually carry on as if this way of presenting is completely normal.

What you'll end up with here is a presentation that looks and feels very much like PowerPoint. It is very linear in nature, but it subtly introduces Prezi's abilities to zoom in on important details. We aren't going to worry about showing off the ability to enter YouTube clips, Prezi Meeting, and non-linear designs; we're just going to make people go, "Oh! I like that!"

If you wanted to be a bit more obvious that you aren't using PowerPoint, you could also zoom out to show a full overview at the end of your presentation. You can see, in the following screenshot, that we've zoomed out to show all our slides and to ask if there are any questions:

If your business isn't used to seeing Prezis, we guarantee the one question you will definitely get at this stage is, "How did you make that presentation?" Once that question is asked, you can start to introduce more of Prezi.

Building a PowerPoint presentation

From the heading of this section you're probably thinking, "They've finally gone mad. Over 200 hundred pages and now they want me to use PowerPoint!" Again, please just go with us on this one. We promise it won't be a waste of time.

Let's take the same slides we saw just now. We already have them in PowerPoint, so why don't we use that for our presentation? We'll just insert a Prezi onto one of the slides to show off some zooming. The slide with the graph would again be the perfect candidate to do this with.

Slide Dynamic

There's a nice Prezi plugin for PowerPoint that's been developed by some clever people at a company called Slide Dynamic. It does come at a price, but you can find more information at `https://www.presentationpro.com/slidedynamic.aspx`.

This great little gizmo allows you to drop online or offline Prezis into your PowerPoint presentation really easily. What you end up with then is an old tired PowerPoint presentation that people will initially roll their eyes at, injected with a fresh new way to engage your audience.

Before we show you how to use the plugin, grab yourself an old company PowerPoint file and save a duplicate copy of it onto your system. Select the slide you'd like to Prezify and delete all of the others. Save the remaining slide as a PDF file and insert it into Prezi.

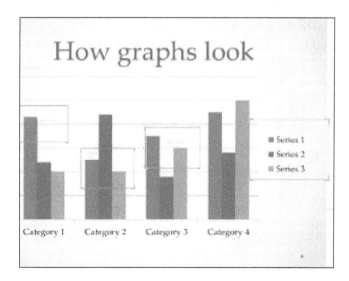

You can see in the preceding screenshot that we've inserted our slide containing the graph. Once in Prezi, we've added frames and paths to zoom in on important details. Make sure you do a good job of prezifying the slide you select.

 Before you follow the steps mentioned in the following sections, make sure you've installed the Slide Dynamic plugin from `https://www.presentationpro.com/slidedynamic.aspx`.

Once it is installed, you'll see the **SlideDynamic** tab at the top of your PowerPoint menu, as shown in the following screenshot:

The following sections show how to use this plugin.

Offline Prezis

To insert a Prezi that's been created in the Prezi desktop application, follow these steps:

1. Click on **File** and select Export as portable prezi….

2. Save the file in the same folder that your original PowerPoint presentation is being stored in:

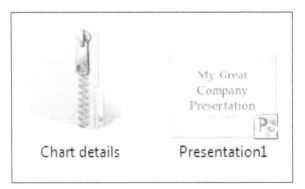

3. Right click (*Ctrl* + click, for Mac users) on the zipped folder containing your Prezi and select **Extract All** to extract the files to the same location again.

4. Open the zipped folder and copy (*Ctrl* + *C* for Windows or *Command* + *C* for Mac) all of the files contained within.

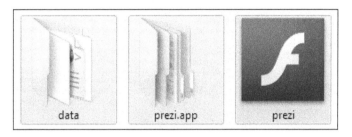

5. Paste (*Ctrl* + *V* for Windows or *Command* + *V* for Mac) the files back into the original location of your PowerPoint file.

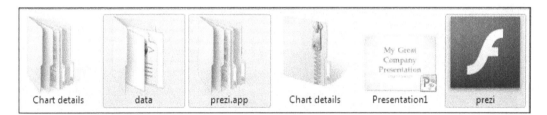

 What you should end up with is everything that your exportable Prezi needs, along with the original PowerPoint slides all in one folder.

6. Now open the PowerPoint file and go to the slide in which you'd like to insert your offline Prezi.

7. Click on the **SlideDynamic** tab at the top and select **Insert offline Prezi**:

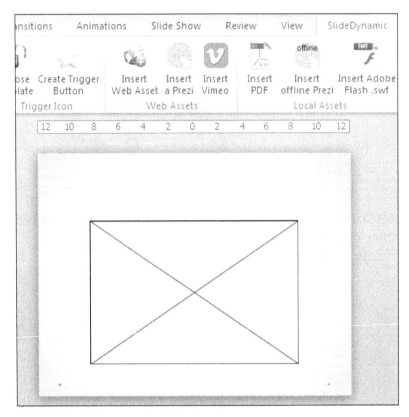

8. Drag the corners of the box that appears to resize your Prezi and fill the entire slide.

9. Go into presentation mode (*F5* for Windows or *Ctrl* + *Shift* + *S* for Mac) to see the Prezi working inside your PowerPoint.

What you should end up with is a very obvious PowerPoint slide show with a little injection of Prezi thrown in.

Online Prezis

To insert an online Prezi is much simpler, but of course you need to have an Internet connection to get things to work.

1. Browse to the online Prezi you want to insert and copy the web URL from the top of your browser.

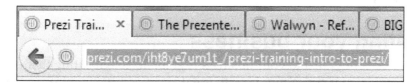

2. Open PowerPoint and locate the slide you'd like to insert your Prezi onto.

3. Click on the **SlideDynamic** tab and then on **Insert offline Prezi**.

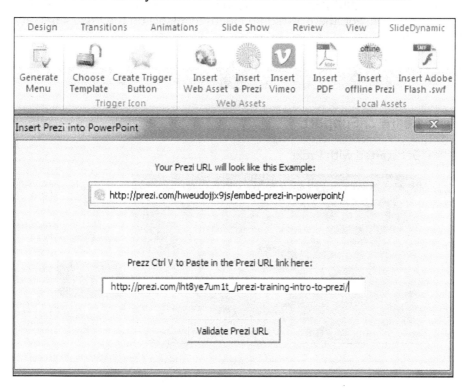

4. Paste the URL into the field at the bottom of the screen that appears and click on **Validate Prezi URL**.

5. Once validated, you can click on **Embed Prezi** and your Prezi will be available to view in presentation mode.

Again, what you'll end up with is a very subtle introduction to Prezi without distracting people too much from the linear format they are used to in PowerPoint.

Educating your business

A part of introducing Prezi to your business is going to be educating them. It includes showing your colleagues how to use it and also how to think and approach designs in the right way.

You'll be happy to know that the Prezi website does have a large amount of useful information in its **Support** pages (http://prezi.com/support). As you can see in the following screenshot, there are some videos available on the Prezi site you can point colleagues to:

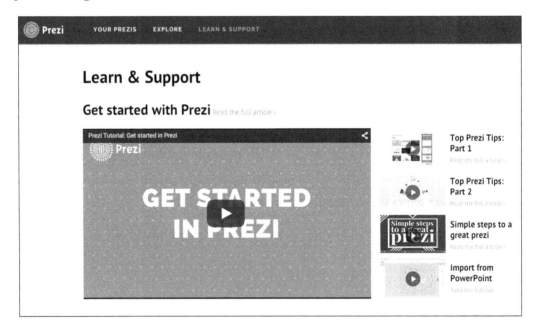

 You can also ask for the help of an official Prezi expert at http://prezi.com/experts/.

Company's how-to guide

It's highly recommended that before you start getting people excited about Prezi, you prepare a very simple "How-to" document that uses some of the basic instructions from the site. The best place to source some useful information is `https://prezi.com/support/1/article/`, which contains lots of useful information on all of Prezi's features.

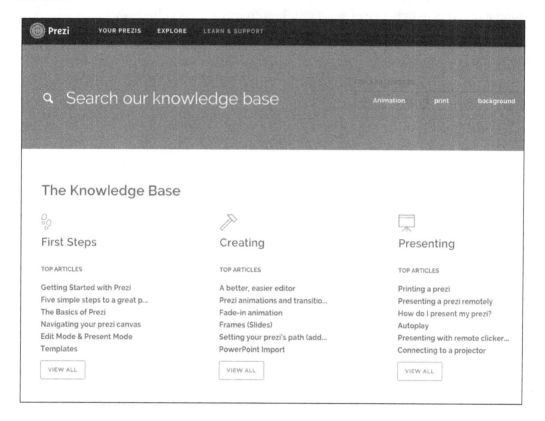

Once you have a big group of colleagues who all want to know more about Prezi, you can hand them this book. See, it was totally worth the investment!

Summary

Hopefully you've figured out by now that it's not just about getting Prezi through the door of your business. It's about slowly introducing its features, winning over the mindsets that have been so used to linear presentations and more than anything being fully prepared to create a Prezi at a moment's notice, without stomping over your company's branding guidelines. If you take the time to prepare now, you'll stand a much better chance of successfully introducing Prezi into your business.

In the next chapter... Wait, there *is* no "next chapter"! Go forth and be a Prezi master. Good luck!

Index

Symbols

3D backgrounds
  about 50
  multiple 3D backgrounds 52, 53
  single 3D background 50, 51
3D canvas 12

A

Adobe Dreamweaver 229
agriMORE
  URL 162
Android
  Prezi application, using 259-267
  voice narration, recording 153, 154
animations
  about 48, 49, 126
  fade-in animations 130-133
API
  about 227
  requisites 228
  URL 227
  using 228
  working with 231
Audacity
  URL 140
audio
  adding 140
  audio libraries, URL 136
  background music, adding 140-142
  common problems 145
  example uses 159
  getting, into Prezi 158
  using, for presentation 145
  voice-over, adding 143, 144

audio, common problems
  background music, for one path step 149
  on mobile devices 152
  uneven volume levels 146-149
audio, example uses
  less text 159
  narration 159
  translation 159
Audio Recorder
  URL 158
avatars
  about 282
  working with 282-284

B

background music
  adding 140-142
  including, for one path step 149
  music and voice-over, combining 150-152
BIG picture technique
  about 13, 19-25
  URL 21
built-in video player
  considerations 164
  file size restrictions 164
  Prezi design, copying 165
  Prezi design, determining 165
  Prezi, viewing online 164, 165
  technicalities 163, 164
bullets 47, 48

C

Camtasia
  URL 292

Cascading Style Sheets (CSS)
  about 62
  Prezi graphics, customizing through 62, 63
CMYK color standard 60
cocreating, Prezis
  avatars, working with 282-284
  Prezi, sharing 278-281
  with other users 278
color schemes
  about 58
  creating 59-61
company Prezi template
  backing up 323
  creating 319
  frame templates, creating 321-323
  Theme Wizard, using 320, 321
custom logos
  uploading 73, 74
custom sounds
  creating 137-140

D

design steps, Prezi
  about 7
  layers 12-15
  planning 7
  style 8
dimensions, images 113
doodles 37

E

Easy Voice Recorder
  URL 153
effects
  about 126
  using 126-128
embedding, Prezi for online delivery
  code 211-213
  performing 210
  sizing 211
  user experience 211
example case studies
  about 301-308
  multimedia tie-in 308, 309
  visual appeal 309-313

F

fade-in animations
  implementing 130-133
font colors 47
fonts
  editing 64, 65
  reference link 65
frame
  about 10, 11
  editing 66-71
free audio libraries
  reference link 137

G

Google image search
  advanced image search 111, 112
  advanced image search, options 112, 113
  limitations 114
  standard search 113
  using 111
Graphics Interchange Format (GIF) 103
grouping 42-44

H

HEX color standard
  about 60
  reference link 67
highlighter tool 41
HyperText Markup Language
    (HTML) 211, 229

I

images
  direct uploading 107, 108
  image search methods 115
  inserting 108-110
  limitations, of inserting from web 111
  searching 107
  searching, from other online sources 114
  searching, with Google image search 111
  vector image, creating 121, 122
  vectorizing, with software 116-120
  zooming 111

iMovie. *See* **Windows Live Movie Maker**
indents 47, 48
Inkscape
  URL 117
interactive Prezis
  about 201
  benefits 226, 227
  using 203, 204
  working 201, 202
Interactive Whiteboard (IWB) 201
iPad screen 13
iPhone
  Prezi application, using 259-267
  voice narration, recording 156-158

J

Joint Photographic Experts Group
  (JPEG) 103

K

Keynote 77

L

LAME
  about 137
  URL 137
linear presentations
  about 3
  advantages 4, 5
lines
  editing 40

M

marketing
  Prezi, using 298
menu
  base HTML file, creating 232
  coding 238, 239
  creating 232
  JavaScript, implementation 233-237

styling 240-244
  submenus, creating 245-247
Microsoft PowerPoint 1
Mind Mapping
  about 16-19
  list, writing 17
  working, with Prezi 19
mobile devices
  audio, getting into Prezi 158
  voice narration, recording 152
  voice narration, recording on
    Android 153, 154
  voice narration, recording
    on iPhone 156-158
motion
  creating 32, 33
multiple 3D backgrounds 52, 53
My Content feature 71-73

N

nonlinear presentations
  about 2-4
  advantages 4, 5
  Prezi, using in 5, 6

O

online collaboration 297
online Prezi, for online delivery
  BIG picture technique, using 221-223
  designing 214
  information, highlighting 217
  information, highlighting with
    color 219, 220
  information, highlighting with frames 218
  instructions, adding 214-216
  narration, adding 217
  timing 221
online sources, for images
  advantages 115
  best image source, deciding 114
  using 114

P

path
  about 31
  adding 34-36
  editing 34-36
  removing 34-36
Portable Document Format (PDF) 103
Portable Network Graphics (PNG) file 102
PowerPoint
  about 77
  in business 315, 316
  presentation, building 326
  Slide Dynamic, using 327, 328
  slides, inserting 324-326
  using 323
  versus Prezi 316
present button 54
Prezi
  about 1
  advantages 186
  benefits 105
  business support 332
  design steps 7, 15
  drawbacks 106
  explore page, URL 135
  for Android 259-267
  for iPhone 259-267
  guidance 333
  hurdles 317, 318
  issues 26, 27
  neural networks, building 21-24
  online link, sharing 197-199
  opportunities 319
  planning 6, 7
  portable Prezis, sharing 199, 200
  presenting, remotely 284, 285
  sharing 196, 197, 278-281
  URL, for guide 333
  using, in nonlinear presentations 5, 6
Prezi, for online delivery
  access control, setting 206, 207
  building 206
  embedding 210

  name and description, adding for search
    engines 209
  online design 214
  sharing 208, 209
Prezi iPad application
  about 252
  Prezi viewer, using 254
  using 253
Prezi, planning
  aspect ratio, modifying 190-192
  aspect ratio, using 193
  correct ratio, using 195, 196
  frames, designing as per projector
    screen 193-195
  importance 187
  overlapping content, handling 187-190
Prezi viewer
  Edit mode 257, 258
  Show mode 258, 259
  using 254-257
Prezume
  about 298, 299
  URL 299
problems, in importing slides
  alternative solution 100
  animations 98, 99
  low-resolution imagery 96
  pixilation 97
  spell check 98
  text 97

R

raster file formats
  GIF 103
  JPEG 103
  PDF 103
  PNG 103
raster graphics editors 103
raster image
  about 101-103
  file formats 103
Red Bull STRATOS
  URL 182

remote presentation, Prezi
  managing 288-291
  setting up 285-287
  tips 291, 292
requisites, Prezi API
  HTML editor, using 229-231
  web servers 228
RGB color standard 60

S

sales generation
  in business 300, 301
  pitching 300
  with Prezi 300
screen blackout 200
screen capture software
  URL 292
  using 292
shapes
  about 36
  basic doodle of mail character,
    creating 37-39
  editing 39, 40
  lines, editing 40
shared folders
  folder, creating 272-274
  folder, deleting 277
  folders, managing 274
  using 271
  viewers, adding 274, 275
  viewers, removing 276
single 3D background
  creating 50, 51
Slide Dynamic
  offline Prezi, inserting 328-330
  online Prezi, inserting 331, 332
  URL 327
  using 327, 328
slides
  about 77
  for businesses 78
  importance 78
  in Prezi 78, 79
  slide-based software 78
slideshow 2

slides, importing into Prezi
  as PDF 94-96
  content, positioning 85, 86
  import, checking 85
  in less time 93
  Insert PPT function, using 80-84
  missing content, importing 87-90
  slides, modifying 84
  slides, placing on Prezi canvas 91
  slides, zooming in 91-93
  slides, zooming out 91-93
  with Insert menu 79, 80
Small Web Format (SWF) 105
Smart Voice Recorder
  URL 153
Smoothboard IWB
  URL 201
SmoothConnect 201
sound
  benefits 136
  using 135
  sound files, searching 136, 137
spell checker 45
spin effect 33
styled symbols 41
style, Prezi
  about 8
  frames 10, 11
  zooming 8, 9
submenus
  creating 245-247

T

tablet
  Prezi, presenting 267
  used, for projecting Prezi 268
templates 29-31
text drag-apart feature 45, 46
text editor 45
Theme Wizard
  using 320, 321
training environment
  creating 160
  customers 160
  example 161, 162
  testimonials 160

U

undo button 63
uneven volume levels
  adjusting 146-149

V

vector file formats
  about 105
  PDF 105
  SWF 105
vector image
  about 101-104
  creating 121, 122
  file formats 105
  hand-drawn images, vectorizing 123
  tips 124, 125
Vector Magic
  URL 121
video presentations
  adding 292-295
videos
  best clip, searching 169, 170
  customer scenarios 183
  editing, in YouTube 172
  experts, using 183
  inserting, in Prezi 182
  other sources 181
  playing 165
  playing, along path 166
  playing, by user 166, 167
  positioning 168
  questions, using 183
  uploading, to YouTube 171, 172
  using, from YouTube 169
  Vimeo 181
  Windows Live Movie Maker, using 181
Vimeo 181

voice-over
  adding 143, 144

W

web presence
  easy incorporation 299
  Prezi, using 298
  Prezume 298, 299
  storytelling 299
whiteboard-brainstorming tool
  about 297
  digital presence 298
  easy sharing 298
  visuals, adding 297, 298
Windows Live Movie Maker
  about 181
  URL 181
  using 181

Y

YouTube
  account, creating 170
  Annotations menu 176
  Audio menu 175
  Captions menu 177-181
  enhancements area 173
  videos, editing 172
  videos, uploading 171, 172
  videos, using 169
YouTube, enhancements area
  filters submenu 174
  Quick Fixes menu 173
  special effects submenu 175

Z

zooming feature 8, 9

Thank you for buying
Mastering Prezi for Business Presentations
Second Edition

About Packt Publishing

Packt, pronounced 'packed', published its first book, *Mastering phpMyAdmin for Effective MySQL Management*, in April 2004, and subsequently continued to specialize in publishing highly focused books on specific technologies and solutions.

Our books and publications share the experiences of your fellow IT professionals in adapting and customizing today's systems, applications, and frameworks. Our solution-based books give you the knowledge and power to customize the software and technologies you're using to get the job done. Packt books are more specific and less general than the IT books you have seen in the past. Our unique business model allows us to bring you more focused information, giving you more of what you need to know, and less of what you don't.

Packt is a modern yet unique publishing company that focuses on producing quality, cutting-edge books for communities of developers, administrators, and newbies alike. For more information, please visit our website at www.packtpub.com.

Writing for Packt

We welcome all inquiries from people who are interested in authoring. Book proposals should be sent to author@packtpub.com. If your book idea is still at an early stage and you would like to discuss it first before writing a formal book proposal, then please contact us; one of our commissioning editors will get in touch with you.

We're not just looking for published authors; if you have strong technical skills but no writing experience, our experienced editors can help you develop a writing career, or simply get some additional reward for your expertise.

PUBLISHING

Mastering Prezi for Business Presentations

ISBN: 978-1-84969-302-8   Paperback: 258 pages

Engage your audience visually with stunning Prezi presentation designs and be the envy of your colleagues who use PowerPoint

1. Turns anyone already using Prezi into a master of both design and delivery.

2. Illustrated throughout with easy to follow screen shots and some live Prezi examples to view online.

3. Written by Russell Anderson-Williams, one of the fourteen experts hand-picked by Prezi.

Prezi HOTSHOT

ISBN: 978-1-84969-977-8   Paperback: 264 pages

Create amazing Prezi presentations through 10 exciting Prezi projects

1. Amaze your audience and keep them engaged during your presentations with Prezi.

2. Create interactive presentations from scratch by adding images, animations, and more.

3. Learn Prezi through ten exciting projects in this step-by-step tutorial.

Please check **www.PacktPub.com** for information on our titles

Instant Prezi Starter

ISBN: 978-1-84969-702-6   Paperback: 56 pages

A user-friendly, step-by-step introductory guide to using Prezi, a web-based presentation application program ideal for engaging your audience

1. Learn something new in an Instant! A short, fast, focused guide delivering immediate results.

2. Amaze your audience and keep them engaged during your presentations with Prezi.

3. Learn with the help of practical resources for awesome examples and inspiration.

Prezi Cookbook

ISBN: 978-1-78355-183-5   Paperback: 296 pages

Over 100 simple but incredible recipes to create dynamic, engaging, and beautiful presentations using Prezi

1. Create eye-catching presentations that zoom and turn.

2. Create interactive presentations from scratch by adding images, animations, frames, and more.

3. Step-by-step guide to understand how to make great Prezi presentations.

Please check **www.PacktPub.com** for information on our titles

www.ingramcontent.com/pod-product-compliance
Lightning Source LLC
Chambersburg PA
CBHW062051050326
40690CB00016B/3059